Mind
Happiness

MW00695817

Volume I:

The Quickest Way to Happiness and Controlling Your Mind

by Sean Webb

Contact Info:

sean@mindhackinghappiness.com

To my wife and son

Thanks to everyone mentioned in this book for your personal advice, guidance, scientific research, stories and support.

And special thanks to George Cornelius who caught a ton of my mistakes.

Mind Hacking Happiness

Introduction

Science tells us that I have 8.5 seconds to get your attention. That sucks, but that's the average attention span of a human mind in today's world. If I go beyond that 8.5 seconds, it's a possibility you'll already be thinking about something else that could distract you from this amazingly awesome content. Of course, our human attention spans didn't always used to be only 8.5 seconds. But thanks to changes that have occurred in the human mind over the last half century, now they are. If you're interested, on a comparative scale, our human attention span is now shorter than that of the common goldfish, which has a full nine seconds of attention in comparison. It's already been 8.5 seconds since you've started this book. Have I lost you yet?

Just getting your attention isn't my only challenge, of course. Beyond just capturing your attention, I need to then keep your attention. Because **every** 8.5 seconds your mind is going to be looking for something new to pay attention to. Another idea. Another thought. Another input. These can even be internal distractions (and usually are). **"Hmmm. What do I think about what the author just said? Wow, I'm glad my mind isn't that out of control. He must be talking about other people."** This human attention span thing is a big problem for us because of how it reinforces our brains to keep repeating its bad habits, and how those bad brain habits affect our overall happiness.

Another 8.5 seconds has passed. Stay with me.

Look, cutting to the chase, here's the scoop on why you need to pay attention to this book: This book is going to help you supercharge your mind in a way you never knew was available, and the result of that power increase is going to change your life in a way you never knew was even possible.

I realize that's a pretty heavy claim, but after seeing the initial feedback from early readers of this book, seeing the personal success levels of people who have employed its strategies, and having been surprised by the affects that this simple little book has had on people's individual lives, it's one I feel confident in making.

Before I wrote this book, I was just a regular guy with some unique theories of how the human mind worked, and some ideas of how we might approach making the human mind operate better. After I published this book (and wrote this updated introduction), I'm still that regular guy, but now I'm a regular guy who gets invited to speak at prestigious science conferences and guest lecture at major universities on how the mind actually works, and how and why we humans do what we do in most decisions that we make in life. In addition, I was also invited into the cutting edge world of artificial emotional intelligence development, where my model of mind and emotions is being consulted to help create real world emotional reactions for artificial personalities, computer programs, and androids. Yeah… C3PO, here we come.

But while creating artificial emotions and simulated android minds are cool, it's the personal human benefits that I appreciate most from being someone who can explain the human mind to people. For example, beyond raising the happiness levels in thousands of people worldwide who have read this book, there are some who have read this book have completely conquered their lifelong substance addiction issues as a bonus. And so as a result we're now assembling an addiction management program based on this work specifically for that purpose. Still others who have read this book have reportedly conquered their Post Traumatic Stress Disorder. And so now we are working with a small group of vetrans to develop a program to specifically address the challenges of PTSD. Yet others have written to say they ended years-long engagements of going to psychological counseling, not because they got pumped up by reading this book and thought they didn't need counseling anymore, but because this book showed them the inner workings of their mind so well, that they were able to figure out the sources of their deepest unresolved issues, resolved them, then ran out of things to say at their regular therapist appointments. People have improved their romantic relationships with this book. People have forwarded their professional career success with this book, and/or attained a healthy balance between their personal and professional lives. People have simply silenced the noise of their minds and increased their overall happiness levels with this book.

That's how powerful the contents of this book can be if you dig in to what is presented here.

So why did I select the words "mind hacking" for the title of this book (and the website and our free online courses)? Well, the word hacking was popularized most recently in the world of technology, where the art of hacking is the process of understanding the fundamentals of a technical system so well that you are able to alter some variables and get a nonstandard result through what is normally a very standard process. To cut through the fluff yet again, the fact is that your mind is very hackable, and it's completely safe to do. You can't accidentally brick your mind like you can an improperly hacked computer system. It's a simple fact that if you understand your mind well enough, it's very easy to hack your mind into the nonstandard result of having it operate at a supercharged efficiency, and experiencing extreme levels of happiness without changing a single external condition of your life from what it is now.

As a heads up, this is a **different** type of book on happiness than any other happiness book you've ever read. It will also probably be the most life-changing book on happiness you've ever read. I know that's a pretty big claim to make as the author of the book, but frankly, **I have a lot of faith in you** to take the information here and use it to your advantage. I know you're smart because you read. I know you're willing to consider making changes in your life because you picked up a personal guidance book. I know if you get the right tools, there's no stopping you from achieving your goals to increase your personal happiness. I'm about to give you those very tools.

Plainly stated, this book is going to tell you how **your** happiness works. Your **personal** happiness. In general, it's the first book on happiness to reveal exactly how happiness works in the human mind. Of all the happiness book written previous to this one, not one of them has explained how happiness actually works, and no book has ever laid out for every individual reader how their personal individual happiness works. "Really," you say? "This book explains my personal happiness?" In a word, YES. Yes it does. And you'll agree with me when we're done.

Now, I know what you're thinking: "How can a book explain everyone's individual happiness for every reader who reads it? Isn't everyone an individual and aren't we all a bit different?" Yes, you are an individual, and no one in the world is quite like you. But the fact is that all human brains work basically the same way, so the stuff in this book definitely applies to you. And as we go along you'll see how your individuality makes your happiness requirements both unique and exactly the same as all other humans, simultaneously.

You don't know it yet, but you're about to become a member of a very exclusive club. It's the exclusive club of people who **truly** understand how their human minds work in a way that they can then take control of their minds and thus get the most out of their minds. Believe it or not, there aren't a lot of people in this club. Most of history's past members have been considered the world's leading thinkers and doers in their fields of science, music, art, religion, philosophy, medicine, etc. But we're about to expand that club's membership dramatically, to include you, so you can then be amazing in whatever you want to do. This club contains the happiest people in existence, with the most powerful minds in existence. In just a short while, you will be a life member, exercising a control over your mind you never thought was possible, enjoying the benefits of that internal power you never knew was available, including being able to increase your personal happiness as an act of will.

As a last quick note, while all of this sounds like new information about your mind and how it works (which it is), please know that what's presented here is also supported by the latest cognitive neuroscience and psychology (some of which is referenced in the book), and is also ironically congruent with common sense and what many of the ancient sages had to say about what it is to be human and to be happy. Sages like Aristotle, Seneca, Spinoza, Einstein, and even Jesus of Nazareth and the Prophet Muhammad. What you're about to read is current in the world of understanding our minds, understanding happiness, and understanding the crap that stands in the way of our happiness, which is one of the critical steps to increasing our happiness; removing that happiness-stealing crap in this brand new way.

Although many things about our mind have been proven in studies, science has yet to put together the big picture. This book gives you that big picture to understand your personal mind. If you command that understanding, you'll be able to do a couple of pretty amazing things. First, you'll be able to better understand the things that cause your pain and suffering (what I call in this book your "inner bullshit"), and second, you'll be able to use that new understanding to take more control of your pain and suffering, and even "turn it down" to a certain extent, thus increasing your personal and collective happiness. We need more happiness in you, and we need more happiness in the world in general. If we increase your happiness, the happiness in the world increases by default. And the more people we touch, the happier the world gets in these crazy, crazy times.

About the Author

Regarding who I am, which is a question you should always ask about the author of any nonfiction book, I'm just like you. I'm an explorer of this world who is simply looking for a way we can all live happy lives, and help others live happy lives as well. Before I fell into the science of making people happier and more effective in life, I started my career as a tech geek working complex systems at the world's leading supercomputing company. According to a biography of entrepreneur Elon Musk, my first employers "hoarded the elite geeks of Silicon Valley." I don't know if I was an elite geek, but I do have a mind that figures out complex problems very quickly, and I have solved complex problems in technology a number of times, even once figuring out some things that allowed me to speak at Kennedy Space Center in front of a room full of NASA engineers. That was cool. Setting that foundation, I see happiness as a complex problem that can be immensely simplified if you know what you're doing. That simplified explanation is exactly what I present here.

One Last Thing . . .

If you do decide to read this book, and it does help you understand your mind better, I'm gonna ask up front that you review it and share it with your friends and colleagues and on social media.

Thanks to the collapse of the traditional publishing model, I've decided not to go that route and to effectively self-publish, hiring my own editors, cover artist, and self-marketing the book. So I've elected to let the quality of the content, how well it helps people, and the reviews it gets online, determine its success. **You are my only marketing team.** Don't desert me when you're done with this book. Your recommendation to others is going to be the only way people will find out about how to take control of their minds and thus take control of their lives and make this world a better place for all of us. If this book helps you, **please do share it, review it, pass it on to your friends,** or however you'd personally like to help share happiness with others.

May this book find you happy and well. And may it make you happier and healthier after you've read it.

Section I

What You Need to Know

1. What You Need to Know

One of my favorite quotes of all time is from Ralph Waldo Emerson. It was a spring day in 1849 when he picked up his pen and wrote in his journal, "I hate quotations. Tell me what you know." I like this quote for two reasons. First, because of its irony of being a quotation that speaks of hating quotations. But second, because of its direct and to-the-point message about being direct and to the point. "Tell me what you know" implies a yearning to hear the direct no-nonsense thoughts from whoever is speaking about whatever topic is being discussed.

And so in the spirit of telling you what I know in a no-nonsense fashion, I am about to share with you some pretty amazing shit, if you'll excuse my French. In short, I am about to hand you the keys to the kingdom of your own mind. Now, I realize that may not sound as super-awesome as it actually is, but in fact, this gift may be the most important gift you will ever receive. Because being handed the keys to the kingdom of your mind means that you get to rewrite the rules to the game of life itself. And believe it or not, that's not an exaggeration.

A Personal Story

For me, this journey started with an unexpected feeling of discomfort I had on my front porch one day about twenty years ago. I was looking out over a manicured lawn that was surrounding a beautiful house I had just purchased by myself at the ripe old age of twenty-seven, and I was thinking, "This is it. I made it." Or at least I thought I had at that moment. It was a pretty overwhelming moment, actually. I'd just signed the papers the day before on my new house, which sat on a double-size corner lot in an upper-middle-class neighborhood in the suburbs of Atlanta. The neighborhood was one I'd never imagined I could ever live in, let alone purchase a house in by myself without a cosigner. This was a big deal for a guy who was brought up in poverty and on government assistance for most of his childhood, because growing up I never really knew what money was, or how it was to have any. I had always lived in small houses or apartments along with the insects and rodents that lived there with us. I always rode in old rusty cars that sometimes wouldn't start, and I almost never had anything but the crappiest food available. I hung out with the wrong crowd, roamed the streets by myself in the middle of the night, and experienced a meal inside a jail cell before I could even drive a car.

But here I was. A little over ten years from the poorest days of my life, and now I had a high-paying job, which allowed me to own a nice house filled with hand-carved imported furniture, a complete state-of-the-art home gym, and a gloss black Yamaha piano. There was a classic 1969 Firebird convertible, banana yellow, parked in one stall of the garage, and a new Limited Jeep Grand Cherokee in another. A third space held a sleek red motorcycle that could go from zero to sixty in about three seconds flat (just because I loved speed), and I had a flashy speedboat parked in the driveway behind that. A new big screen and stereo system were being delivered by truck shortly, so I was waiting on the porch for the installers, soaking the whole scene in.

In those short ten years, I had graduated in the middle of my class in high school, served an enlistment in the U.S. military, put myself through college, and stumbled into a high-paying career in the supercomputing sector. And now I was standing on the front porch of a house I owned, basking in that glory. "This is it," I thought. "I've made it." But those words in my head hadn't really even faded into echo before another thought rose up and interrupted them. The positive feeling of accomplishment being supported and fueled by the material evidence of the scene around me was now pierced by a new invading interrogative that would not be denied an audience. This new thought threw everything else aside. It was accompanied by feelings of profound emptiness and uncertainty, and even a small bit of dread. The thought by itself seemed innocent enough. "What now?" my inner voice asked, as I looked around surveying my new kingdom. Though the question sounded innocent, the thought arose in a tone that suggested this amazing scene wasn't yet complete. As if there was something missing from the equation that would deliver the feelings of satisfaction and happiness that should have come at that moment.

Searching, I looked out over the open grass next to the house. Maybe it was an attempt to answer the question that interrupted my perfect moment when I started thinking, "I could put a gazebo near the trees over there, with a path out to it. With a light and a fan and wire it into the sound system. That would be nice." But even as I thought about the new idea, I knew the emptiness which accompanied that new thought wasn't looking for a gazebo as an answer. That new thought, which was now drowning out all others, came from somewhere deeper within me. And it was looking for something much more meaningful than a new sports car, season tickets, or another trip to Vegas could provide.

It was at that moment that something within me clicked. This hadn't been the first time something clicked in my mind that would then change the direction of my life. The first time was when I was lying soaked and shivering uncontrollably on the edge of a riverbank late at night in northern Indiana in the freezing rain, looking out over the river that had almost taken my life moments before. My car, which got me to that scene, was now lying at the bottom of that river, where I would have also been if it had not been for a television episode I once saw as a kid. I'll tell that story a little later so we don't lose track of this one, but what I experienced on that porch that day was as profound as almost dying, and certainly equally as important, as you will soon understand.

The thing that clicked as I waited for the delivery truck carrying my stereo system was a realization about happiness. Because at that moment I realized that I had attained all the things I was told I was supposed to attain to be happy, but there it was; that empty feeling and that "what now?" question taunting me like my best efforts to attain happiness hadn't been good enough. "Holy shit," I thought. "I have everything I ever wanted, and I'm still not happy." But how could that be? I had crawled up from poverty out of a horrible childhood without any help, to educate myself, apply myself, and work hard at every job I filled, including when I was slinging pizzas and waiting tables. I worked hard to make friends, learned how to have great romantic relationships, and I developed what I thought was a meaningful relationship with God. I was living the American Dream. There was no part of my life that wasn't filled with a good answer.

But there it was. The empty feeling told me in no uncertain terms all these things around me would not be delivering the happiness I was looking for, and the "what now" question was evidence that I had no idea what I was looking for beyond what I had already attained. So I had spent ten years working, studying, starving, striving, and constantly jumping out of my comfort zone, only to learn that all my financial, professional, and personal success had been in vain in delivering happiness. Something was missing.

And so that day I started again at square one on my quest for happiness. I took a step back, and said to myself, "Self, you're gonna get to the bottom of this happiness thing so you can quit wasting so much time. You're motivated, you have a mind for simplifying complexities, and heck, you spoke at NASA once, right? So this happiness thing should be a cinch." Or so I thought.

It wasn't easy. And it didn't come quickly. That said, twenty years later . . . after reading a ton of books on happiness (some good and some not so good) . . . after exploring numerous ancient wisdom practices where I discovered what I consider to be the-holy-shit-of-all-discoveries . . . after researching the very latest in emotions science, emotions neuroscience, consciousness science, and even quantum physics (going as far as to have had multiple beers with a man who was nominated for the Nobel Prize for proving quantum entanglement) . . . after doing some deep research into my own mind and finding something about mind that all the experts had missed . . . and after reducing two decades of work into a simple system to increase happiness, which I then shared with others whose lives changed toward awesomeness . . . after all that, I think I can finally say I've figured out happiness.

Personally speaking, I can report that I'm completely happy, and I even have an fMRI brain scan to prove it. But beyond figuring out just my personal happiness, something else happened along the way that helped make mastering happiness a slam dunk for absolutely everyone reading this book. Because while trying to figure out how happiness worked so I could selfishly experience more of it, I actually stumbled into a deeper understanding of how the human mind itself works. This not only granted me access to an unlimited supply of on-demand happiness, it took me to the place well beyond happiness, and showed me how the whole happiness process works within the human mind in general. And I think using this knowledge can take you to that place well beyond happiness also. Not only that, but I think it can quell your overall pain and suffering, and unlock the hidden power of your mind that you had no idea was even waiting to be discovered.

That's why I intend to share with you the keys to the kingdom of your mind. Because when you accept those keys, you will certainly have the freedom to increase your happiness levels if you wish. But having those keys will do a bunch of other cool stuff for you also.

The Power of Our Minds

We don't think about it very often, but it's our mind that creates our whole life. You could say our mind **is** our life, or at the very least it is how we experience every single moment of our life, and it is what we use to make the decisions about where our life takes us. If you want to get technical, there is absolutely nothing in life that we could ever experience or do without the assistance of our mind. When we look at a sunset, our mind is where we see it. When we listen to an amazing piece of music, our mind is where we hear it. When we stop to smell the flowers, or taste a good meal, or stand in wonder of how amazing the water feels on our back as we take a hot shower on a cold winter's day, it is in our mind where all that magic happens. And that's only where the magic of our mind starts. Our mind is where every one of our thoughts is generated. Every one of our opinions. Every one of our perceptions about how we see the world and all that happens in the world. Every time we cash a paycheck, it's because of our mind. Every time we vote in an election. Every time we give a hug. Every time we pray to God. And that's just stuff connected with our waking consciousness.

When we dip below the surface of our waking mind, that is where we find the real power that determines how good our life actually is. It's our subconscious mind where every one of our emotions is formed. Happiness. Sadness. Anger. Fear. Disgust. All emotions spring forth from our subconscious mind, and it's our subconscious mind that determines how often we feel those emotions. It's our subconscious mind that also creates the undercurrents of influence that fuel our inner voice to either support us, or tear us down and criticize us. It's our subconscious mind that controls how healthy our bodies are to a large degree, and how much stress we feel about life, which also by the way, directly impacts our health. Believe it or not, our subconscious mind even helps determine how old we are when we die. We will look at that published science shortly.

And so when we're talking about handing you the keys to the kingdom of your mind, what we are talking about isn't just some weak sauce of tips and tricks you can try to employ in an attempt to marginally change your life for the better. These mind keys aren't the keys to some positive thinking or law of attraction crap you may have heard about previously, where you try to think a certain way in contradiction of your subconscious mind in hopes that life will magically give you everything you want by simply thinking about it. No, that stuff is bullshit, and we'll present the proven science of why it's bullshit later in the book.

When we're talking about giving you the keys to the kingdom of your mind, we're talking about the keys to getting in deep. We're talking about the keys that can allow you to get into the control room of your mind, where the real power of your mind resides. We're talking about the keys that can turn up your intelligence, turn up your health, and open the door to the very room where your internal happiness is stored. Have you ever noticed that your mind Scrooges on happiness, hoarding like it's something you need to earn after you've aligned all the stars in the universe, so that your mind can then trickle out some happiness to you from under the door? Here you go. Here's a little happiness for you. Now go run some more errands for me, and I'll give you some more happiness. Excuse my French, but **fuck earning happiness from your own mind!** That happiness is yours, and you can open the happiness door and stroll right in if you have the keys.

If you've always thought your mind is simply out of control and there's nothing you can do about it, and you believe that you just need to deal with whatever your mind gives you at any particular moment, I'm here to tell you that's bullshit. If you think you can't get your mind under control, and indeed get your emotions under control, there's a lot you need to know about your mind. Getting the keys to your mind is a game changer. They give you access to the most ancient secrets of mind, where you can take control of your thoughts and emotions, and reshape your entire life.

How many times in our lives have we heard someone say this? You can do anything if you put your mind to it. Have you ever wondered if that statement was just an overblown cliché? I think I remember hearing my mom say it when I was in preschool. I certainly heard it again a few times in elementary school from the teachers, and maybe a couple times in high school. I used to think the idea was just something we tell our kids even though most of us don't really believe it. But it turns out the statement is completely true. We **can** do anything we put our minds to. The only thing that makes us doubt the idea is because no one has ever taught us how to develop control over our minds, so as to put the full power of our minds into gear. That's the rub with the "you can do anything if you put your mind to it" idea. It's the "and here's exactly how you do that" part that's missing.

Without even knowing you personally, dear reader, I know absolutely no one has ever explained your mind to you in a way that allows you full control over it. I think it sucks that no one ever handed you an owner's manual for your mind so that you could use it to its full potential. Your mind happens to be one of the most powerful tools in the universe, especially when it comes to the task of creating an amazing life for yourself. You should have a manual for it. You should know how it works under the hood so you can use that knowledge to do things that you may have thought were impossible until now.

Cutting the Bullshit, Big and Small

As a simple example of something that sounds impossible but isn't, how important and awesome would it be for you to be able to get into your mind, grab a control dial, and turn down the intensity and frequency of your life's bullshit?

Wait. You know what your life's bullshit is, right? It's that stuff that makes your life less awesome than it could be if the bullshit didn't exist, and it's the stuff that blocks your happiness and joy from flourishing every moment of your life, except . . . the bullshit. On a grand scale, your life's bullshit can be defined as absolutely anything that bugs you . . . about absolutely anything... **ever**.

So your life's bullshit includes the small stuff, like when you get upset when someone cuts you off in traffic. Or when someone you're talking to says something that rubs you the wrong way. Or when you see something on the news or online that makes you sad or fearful or angry. Your life's bullshit is when you look in the rearview mirror to see the asshole behind you driving so close you can see his nose hairs. It's when your significant other forgot [whatever it was] . . . for the third friggin' time. It's when all you want to do is to call and speak to a human being, but all you get is an automated voice asking you to repeat what you just said because the computer behind that automated voice didn't understand you. Again: "Customer service representative!"

But more than just the trivial stuff, your life's bullshit also includes the big stuff. Like when your romantic relationship isn't going well, or it's ending, or when it bugs you deep down that you don't even have a romantic relationship at the moment. Your bullshit is the fallout when you lose someone you love from your life. Your bullshit is when you're worried about losing your job, or you're worried because you're not making enough money to pay the bills or save for retirement. Your bullshit is worrying about your health to the point that the worry itself makes you sick when you would be perfectly healthy otherwise. Your bullshit is when you look in the mirror and hear that critical voice in your head that tells you you're not good enough, not smart enough, not pretty enough, not talented enough, not thin enough, not rich enough, not sexy enough, or not deserving enough to be able to live a happy life. Your bullshit is when that voice second-guesses your decisions. "I should have done [this]." "I should have said [that]." "I wish I could act differently in [this way]." "I can't believe I ate two pieces of cheesecake. I'll be wearing that tomorrow. I'm such a dumbass."

Basically stated, your bullshit is when you look out upon the world and think [whatever it is] should be different.

So your life's bullshit is anything that distracts you from being happy absolutely all the time. If we need a gauge on how much bullshit we humans generate, the list of words we use to describe negative feelings and emotions is almost twice as long as the list of words we use to describe positive feelings and emotions. Science calls that our negative bias. So it seems we're a big bullshit generating crowd, and we might appreciate a big left crank on that bullshit knob.

But alas, everyone has some life's bullshit, right? There's no getting rid of it. There's no turning it down. Well, at least that is what we are told. Because that's just the human experience, right? That's just the way life is, and we just have to accept it. It's all just ups and downs. Right?

Well, I suppose that's true for someone who doesn't hold the keys to their mind, but that's not your future.

That "we just have to live with it" crap is one of the biggest lies ever perpetuated on the human race by the human race. Because having life be a number of good moments interrupted by the regular delivery of a dump truck of mental bullshit about whatever just happened (or about what happened years ago but we're still carrying it around unresolved) doesn't have to be the case. And life can actually be awesome all the time. Because, although I don't relish playing the role of Captain Obvious, along with all the awesome stuff your mind does with sunsets, and hot showers, and hugs, the simple fact is that it's your mind that also creates 100 percent of the bullshit you have ever and will ever experience in your life.

"No, wait," you say. "My mind reacts to the bullshit. It doesn't actually create it. Other people create it. I just have to deal with it."

And Captain Obvious's reply to your reaction is, "No. You are wrong, sir or madam. Flat out."

You Create Your Own Bullshit

Other people and world events don't create your bullshit. You create 100 percent of your own bullshit based on your mind's reactions to world events and what other people do or say. And when we look at our bullshit moments on slow motion replay, there's really no denying that. The simple fact is that the last stop between something happening in the world and your reaction to it is always your mind. And it's your mind in particular that adds the negative reaction to any given scenario you experience. The last stop between someone doing something that bugs you and you getting bugged about it **is your mind**. The last stop between someone doing something that might anger you and you getting angry about it **is your mind**. The last stop between something happening that might scare you and you reacting in fear **is your mind**. The last stop between something happening that can make you sad and you getting sad about it **is your mind**. It's a really weird thing to think about, but it's true.

Let's take a breath here. Because this is a huge concept that will change your entire life if you let it sink in before taking the next logical step in the progression. What needs to sink in is both scary and amazingly empowering at the same time. The scary part is the huge responsibility I've just handed you by pointing out the fact that no one in the world can make you angry except you. No one in the world can make you sad except you. No one in the world can make you afraid of anything except you. Every negative thought, every negative emotion, and every negative reaction that has ever passed through your mind didn't simply pass through your mind, it was created by your mind.

Taking Control of Your Mind

The great news encapsulated in all this is that when you take full control of your mind for the first time in your life, all of those same scary statements become amazingly powerful and scientifically valid affirmations. Because after the point at which you take full control of your mind, that no one in the world can make you angry **without your permission**. No one in the world can make you sad without your permission. No one in the world can make you afraid of **anything** without your permission. In fact, all the negative, destructive, and detrimental stuff that your mind generates at home, at work, out shopping, or wherever, can indeed be turned down at will if you know how. It's **your** mind. You can take control of it if you choose to, and train it to give you responses that are empowering and useful rather than reactions that are upsetting and a waste of your life. You have the choice to turn down that inner critical voice that saps your confidence. You have the power to cease the reactionary thoughts and actions that cause you heartache and complicate your life with additional challenges you need not be forced to deal with. There is a way to get into the control room of your mind and turn that crap down, if not turn it off altogether. And when you do, you will realize some amazing and immediate life benefits.

For instance, did you know when your mind reacts negatively to something, the first thing your brain does is turn off ten to twenty IQ points as a result? This is a physiological function of your brain designed to help you survive threatening situations by turning off less critical systems and shunting energy to your survival systems. After all, if we encounter a deadly snake, we don't need to think too deeply to figure out how to run away. So when we experience negative emotions like anger, fear, or even just high stress, our brain turns off the prefrontal cortex, otherwise known as our thinking brain. But in today's more complex and developed world, that physiological reaction has a life-shortening effect rather than a life preserving one. Unlike 150 years ago, many of today's challenges require us to use our thinking brain to calculate the quickest and best resolution to those challenges.

The longer we don't resolve our challenges, the longer they create stress for us, creating a snowball effect that keeps our thinking brain out of the loop, keeping us stressed out. And if you didn't already know, stress is a killer. It's estimated that over 75 percent of hospital visits are caused by stress related issues. That means up to 75 percent of hospital visits are caused by reaction of the mind. The mind creates stress. Stress sends you to the hospital. There you go. Stress steals years off our lives, increases inflammation in our bodies, which leads to things like high blood pressure, heart disease, and cancer. In addition, stress creates cortisol in our bodies, which kills our brain cells and synaptic connections slowly over time, contributing to cognitive decline and leading to ailments like dementia and Alzheimer's. Numerous studies have shown our mind's creation of our internal emotional landscape influences our respiratory, immune, cardiovascular, gastrointestinal, and endocrine systems. So how your mind works, and getting it to work better, is imperative. There's no doubt you need to take control of your mind which controls all these critical influencers.

The implications of you accepting the keys to your mind are invaluable. In the short term, you'll be able to turn your inner bullshit down, you'll reduce your stress levels which will improve your health, and you'll learn the most effective method of taking back control of your mind during the times that you've accidentally lost control of it. Some published science out of UCLA will help us with that one. As a result, you will learn how to get those 10 to 20 IQ points back in those critical times when you need them the most. Over the long term, you will learn how to take complete control of your mind, and thus complete control of your life. And at that point, you'll be all Zen. You'll be all badass Jedi like Samuel Jackson. No one will throw off your mojo. Ever.

The Next Logical Step

If we can let all that sink in for a moment, we're ready to take the logical next step. That logical next step is to lay out the tools you will need to get your mind under control for the first time in your life. The process flows like this: First, we introduce you to the control room of your mind. The control room is a small but infinite space within your mind where you can observe and take control of the rest of your mind. After showing you that control room, we then explain to you how the rest of the mind works as you actually watch your mind operating from that control room. It is here that you will learn exactly how your subconscious mind works, including specifically how your emotions work, and where the subconscious motivation comes from that prompts your inner voice to be constantly active.

From there, we will discuss some of the invisible control knobs and levers that are available for you to manipulate and control your mind on a macro level. While discussing the control mechanisms, we'll learn some tips and tricks of neuroscience to use the body's own hard-wired brain physiology to your advantage. Thanks to the latest discoveries in neuroscience, there are some cool brain-wiring hacks that will become useful, such as getting the right ventrolateral prefrontal cortex (RVLPFC) speaking to the medial prefrontal cortex (mPFC) to down regulate your amygdalae. This is a really fancy way of saying there's a mind hack that will physically turn down some of your life's bullshit in real time at any moment you wish. (And don't worry, we will simplify the details of the mind manipulations into easy-to-understand concepts without specifying the brain regions from this point forward. This is the last time you will hear the words right ventrolateral prefrontal cortex. Just know there's a bunch of cool science we'll touch on.)

Finally, after getting you the tools to increase the quality of your day to day life, we'll slip into the calm space called open awareness, where we expand and fine tune your control of your mind. It is here that many, **many** rooms within your mind, which you didn't even know existed will be opened to you. It is here that your stress levels will be reduced, your processing of basic and complex emotions will be more conscious and effortless, and a joy of having a higher level of control over your entire existence will wash over you. If you are like many study participants, you may experience increases in IQ, creativity levels, focus, verbal and spatial intelligence, short term and long term memory, and increased overall feelings of well-being. And as awesome as all **that** sounds, the coolest part of this process is what happens next.

What happens next is something called neuroplasticity. Neuroscience, aka the science of the brain, is only a few decades old. But while this brand-new science is still in its nascency, one of the coolest things that neuroscience has discovered is this process called neuroplasticity. Let me explain neuroplasticity in terms we can all agree with moving forward. The scientific community used to be believe that the brain was static. We knew that our brains grew from nothing to fully formed while we grew into adulthood, but after we were adults, it was assumed that our brain never changed, that new brain cells were never born, and whatever brain we wound up with was the brain that we were basically stuck with for the rest of our lives. Here's hoping that you get a good one. It's your turn to roll the dice. Come on, seven! But all that science turned out to be a pile of bad assumptions.

In truth, science recently discovered that our brains act just like our muscles do, in that they can change over time depending on how we use them. With our muscles, we know that if we work them more, they get stronger and bigger in the specific areas that did the work. And we know if we work our muscles less over time, they atrophy, getting weaker and less efficient as time goes on. Well, it turns out the brain works exactly the same way. After hundreds of studies done all over the world, we now know the brain can and does change in both form and function depending on how we use it, including how we specifically use our brain via that cool interface called mind.

It's proven empirical science to say we can literally change the structure of gray matter in our heads by thinking differently. In fact, Dr. Richard Davidson, who is one of the world's most respected cognitive neuroscientists, and who helped create the entire field of what is now being called Contemplative Neuroscience, and who is the founder and chair of the Center for Investigating Healthy Minds at the University of Wisconsin—Madison, gave a Google Tech Talk in 2009 where he stated plainly, "The brain is the organ that is built to change based on our experience, more than any other organ in our body." He then followed that statement with this one: "It is clear that the intentional deployment of specific mental training strategies can induce plastic changes in the brain **which endure and can transform cognitive and emotional styles**." And if that wasn't definitive enough, about 2 minutes later Dr. Davidson dropped this bomb: "It turns out that there is no more effective way to produce localized and specific changes in the brain than behavioral or mental interventions." Otherwise stated in conversational English, science has proven that the way we decide to use our mind has the capacity to change our brain in the most targeted way available. There is no more effective way to change the brain than by **changing it willfully**.

Dr. Davidson then clarified that behavioral or mental interventions can produce more specific biological changes in the brain than any other currently known intervention, including being more effective than any pharmaceutical drug, or any other FDA approved medical therapy. He said all this in a talk titled, "Transform Your Mind, Change Your Brain." You can find it on YouTube. We may touch on some of Dr. Davidson's work in later chapters, but for now this scientific position supports that when we use our mind to turn our BS down and turn our happiness up more and more often, the brain can actually start to change so as to help us repeat that process automatically with less and less effort. Thus, over time, just as our brain helps us get better at playing the piano with practice, or get better at crossword puzzles with practice, or get better at basketball with practice, our life can be lived more happily with much less effort the longer we practice happiness. After a while our life becomes happy at a subconscious level, which then creates happiness in our waking consciousness most, if not all, the time.

My dear friend Meng Tan calls this "raising our happiness set point." Meng is Google's "Jolly Good Fellow" turned mindfulness teacher, famous for creating Google's wildly successful internal mindfulness program Search Inside Yourself. Meng discusses raising our happiness set point at length in one of his most recent books, titled Joy on Demand. It's a good book. You should probably read it. You may want to keep a notepad handy for a few reading or viewing recommendations as we move along. There will be several.

Although it sounds incredible, dramatically increased happiness levels through mind development are exactly what people are finding after employing this new mind hacking method I'm outlining for you here. People can't help but experience drastic improvements in their life when they hack their mind, because unlike every other approach available, we are using the brain's existing wiring to our benefit. And when the change occurs, it can be a night and day difference. Just one real world example from hundreds is a lady who came to see me named Katherine.

A Real Life Transformation

Katherine is a retired executive who came to me after watching a video I produced about a small portion of one of the following chapters. We sat together one afternoon for about five hours without a single break. It was intense. But at the end of that five hours, she had most of what you and I will discuss over the next number of chapters. The reason Katherine felt so compelled to come see me was because she was struggling with a number of issues that were sucking the happiness out of her life. A couple of the largest issues were connected with her family relationships. She and her immediate family were not getting along, which caused her not to be able to see her grandchildren very often even though they lived just a few blocks away, and she had been plagued by a pattern of negative thoughts in her mind about . . . well, it sounded like just about everything. She was not a happy person. She didn't like this or that about some decisions her children made about her grandchildren. She was upset about her neighbors on one side. Her unruly dog was even pissing her off during their regular walks. In summation . . . and I can only say this because this isn't the case anymore . . . her mind was a mess, and it was ruining her life.

After we spoke that one afternoon, I didn't hear anything from Katherine for about two weeks. But then she sent an e-mail and asked if we could talk on the phone. "It clicked!" she told me. "I had taken the dog on a walk down to the police station to ask a quick question, and as I was focusing on whatever I was upset about, the dog suddenly lunged at one of the officers and started barking and pulling. This put the officer on his heels a bit while I was trying to control the dog . . . and that's when it all just stopped. I saw it all in slow motion. I saw what was going on with the dog, I saw what was going on in the police officer's mind in reacting to the dog, and I saw my negative reaction to the whole ugly scene in real time as my reaction was happening in my mind." She broke down the details for me, which were accurate from my best assessment not having been there. It seemed she certainly understood the workings of her own mind at that point. And then she said this: "Nothing has been the same since that moment." I asked her what she meant by that. She replied, "I see it. I see my mind, and what was causing all my anger. And nothing has bothered me since." You could hear it in her voice over the phone that she was a changed woman. But did that change last over time?

Fast forward two years later. Katherine's life has been completely transformed. Her mindset has totally changed. The issues she'd previously experienced with her immediate family are gone. She now gets to see her grandkids multiple times a week, and it's a pleasure for the family when grandma is around. Her neighbors no longer annoy her. Her thoughts no longer have a negative spin. Her Facebook posts are filled with nothing but love and inspiration, and she's regularly posting links to cool stuff associated with the positive side of life. To top it all off, she now spends every Saturday morning at the local farmer's market, rain or shine, with a FREE HUGS sign handing out warm embraces to anyone who wants one. I shit you not. She's so happy it annoys people. So the change seems both dramatic and permanent. It's been over two years since her metamorphosis. And counting.

This is just one story of dozens of amazing transformations that have occurred when people learned how to see their mind operating in real time and take control of it. And it's one of hundreds of stories that also tell of milder general improvements in people's lives about increases in their levels of overall happiness using these same methods. Even before sending this book off to the editor, I received a text message from someone to whom I'd sent some early chapters. This is quoted from my iPhone. "Because of what I learned from you Sean, I have just signed a lease on opening my first business without a shred of fear. My mindset has transformed and I truly attribute your nudge for pushing me over the edge." I replied to him with additional advice that what he learns from this book will help him recover faster from potential business setbacks, and give him the tools to more effectively interact with his future team members and customers. He then replied back, "The recovery time is the biggest thing I've really noticed a change in. Things that used to eat at me are now just fading thoughts. I wouldn't be in this position without that ability. I feel like I have an advantage in every interaction. You did an amazing job in illustrating that lesson for me."

As diverse as these two real life examples are, don't worry. You don't have to be someone who winds up holding a FREE HUGS sign at your local farmer's market, and you don't have to open your own business. You can choose to use this new science exactly the way you wish. From newbie to master, you can take what you learn here to control your mind and improve your happiness game as much or as little as you want. Katherine took it to free hugs at the farmer's market. Where will you take it? Will you turn your fear knob down and finally create that successful business you always wanted to start? Or do you like your job and just want to have a better personal life? Will you grab your pessimism lever and slide it to off? Or will you just turn your anger down a little bit and reduce your blood pressure while you're at it? With this stuff, you can choose to use it to simply enjoy life more and be happier without changing anything else. But I'm interested. Please stop by MindHackingHappiness.com after you've read this book and let us know how you're using it. Your story might just help others.

Happiness Is in the Mind

It is an undeniable truth that happiness is found nowhere other than the mind. And no external circumstances need exist for that happiness to flourish. It is a choice of how you use your mind once you understand how your mind actually works. Knowing how your mind works is the most important piece of information you will ever receive, because it is within your mind that the secrets of how to live a completely happy life are hidden. It doesn't matter what your life's circumstances are if you are someone who knows how to not let your life's circumstances ruin your day. And when you develop your mind to that point, you will understand why all the empirical science on happiness shows conclusively that life's external conditions don't affect our happiness meter much at all.

Science has shown in hundreds of studies that things like success in business and accumulation of wealth do not provide happiness. In fact it's the opposite that's true. It's actually happiness that provides for things like success in business and accumulation of wealth. Similarly, having happy, healthy, well behaved kids doesn't provide happiness. Happiness provides for happy, healthy, and well behaved kids. Great romantic relationships don't provide happiness. Happiness provides the building blocks for great romantic relationships. It turns out we've had this happiness thing backwards all along. Happiness needs to come first. And I'm going to show you how to create it.

We are about to open up the deepest secrets of the mind for you so that you can hack into your mind and increase your happiness levels across the board. Happiness expert Thich Nhat Hanh, a Vietnamese Buddhist monk who attracts audiences from all over the world, puts it this way: "There is no way to happiness. Happiness is the way." By the time you finish this book, you will not only understand exactly why that is true, but also how exactly you can make happiness your way.

So let's get this party started. In the next chapter we will briefly discuss the control room of the mind, and then move into the very important concept of self. (That chapter is all about you, by the way.) After self, we'll show you, for the first time in history, exactly how and why all your emotions come to be, which will grant us a look under the hood at your subconscious mind and how that works. Then in Section II, we will discuss how to push some buttons, turn some dials, and yank on some levers to start using your brain's existing physiology to get your mind working the way you want it to. That right there will be enough for you to dramatically change your life for the better. Are you ready for my TV infomercial voice? But wait, there's more!

After we get you the tools you need to take charge of your mind and make your life awesome, if you continue to Volume II, we'll take a left turn and dive into the deepest secrets of mind. The good stuff. The ancient stuff. The stuff the world has been trying to figure out throughout all of written history. It is there (and I never thought I would have an opportunity to say these words the moment I saw Lawrence Fishburne perfectly deliver them in the movie The Matrix, but here we are) . . . it's there that I show you how deep the rabbit hole goes. That's where I will explain to you some mind secrets of the ancient wisdom traditions, including the very path to to the fabled Nirvana, which is the mind state where an uninterrupted bliss can occur. No shit. I'm not even kidding. More on that later.

For the moment, let's just take a huge step toward you learning how to control the most powerful tool in the universe. Our next stop is the control room of your mind.

Chapter 1 Takeaways

1. Happiness comes from within our minds and no other place.

2. All the stuff that blocks our happiness comes from within our minds also.

3. It is possible to take control of our minds and change the mix of happiness and non-happiness that's created.

4. This change in the mix can become permanent over time, thanks to neuroplasticity.

5. Science supports all four of the above takeaways.

Chapter 1 Reflection

1. Have you ever contemplated how happiness is sourced from your own mind?

2. Have you ever contemplated that the things that block your happiness come from within your own mind also?

2. The Control Room of Your Mind

Rule your mind, or it will rule you.

—Horace

In Chapter 1, we pointed out the really obvious fact that both our happiness and the crap that blocks our happiness comes from within the confines of our own minds. So without a doubt, controlling our minds is the single most important thing we can learn in the course of a human lifetime. The good news is that controlling our minds is easy when we familiarize ourselves with the control room of our mind. Of course, there isn't a real room in your mind with walls, a ceiling, and a door. There's no actual sign. It's more of a virtual space than a room, but it's there, and this virtual space is called meta-awareness.

Meta-Awareness

Don't let the fancy term scare you. You already use meta-awareness daily even if you didn't call it meta-awareness. In fact, the last time you caught yourself in a daydream and refocused your attention to something else, you were in the control room of your mind called meta-awareness. Meta-awareness is simply the ability to take notice of what your mind is doing at any given moment. It's an awareness of your awareness. The Greek word meta means "beyond," so meta-awareness literally translates to "beyond awareness." It's an awareness that is a step beyond. It's not just paying attention to something. It's paying attention to what we're paying attention to, turning our mind back onto itself, looking to see what our mind itself is doing. It's in the control room of meta-awareness that we can take charge of our minds and change what our minds are doing. Let's look at an example.

Let's imagine we're standing in a kitchen together looking at a bowl of ripe red apples. You see the apples. You see the color of the apples. You see their texture. You see the way the apples are stacked so they don't fall out of the bowl. You may even have a thought that you'd like to grab an apple as a healthy snack. From there, another thought might come. "Should I ask Sean if he wants an apple? Would it be rude just to reach down and grab an apple as he's talking?" All this stuff happens in your awareness. You're simply watching the play on the stage of your mind, following whatever thoughts come. In general, your awareness can be consumed by objects, people, sensations, thoughts, feelings, emotions, memories . . . whatever it is that engages the mind in activity. But when you turn your awareness back onto the mind itself, that's meta-awareness. It's the moment you realize you're thinking about the apples, and not about what I'm saying. And in that moment you've noticed you're attention is off track, you've entered your mind's control room. Now you have the freedom to refocus your attention. And now you can take control and keep your attention focused. That's exercising power over the mind, and it's why I call meta-awareness the control room of the mind.

A Quick Mind Exercise

The control room of your mind is made possible because of how your mind works under the covers. We'll get into greater detail of how it works later in the book, but the most basic characteristic of your mind, which is what allows the control room of our mind to exist, can be exhibited by doing a quick mind exercise, with two parts. I'd like to invite you to do this exercise right now. Do this as long as you're not driving somewhere or doing something else that requires your attention. Ready? Here's Step 1: Picture an elephant in your mind. It could be a real elephant, a cartoon elephant, a child's drawing of an elephant. It doesn't matter. Okay, now change the elephant you see from whatever color it currently is in your mind to make that same elephant pink with purple polka dots on it. Can you see it? Can you see your pink elephant with purple polka dots on it? Great! That's all we need for Step 1 of this exercise. Thanks.

Step 2 is to now take a look at what just happened in your mind. Let's do that together.

So what just happened there in your mind? More specifically, who in your mind provided you that image of the elephant you saw? Wait, what? Why did I just ask who just provided that image? Wasn't it you who created the image of that elephant? And wasn't it you who then turned that elephant pink with purple polka dots? Well, we like to leap to the conclusion we did all that magic because that answer doesn't require any more thinking about it. We just tell ourselves, we did that. We created that image of the elephant, and then we turned that elephant pink and put some purple polka dots on it. But the reality of that process is a little more complex than that. The more accurate assessment of that process was that you heard the words "picture an elephant in your mind," and then poof, a moment later, an image of an elephant magically appeared. But the fact is that we, in our top level of consciousness, didn't actually make that elephant image appear. That elephant kinda just appeared on it's own. Like magic. But it wasn't magic. It was the science of multiple levels of consciousness within our minds.

As a warning, you're about to learn the weirdest truth that exists about your mind right here up front in Chapter 2. So don't freak out. This truth actually explains a lot of stuff that perplexes us about being human. Just strap yourself in for a moment.

The Levels of Consciousness

Okay, so, here's the weirdest thing you'll ever learn about your mind. That weird thing is that we have multiple levels of intelligent consciousness cohabiting within our minds. Our top level of consciousness, which is the consciousness we most often consider as us, is our waking awareness. It's the consciousness you are experiencing right now as you hear these words, and as you experience the ideas your mind is creating in response to them. It's the consciousness from which you are seeing the images of your immediate environment, hearing the sounds of the noises around you, feeling the sensations you feel from your skin and other sense input streams, and even experiencing and directing the thoughts passing through your mind at this very moment. That is your waking consciousness. That's your experience of **you**.

But that waking awareness is not the only level of consciousness that exists in our brains. There are other levels of consciousness that exist below our top-level consciousness. For instance, when the idea "picture an elephant in your mind" entered your awareness, if you were playing along, your intention then asked for an image of an elephant to be imagined, or brought up from memory somewhere. It wasn't your top level consciousness that actually performed that action however. That was performed at a lower level of consciousness just below your waking consciousness, which psychology calls part of our subconscious. You simply asked for the image of the elephant to appear. After that moment, a different level of consciousness in your head actually performed the task of retrieving the image of that elephant from memory, or imagination, or wherever it came from, which then magically, and probably immediately, appeared in your mind.

Then what happened next? I asked you to paint that elephant pink with purple polka dots. More accurately stated, I asked you to envision something that doesn't exist in our real world, which you couldn't possibly pull from memory. And what happened? Did you physically paint the elephant pink with purple polka dots with a paintbrush, or did it magically happen in your mind again? Again, that's not magic, it's the science of other levels of consciousness in your mind working to provide you exactly what it was you were asking for at that particular moment in time.

The Workings of Consciousness

When we asked our minds to paint our elephant pink with purple polka dots, multiple levels of consciousness in our mind then went to work to deliver that second request. First, someone a few levels down needed to pull from sense memory what pink looks like, someone else needed to recall what purple polka dots are, and how those might look together if they were to be placed on the image of our elephant, and then all those pieces got forwarded to the consciousness level right below our regular waking consciousness, which ultimately assembled all the information together to create our never before seen pink elephant with purple polka dots. And we, from our top level waking consciousness, simply saw that new image in our minds. But our top level waking consciousness didn't actually do the work. The other consciousness levels in our brains did.

So the freaky thing we're talking about that any psychological sciences professor will tell you is old news is that there is more than one decision maker inside your head besides you. But don't worry. You're in charge of everyone, or at least you will be soon.

Before you go off denying there's more than one thinker in your head besides you, science has proven that we all have multiple levels of consciousness at work constantly. One easy example of this phenomena in action is in the study of split brain patients. Some people who are afflicted with certain types of seizure disorders sometimes need to be treated by cutting all the connecting tissue between the right half and the left half of their brains to stop the seizures. And most of the time, this treatment works, but it has some side effects and creates what is called a split brain patient. In short, it leaves the individual with two perfectly working halves of their brain which can no longer talk to each other. In experiments on consciousness with these particular patients, when they are asked to write out an answer to any particular question, such as "what would you like to do as an occupation," one hand which is controlled by Brain Half 1 will write out "doctor," while the other hand controlled by Brain Half 2 will simultaneously write out "race car driver." One brain provides two different answers to the same question from two equal but separate halves of that brain. Similarly, other consciousness experiments show when those same people are shown an object with one eye covered up, so that only one half of the brain knows what was seen, when both sides of the brain are asked what was shown by asking both ears, only one half of the brain can answer questions about the object while the other half can be measured under brain scanners to be completely confused by the question. That type of brain behavior is the brain exhibiting two completely independent consciousnesses trying to give two completely independent responses. One consciousness saw the object. The other consciousness simply responds, "What object? I didn't see anything." So multiple levels of consciousness in our one brain do operate simultaneously, which then come together to contribute to what we experience as our single waking consciousness. It's only because we perceive the one at the very top level that we can be tricked into thinking there's just one consciousness in there.

Nope. There's more than one, and you can actually control more than one level of consciousness when you develop a deeper control of your mind. More on that later.

So why did we need to dive into a discussion about multiple consciousness levels in our minds right off the bat? First, it's going to help explain a lot of stuff later in this book, and especially in Volume II. But most importantly, going back to the topic of this chapter, in its most basic description, the control room of our minds called meta-awareness is simply another level of consciousness that's available to us any time we wish to use it. But instead of being a level down into the mind, it's actually a level up above the mind where we can see more of the mind and what it's doing.

The key to taking better control of your mind, and thus better control of your life and happiness, lies in your ability to enter the control room of your mind at will. It lies in your ability to enter meta-awareness at will so you can observe what your mind is doing and change what it's doing if it's not doing something that serves you. You accomplish this by intentionally raising your awareness out of the noisy business of your mind into a higher level of consciousness looking down into the mind. The words **higher consciousness** are not a hippy bullshit term anymore. They are a scientific term connected with the multiple levels of consciousness that have been identified in the human mind. You just need to learn how to slip into these higher levels of consciousness at will, rather than by accident, so as to start using them to control your mind more often.

Why Else This Is Important

All that said, there are also other important reasons we need to know about our multiple levels of consciousness. First, knowing what we mean when we say the word **mind** gives us a much better chance of success when we actually go to control our minds. We need to know what is going on under that umbrella term subconscious if we want to shut down the subconscious crap that steals our happiness. Second, knowing there are multiple levels of subconsciousness awaiting our commands gives us an idea of how much hidden horsepower is available to us that we haven't been using. Our elephant exercise proves there are multiple levels of consciousness ready and willing to assist us with whatever we want to do. And beyond just painting imaginary elephants, our subconscious minds are powerful. As we'll soon learn, our subconscious minds control many of our actions and behaviors, and even the physical health of our bodies to a large extent. Why would you not want control of **that**? Third, in seeing that our multiple levels of consciousness do indeed work to serve our needs, we are reminded that our minds work for us. We don't work for them. This is a hugely empowering realization that you no longer need be a victim to whatever bullshit negativity your mind creates for you in any single moment. You're in charge, proven by the fact your mind will do what you tell it to do when you give it specific commands.

If you've been letting your subconscious mind run your life, it's time for your wake up call. There is a way to take better control of your mind and get your mental house in order. And until you do, your life is going to be filled with a bunch of intermittent bullshit that you shouldn't have to deal with. And this bullshit is what holds you back. It's what steals your thunder, saps your courage, and sucks the life out of your soul. I say fuck that. You're done with that. That's yesterday. Welcome to today.

Now . . . before we move forward and discuss how to take better control of our minds, there is a small tangent we need to take here. Because you're undoubtedly going to run into someone someday soon who tells you, "You can't control your mind. Control of the mind is an illusion, dude." Being fans of better living through science, we need to acknowledge there's some bad brain science out there which suggests we're not really in charge of our minds at all, and that our conscious control is an illusion. But the fact is, that's just bad science. We'll discuss the faults of that science in Volume II, and explain why the assumption that we don't have control of our minds is flawed, and what those scientists missed. The truth is that the psychological science is conclusive that we can indeed change how our minds work if we want to, and use our minds to alter what our subconscious is trying to push into our waking consciousness if we choose.

Not only is our consciousness not an illusion, the most important function of our multiple levels of consciousness is that it allows for our mind's control room to exist. Our regular waking awareness, where you and I are both sitting at this very moment, is a level of consciousness. We experience the world and our thoughts about the world in that consciousness, and we're usually caught up in the flow, whether it's reading or listening to a book, or being caught up in a daydream, or even actively thinking about a situation in our lives. Our mind decides where to go next based on what is handed to us from our subconscious. Twenty-five hundred years ago, Buddhism started calling this pattern our Monkey Mind. Sometimes we even fling virtual poo at other people and ideas when we're in this level of consciousness. (I love mentally flinging poo sometimes. But it makes your mind smell like shit.)

Getting into meta-awareness is our insurance policy against letting our mind fling too much poo. When we find ourselves daydreaming, it's a fact that we slip out of our daydream awareness into a higher consciousness that our mind is in the process of daydreaming. We stop being caught up with the fantasy, and see what our minds are doing at the moment. And that's when we can exercise control. We stop the daydream and do whatever is next. In that moment, our minds are no longer deciding where we go next. We are.

Although most the time we slip into our mind's control room accidentally, there's a big secret about the control room of your mind you need to learn. Because the fact is that you can actually enter the control room of meta-awareness at will if you want to. Would you like an example? What is your mind doing at this very moment? Are you simply reading or listening to this book while thinking about meta-awareness, or are there other thoughts or feelings vying for your attention within? What is going on in your mind? What other thoughts are trying to interrupt you reading or listening to this book at the moment? Are you waiting for sleep to occur if you're lying in bed? Are you paying attention to traffic if you're driving and listening to the audio version? Are you also thinking about what you need to do later in the day or some time tomorrow? Wow! Look at what your subconsciousness is serving up to you now that we've introduced those ideas? Are you a little distracted now? What is your mind doing now?

The simple fact that you just looked at your mind to check, means you just slipped into meta-awareness. You intentionally looked at the contents of your mind and took note of them. So you already have the ability to willingly put your regular awareness aside and enter a basic meta-awareness. Great job! We'll make this particular talent super useful for you shortly.

It's a fine line to draw, but that little shift between awareness and meta-awareness makes the monumental difference between you being on the leash of your mind, vs. having your mind be on that leash. Shifting into meta-awareness gives you an active view of what your mind is doing, and as a result also gives you the opportunity to change what your mind is doing if you so choose.

The key to mastering happiness throughout an entirety of a human lifetime lies in the ability to enter and stay in the control room of meta-awareness at will. For most of us, meta-awareness pops up unexpectedly, like when we find ourselves daydreaming, or when we get distracted and find ourselves driving or walking in the wrong direction. I can't tell you how many times I've exited my neighborhood on the way to go somewhere and find myself driving somewhere else by habit. Usually shortly after I make the first wrong turn, I "wake up," realize I'm not focused on my path, and then I exercise control to redirect my awareness to getting on the right path to my destination. But entering meta-awareness does not have to be an accident. And in fact, maintaining meta-awareness **purposefully** is our passport to controlling the mind at any and every moment of our lives.

Is This a New Idea?

Now, entering meta-awareness intentionally may sound like a new idea, but it's not. In fact, the idea of using meta-awareness to make life better is as old as time. The ancient practices of contemplative prayer and meditation are all about entering meta-awareness intentionally. As we'll discuss later in the book, contemplative prayer and meditation have touched every major religion in history. So every major organized religion once used meta-awareness as a tool for finding an accelerated path to God (which of course, delivered those religious folk into spiritual bliss, aka happiness). In fact, many religions still use meta-awareness today to find spiritual fulfillment, including Christianity, Islam, Judaism, Buddhism, Taoism, etc., although they don't call it meta-awareness. We will discuss the deeper secrets of meta-awareness and things like prayer and meditation as potential tools later in the book. But you don't need to be religious to use this science. What I'm trying to communicate here is that meta-awareness isn't such a new idea. It's actually a super old one, and possibly as old as humanity itself.

Some contemporary teachers call meta-awareness mindful awareness, and they make it the basis for their mindfulness coaching programs. Mindfulness is huge in business right now because published studies show mindfulness increases focus and creativity, reduces stress, increases emotional and cognitive intelligence, increases productivity, and can be a huge positive effect to a company's bottom line. Modern science is giving us an alternative path into the control room of meta-awareness, and as a bonus it's providing us some amazing study results that show its effectiveness in improving life through taking control of the mind. Wow! Who knew that if we took control of the mind that creates our whole life that our life could get better? Go figure.

No worries, kemosabe. We'll become more familiar with this meta-awareness thing as we move forward. It's not that tough to master, given what you're about to learn about how to hack your mind.

In conclusion, the human mind is like a curious child. It's fun-loving, inventive, and wonderful to watch at play, but just like a curious child, at times the mind is certainly in need of a little discipline, and we definitely should never let our mind run the show of our life without supervision. When we discuss how the mind works, you'll understand why a mind left unsupervised is a recipe for endless mistakes, and a great deal of pain and suffering (and not just our own pain and suffering—the negative effects your mind has on you can spill into the lives of other people as well). The quote by Horace used to open this chapter said it best over 2,000 years ago, "Rule your mind, or it will rule you." Well, now at least you know where the control room of your mind is located, so we have that going for you, which is nice. And now that you know you can enter that control room at any time by turning your awareness back onto the mind itself, it's time to move into explaining how your mind works so you can familiarize yourself with all the mind controls at your disposal. To do that, we'll start with the most important and influential component of mind, which also happens to be the biggest secret in the universe.

Chapter 2 Takeaways

1. Multiple levels of consciousness are at work constantly in our minds, most of them serving our needs.

2. There's a control room of the mind. It's called meta-awareness. And it's the virtual space in the mind where you see what your mind itself is doing. It is simply a higher level of consciousness in your mind.

3. When you intentionally enter the control room of meta-awareness you can control and change what your mind is doing to better suit your needs.

4. The idea and use of meta-awareness predates written history.

Chapter 2 Reflection

Can you remember the last time you entered meta-awareness and changed what your mind was thinking about?

3. The Biggest Secret in the Universe

Know thyself, know thy enemy.

A thousand battles, a thousand victories.

—Sun Tzu

The most liberating moments in life come when life itself shows us unexpectedly that we are not who or what we think we are.

In Chapter1, I promised you a tale about a life-threatening incident I experienced that changed my life. I'd like to share that story now. If you've never heard a first person narrative of what it's like to be completely alone and only moments from death, with no one there help you but yourself, let me now take you for a short ride in a car that wound up sinking in a dangerous and deep river late at night, with me trapped inside. This is certainly an unusual, perhaps unique, story, but I think you'll agree it also serves as a wonderful introduction to the biggest secret in the universe.

A Personal Story

It was late. It was well past 11 PM on a weekday night, and I was out driving around in the old beat-up 1973 Pontiac station wagon I'd coaxed back to life from behind the tall weeds in my mom's yard. Although it was old and rusty and had a loud exhaust leak, being a seventeen-year-old male, I tried to make this car as cool as possible. I yanked out the middle bench seat, put some captain's chairs from a custom van up front, and installed a control panel on the sun visor to hold the switches for some funky interior lighting. I thought the lights would give the car more of a limousine feel. Admittedly, it did not remotely feel like a limo at all. It was still just a junker station wagon. But it got me around.

I'd been out that night trying to have some fun and stay out of trouble, with little success. A black friend of mine named Tim and I had gotten into an altercation with some racist jocks from another high school, and after dodging the police we had decided to call it a night. I dropped Tim off at his grandma's house, which was located in an unfamiliar part of town, and headed for home.

It was November. A freezing rain was falling, which made the roads very slick, and I was driving alone in the dark. This was before the time of public GPS systems, and I was trying to figure out how to get back home. I took a turn that I thought would lead me back in the correct direction, when I found myself driving down a hill in a strange neighborhood. The windshield had just started to fog up, so I glanced down for a second to move the heater switch to defrost, while my left foot searched for the high beams switch on the floorboard (which is where that switch is located in older cars). After clicking the high beams on, the road in front of me came alive with light, and I noticed a rather odd sight approaching.

The oddity I noticed was a small white curb, laying directly across the entire road ahead of me. There were no warning signs. No reflectors. No lights. No barriers. Just a curb, what looked to be a practice putting green for a golf course, and then off ahead of that, darkness. There seemed to be nothing beyond the small patch of grass that I could now clearly see had little white sticks poking out of little white holes where people practiced hitting little white balls. That's not supposed to be in the road. Am I seeing things?

As my mind registered the visuals of the scene, time seemed to slow down and almost stop. It was really weird. I was able to process everything with extreme clarity. Even the smallest details did not escape notice. For instance, I remember noticing details of the little white curb that lay directly in the path of the vehicle. Although it looked like it was originally constructed to be a full-size curb, I noticed that it now seemed shorter than it should be. It looked as if the roadway it outlined had been paved over a few times with new layers of asphalt, effectively shortening the height of the curb in relation to the road. Where once a tall, proud, 5-inch piece of solid concrete had been menacingly protecting the grass from any incorrigible and wayward automobiles, here stood a short, embedded, 2-inch-tall, glorified white-paint-holder that simply suggested that... maybe, if it wasn't too much trouble, and if it wasn't your true intention to leave the roadway, that it would be nice for you to think about potentially not driving on the grass. Please?

Whoops, and here it comes. Fwump-fwump. The tires passed over the short curb effortlessly. To expect an automobile as large and behemoth as a 1973 station wagon—a car that can take full-size speed bumps at 40 mph while barely feeling them—to register that a curb even exists, even as you pass over it, is folly. I started pumping the brakes and gripped the steering wheel more tightly. "Oh, shit," I thought.

Now, the "oh, shit" response is something that I think everyone has. It's that response you have when you see that a course of events has been set into motion—over which you usually have absolutely no control—that is going to play out regardless of whether or not it is going to resolve at a preferred conclusion. Like when you go over the top of that first large drop on the roller coaster, or the point where you see the pitcher of Kool-Aid starting to tip off the kitchen counter, and it's already past the point of not tipping off onto the floor. That point of tippage, where you know the pitcher of Kool-Aid is definitely going over the edge . . . that's the oh, shit moment. You know without a doubt that a force of science (gravity in this instance) has taken over, and the rest has already been predetermined, and there's nothing you can do about it. You know that the pitcher is definitely going to fall to the floor and splash it's permanently red-staining sugary sweetness out all over everything.

Now . . . it is at this point of having an oh, shit moment that you typically have two choices. Your first choice is to try and bend the laws of physics, attempting to change the outcome of a course of events that already has a predetermined outcome. That when you see the Kool-Aid pitcher tipping off the table, knowing full well its going to hit the floor, and trying to get over to the pitcher anyway—even though there is no way you will be able to get to it. People who usually make this choice either (1) don't believe they can't change the outcome, (2) don't know they can't change the outcome, or (3) know they probably can't change the outcome, but just want to feel better that they at least tried to change the outcome. But regardless of the effort, the pitcher will hit the floor. Splash. And now you're covered with red Kool-Aid, because you're now much closer to the pitcher than you were when you decided to be the hero. So you failed, and ruined your third-favorite shirt. Yay for you!

The second choice in response to the oh, shit moment, is to let things happen as they are going to happen, and accept the fact that there is nothing you can do to affect the outcome. A lot of people pick this option. This is sort of the lazy approach to the situation. The reasoning goes that since you're not going to be able to get there anyway, at least now you can sit back and watch the pitcher fall, watch the cool patterns in the motion of the liquid Kool-Aid as it leaves the pitcher and splashes the fuck over everything in the kitchen, and watch to see if it nails the dog drinking out of his bowl in the opposite corner of the room. What fun!

I chose the latter of the two oh, shit responses. I figured I was already on the brakes, so wherever that beast of a car was going now that it left to road, it would eventually stop somewhere. Hopefully, not in someone's living room. In my new status as observer of the ride, rather than director of the ride, I glanced out the driver's side window. Well, how about that...? I saw the perfectly manicured holes of what I now confirmed was a practice putting green. The little white flag sticks were still sticking out of the holes, which seemed odd at 11:30 at night. Don't they pull them at night? Won't someone steal them? Wait, what the hell was I thinking? Why would anyone want to steal the little white flags from a practice putting green? That was a stupid thought. Wait, maybe I could steal them. What I could do with some practice putting green flags. The possibilities were limitless.

CRASH! The car decelerated to a near dead stop almost immediately. Well, I didn't expect to stop that quickly. The driver's seat had broken loose and pinned me to the steering wheel, but the seatbelt had done its job, saving me from a cracked skull at least. I looked out the front windshield to see nothing but darkness. No trees. No buildings. No someone's front yard garden gnome. Well, look at that. Why is there nothing but blackness out there? Where the hell am I? I looked down to ensure my headlights were still on. They were, but I still couldn't see anything through the windshield. It was then I looked out my driver's side window to notice that there was a line of solid water resting at an angle where the side mirror was supposed to be. Water? I looked at the windshield again and saw a dead leaf float by bumping against the glass. Wait, what? It was then I realized the entire windshield was covered with solid water. My shocked mind put all the painfully obvious clues together. Holy crap! I drove into a body of water! I quickly transitioned from passive mode into active mode again.

Thinking the car must be sitting nose-down halfway into a small pond (like those found around golf courses), I quickly started turning off the electronics in the car. That car presently held most of my worldly possessions in the back, and it was my only mode of transportation. Salvaging as much as possible from this accident was high on my mind. If I could turn everything off, including the radio, get out, lock the doors, I could come back later to get the car and my stuff. Maybe it could be fixed. My feet started getting wet as water seeped into the car. Oh, yeah. I guess I should start thinking about getting out, before... I looked to the left again and paused. I noticed the water on the driver's window was much higher now, and that it was slowly and steadily rising. Holy shit! This car isn't sitting on the bottom, it's sinking! With me in it! Not good!

I pushed hard against the floorboard, getting the seat to scoot back a few inches so I could move and undo the seat belt. I grabbed the driver's door handle and pushed on the driver's door. It didn't budge. The door is jammed! Primary way out not opening! Not good!

It's funny what the mind does for you when you're faced with a particularly challenging situation. My mind immediately recalled a memory of a CHiPs episode I once saw on TV. You remember CHiPs? Bah-bah-badup-bah! CHiPs was a popular television show from the 1980s that made it okay for middle-aged white women to fantasize about Hispanic men. Eric Estrada was one of the two lead actors who played Frank Poncherello, an attractive motorcycle police officer who helped saved the day every week on and around the highways of Southern California with the forgettable white guy. Personally, I liked his partner Jon, played by Larry Wilcox, but when you take a perma-tanned Hispanic guy with a winning smile and sense of humor, add a motorcycle and a police uniform, in the relatively sexually repressed days of that late 1970s and early '80s, you're gonna have a successful TV show. The dude made women swoon.

Anyway, the episode my mind recalled showed a Ford Pinto driving into a pool, trapping the passengers inside because the pressure of the water outside the car didn't allow the doors to open with air inside. In that moment of being in the car surrounded by water that was keeping my driver's door closed, I actually saw that very CHiPs scene playing out in my head, as I wrestled with my own driver's door, water gushing in against me as I tried to push it out. My subconscious memory was playing the video for my waking consciousness in my head. I can't get out this way, I thought, the water is too heavy. I let the door slam shut again. Fuck, this is getting serious.

The first evacuation attempt having failed, and me having neither Ponch nor Jon from CHiPs coming to my rescue, I knew I had literally a few seconds left to get out of the car before it might roll and land in an underwater position making it impossible to find an exit. I knew the back window and tailgate would only open with a key from outside of the car, so the very last chance to save my life was to open a back passenger window. I climbed up to the back seat (the car was nose-down at a high angle now), and I cranked the knob on the right rear passenger door. Thank God for window crank knobs. The water, which was now up to that window, started flooding in against me. But this was literally the only way left to get out of that car. So I stepped up onto the back of the passenger's seat, then the armrest of the passenger door, and pushed hard through the open window and the gushing water, and stood on the window jamb of the door after I climbed out. The car filled with water up to that open window quickly, but slowed its descent into the abyss as the air in the cargo section of the vehicle got trapped.

It was then that I was finally able to process the full scope of my situation. While I initially thought the car had driven into the edge of a small body of water, such as a water hazard at a golf course, I could see now that the car had actually launched off a short, elevated seawall on the banks of a rather large local river. Although I'd originally hoped to be close enough to jump to shore from the back of the car, it was now clear that the car was floating out into the middle of the St. Joseph River in South Bend, Indiana. This newest discovery was a big problem.

The St. Joseph River is wide, and it runs fast and deep, and has a horrible reputation for drowning people. There are tons of fallen trees and undercurrents that can grab you, pull you under, and pin you there for days until search crews eventually find your body. We'd hear about someone in our area dying that way every year. In addition, the river was highly polluted and everyone was told not to eat any fish caught from it. And here I was sitting on top of a car that was already fifty yards out from shore and floating out farther into this very river every second.

I looked for help from the shoreline. Surely, someone had heard the big crash, come outside to see what had happened, and would be able to call for help. Lots of people had houses on the river. But I didn't see anyone. Then I saw the line of golf carts sitting next to a golf course maintenance building next to the river. The carts were right near where I had driven into the river. So if the practice putting green wasn't enough of a clue, at this point I was pretty certain I had just driven my car into the river at a golf course... at night... in November... in northern Indiana when all the golf courses are closed for the season. And I'm realizing all this as I'm floating out into the middle of a very dangerous river in the freezing rain. Oh, shit.

I didn't even yell for help because I knew there was none coming. I did say the word "help" to myself in a very similar tone that would have sounded like a panicked cry for assistance, had I put any volume behind it, but it was more a joke to myself than anything else. I said it just loud enough for me to hear, "Heeeeelp," then I actually giggled at myself for doing it. One of the things I love about being me is that the world could literally be ending, and my mind will be making some funny ass joke about it, leaving me giggling out my last breath.

Okay, time to quit screwing around. Every moment I wasted was a few more feet added to the swim, so I made a decision and took action. I took my shoes and coat off, and held them in my hands as I jumped from the sinking car. The shock of the freezing water completely enveloping my body was overwhelming. My heart almost stopped. It felt like thousands of needles were poking into my skin, and it was all I could do to get my body to take a single breath again. It didn't want to exhale. Breathe. Don't panic. Just breathe. Keep moving. It will generate heat. Just get to shore.

I immediately started kicking for shore. My breathing finally started to restore itself, if only a little. I looked down into the water as I swam. I was wondering how deep it was, and when I might expect to be able to touch bottom and walk. Thoughts of ancient horror movies entered my head... the ones where whatever evil that is lurking below the surface comes and plucks the swimmer from the surface and drags them under. *Crap,* I thought. Let's not deal with that at the moment. *Keep moving.*

I heard some gurgling behind me. I stopped swimming long enough to turn and look back. The gurgling sounds weren't coming from a monster, but what I saw was certainly a monstrous sight. It was the car, sinking entirely below the water's surface into the river. MY CAR! Disappearing into the depths. The classic fin taillights of the station wagon were the only things left protruding above the water, and as I watched, the last bit of the rear end slipped beneath the surface. Bubbles of air were escaping from various places. Gurlge, gurgle, gurgle. My independence of transportation freedom was slipping away. How was I going to get to work? How was I going to get to school? How was I going to get *home*?

There was a hint of finality to the moment when I saw the car actually slip into the darkness. Not that there had really been an option to stay with the car at the point it entered the river, but the disappearance of the only object that was familiar to me in that whole scene was still disconcerting a bit. Now it was just me, the river, whatever monsters lurked below, and whatever was going to happen after I got up on shore. *Keep moving.*

I was doing okay until about twenty yards out, when I started losing control of my arms. I was shivering so violently, it inhibited my kicking and paddling, and my arms started refusing to leave my chest. I can't make it this far and die now, I thought. I concentrated on moving my arms and legs in a swimming motion as much as I could. Keep swimming. Within the last few feet of shore, where my feet finally touched bottom, I pushed up with all I had left, stood up in the water, and kinda rolled onto the top of the seawall next to the river. I lay there shivering uncontrollably, trying to cover myself with my now soaked winter coat. I knew I'd need it on shore, and I was right. It was freezing cold out, and I was wet in that very cold night air. Any heat my body had left would need to be.

I couldn't stand yet, so I waited for the shivering to subside. It took a few minutes, but finally, it did. It stopped right about the time the freezing rain also stopped pelting me in the face. This made for a bit of a surreal moment. Just as my body relaxed, the clouds parted enough for me to see a few stars. A feeling of immense peace swept over me. It was quiet. Almost relaxing, to a point. I listened to the sounds of the river that had almost just taken my life as I reflected on all that had just happened. Yes, my car and most of my worldly possessions were now at the bottom of the river, and I had no idea how I was going to get home twenty miles away in the middle of the night. But the fact remained... **I had just beat that deadly river with a dramatic death defying escape in**

the middle of the night with absolutely no one's help. It was an amazing experience. "I can do anything," I thought.

Station wagon rescue

Divers Dennis Hurst and Wayne Ryan, members of the Mishawaka Water Rescue team, prepare to recover a station wagon that sank about 80 feet out in the St. Joseph River after it was driven off the bank at the Eberhart-Petro Municipal Golf Course last Tuesday. Lt. John VanBruaene, standing in the water, holds onto a guide cable, while Capt. Gary Dentino hands over the tow hook during the Saturday operation. A Niles teen-ager escaped serious injury in the Tuesday accident.

This empowering cognition was a change in thinking from a kid who had spent his previous ten years as the victim of severe bullying and being a social outcast. I had very little confidence in myself at that time. As hard as I tried to keep a good sense of humor, in the last number of years there hadn't been a single week gone by that I hadn't been punched, kicked, pushed to the ground, spat on, peed on, had my personal items stolen or broken, had my locker at school stuffed with whatever was handy including me (yeah, that doesn't just happen on TV or in the movies), had my private journal read aloud in class while the teacher was out of the room, or simply verbally abused in the school hallways, which at that point was welcomed over any other form of torment as far as I was concerned. This blossoming confidence on the side of the river was a new feeling for me. It seemed that maybe old Sean was lying in a car at the bottom of the river, while new Sean was freshly born into the world, ready to tackle whatever came next.

I'm alive when I should be dead, I thought. So everything that happens after this moment is a bonus. My very sense of self had changed. It was a release of everything in me from the past, and a re-envisioning of everything in the future. And that change in how I saw my self is what propelled me to succeed at what I chose to do for the next ten years. And this brings us to the biggest secret in the universe. Because the biggest secret in the universe is all about this thing inside us we call **self**.

The Biggest Secret in the Universe

The reason the self within us is the biggest secret in the universe is because of how deep the secrets of self go, and how transformative the reality of self is when the full capacity of self is discovered. That night on the river, I experienced a shift in self that created a metamorphosis between being a beat-down, dead-end teenager and becoming a focused professional success in the ten years following the accident. While that might sound intriguing, what I didn't know is that my seemingly dramatic change in self that accompanied almost dying hadn't even scratched the surface of the deepest secrets of self. Those secrets would come later, after I discovered that none of my future professional and financial success would deliver happiness.

As we'll discuss shortly, from a psychological sciences perspective, self touches absolutely every thought process we experience. So learning the basic secrets about your self provides for an amazing amount of clarity about your personal mind and your personal life. But beyond that, when you go even further and discover the deepest secrets of self, something amazing happens.

When a human discovers the deepest secrets of self, the mind changes to grant access to places in the mind that were previously closed off from your regular waking consciousness. When you find the deepest most fundamental you, your mind brings forth a level of knowledge and wisdom that you never imagined was possible. Great sages aren't born. They're developed. And you can be your own great sage, if you discover the secrets of your self.

Moving forward, we are going to discuss self in a few different ways. We will touch on the science of self in the brain, and in the next few chapters we will start to understand how our standard misconceptions about self create all our personal pain and suffering and all our inner bullshit. But for the moment, I want to take you back in time to consider how long the world's most prolific religious and scientific figures have been trying to tell us that the secret of the self is the most important discovery any of us can make.

For instance, from the religious perspective (we'll talk about the nonreligious perspective momentarily), Christians may find it interesting that Jesus Christ taught about the secrets of self in the Gospel of Thomas and in other parts of the New Testament. In the Gospel of Thomas, Jesus made statements like, "Whoever has found oneself, of that person the world is not worthy." That's quite a dramatic statement from the figurehead of Christianity to suggest the world is not worthy of our presence once we have found our self. He also suggested that discovering the secrets of self may be the very path to finding Heaven itself: "If your leaders say to you, 'Look, the [Father's] kingdom is in the sky', then the birds of the sky will precede you. If they say to you, 'It is in the sea,' then the fish will precede you. Rather, the [Father's] kingdom is within you and it is outside you. When you know yourselves, then you will be known, and you will understand that you are children of the living Father. But if you do not know yourselves, then you live in poverty, and you are the poverty." Wow! Telling someone they live in poverty and they are the poverty if they don't know their self... that's some hardcore Jesus, right there. That sounds like the type of Jesus who overturns money changing tables. And while those statements found in the Gospel of Thomas may sound a bit different from what's found in the New Testament assembled at the Council of Trent, the fundamental message of Heaven being found within is Jesus's thing.

So Christians certainly have a directive to understand self. But what if you're part of the 1.6 billion people in the world who consider themselves Muslim? Well, the Prophet Muhammad summed up his thoughts on self in a more direct way: "Whoever knows himself, knows God." There's not really much room for semantic or contextual interpretation of such a simple statement. The idea is repeated more than a few times in Islamic teachings. Here, Muhammad seems to state plainly that knowing self is the key to knowing God and finding Heaven.

The Upanishads, which are the collective texts of Hinduism, state it this way: "One who knows the self puts death to death." Judaism has an entire school of self exploration within it called Kabbalah, which exists so practitioners can better understand their self's relationship to God, the universe, and infinity. Buddhism in all it's various forms is focused on discovering the truth of self to end our life's suffering and attain enlightenment. The founder of Taoism, a great Chinese philosopher named Laozi (Lao Tzu) expressed his thoughts on self this way: He said, "He who knows himself is enlightened." Even the ancient Greek Oracle of Apollo at Delphi has an inscription associated with the secrets of self. It states plainly, "Know Thyself," and is included in a larger extrapolation of that idea from the site. "Heed these words, you who wish to probe the depths of Nature: If you do not find within yourself that which you seek, neither will you find it outside. If you ignore the wonders of your own house, how do you expect to find other wonders? In you is hidden the Treasure of Treasures. Know Thyself and you will know the Universe and the Gods."

These religious authorities were trying to tell us that the secrets to their respective religions could be found within the secrets of self. And when we read them all in quick succession, it kinda sounds like the secrets to all world religions (or at least the ones we mentioned) are the very same, which is; all the answers to everything we might seek, including when looking for God and entry into Heaven, are found within the mystery of self.

I don't know about you, but that blew my mind a little the first time I made that connection. What blew my mind even a little more however, was when I discovered that the messages about self from the world's leading thinkers outside religion also point to the same truth.

It was self-declared agnostic Albert Einstein who said of self, "The true value of a human being can be found in the degree to which he has attained liberation from the self." Christian turned Transcendentalist Ralph Waldo Emerson said this, "Whatever we do, self is the sole subject we study and learn." Agnostic Nobel laureate and German novelist Thomas Mann told us, "No one remains quite what he was when he recognizes himself." Prominent atheist and psychoanalyst Erich Fromm told us, "Man's main task in life is to give birth to himself." Agnostic Matthew Arnold said, "Resolve to be thyself; and know that he who finds himself loses his misery." American novelist Henry Miller said, "There is only one great adventure and that's inward toward self." And it was the Greek thinker Socrates who said, "To know thyself is the beginning of wisdom."

These statements from these nonreligious men are also not to be taken lightly. They sound like definitive conclusions arrived after years of contemplation and review of the most important topic imaginable. These are just a few examples among dozens of similar thoughts from other world-leading thinkers, all pointing toward the secrets of self as being life's most important solvable riddle. (I have an e-mail list for those who would like to receive regular e-mail quotes from these folks on this topic of self. You can find it at MindHackingHappiness.com if you're interested.)

The Need to Know the Self

So exactly what is self? And don't you already know yours? Don't you already know yourself and who you are? I'm not supposed to ask that question, because I already know the answer to it. I already know you think you know who you are. But I also know that even though you think you know who you are, the reality is that you don't, not to the extent the past masters of self are talking about anyway. And that's why self is the biggest secret in the universe.

Everyone thinks they know their self because they know a lot of information about their body and their life, but they mistake that information as being the self the past masters are talking about. And that's where people go way wrong in life unintentionally, because it turns out how we see self is connected to virtually every process in our minds. Self touches and influences almost everything we feel, think, and do during the course of our entire lives. So just like when we're cooking a meal and we accidentally add a spoiled ingredient that taints the whole dish, in this case our unintended spoiled ingredient is our tainted understanding of self, which then helps make our whole human life taste a little worse than it should.

In the following chapters, I'm going to help you better understand the first part of the secret of the self that all the historic luminaries wanted you to know. Along the way, I am going to lead you through a very new, very specific process that will reveal some of the illusions you hold about your self, and usher you toward the space within where you can find the secrets of self that have been hidden from you until now.

But there's a challenge to that process that we need to acknowledge before moving forward so we can be prepared to address it. The challenge we face is connected with the fact that your brain is actually hard-wired to reject the thought that you don't know yourself. We will discuss that science in one of the following chapters, but it turns out our brain requires having a definition of self. As a result, when we bring our existing definition of self into question, it can feel a little weird at first. Negative emotions can even surface as a result. Resistive thoughts can also surface, pushing to distance you from what is being discussed. You may even feel a little weird at this very moment about me telling you that you don't really know yourself. These types of pensive reactions from your mind are normal. If uncovering the secrets of self (which then awards a major level-up in the game of life) were easy, then everyone in the world would have uncovered the answers already. But almost no one has. And while you will soon have the power to choose whether you uncover your secrets, just know as we move forward that this sometimes muddy process of digging into your mind is what will hand you all the keys to your mind, which will then allow you to turn down your life's bullshit and turn up your life's happiness. At the bare minimum, even if you decide this whole path is more of a mental exercise driven by curiosity than your personal path to self-mastery, when we're done you will at least understand what all the greatest masters of mind were speaking of when they discussed the mystery of self.

So let's take our first step along the self path. First, we will look at your mind's current sense of self, which will lay the foundation to understand exactly how your mind creates all your life's pain and suffering. When we get there, I'll show you a quick trick of neuroscience that will allow you to turn down some of that negative crap at will, even as a mind hacking beginner.

Chapter 3 Takeaways

1. Do not go driving with Sean late at night in unfamiliar territory. You may wind up in a river.

2. The biggest secret in the universe is about this thing within us called self.

3. The world's leading religious and scientific minds agree that the secrets to everything are contained within self.

4. Psychologically speaking, the self touches every process of our minds.

5. Although you think you know yourself, you do not currently know your self the way the past masters spoke of self.

6. This idea you don't know yourself may make you feel uneasy, because the brain actually requires a self and rejects the idea that you don't know yourself.

Chapter 3 Reflection

1. Does it feel weird to be introduced to the idea that you don't truly know yourself?

2. Does your mind want to reject the idea you don't know yourself?

3. Can you step into meta-awareness and be open to the fact

there may be more to the story about your self?

4. The Mind's Self and the Deeper Self

Be yourself, but always be your better self.

—Karl Maeser

As a heads up, these next couple of chapters about self are pretty important to understand. I say that because mastering everything we've talked about so far, including entering the control room of your mind, turning down your life's bullshit and turning up your happiness, and discovering the deepest secrets of self all depend on you understanding something about yourself that we're about to discuss. But don't worry. This stuff isn't difficult to understand. I just wanted to give you a warning to pay particular attention, because these next couple chapters will touch each and every subsequent chapter.

The Mind's Self and the Deeper Self

One of the biggest ancient secrets of self is that there are two levels of self within you. The first level of self is your mind's idea of self. This is the only self you are familiar with at the moment. It's the self you feel and believe is you as you walk around all day being you. It's the self that commands the voice in your head that creates thoughts about the things you think and experience. It's the self that experiences and is deeply affected by your emotional reactions. In short, it's your you. Now… spoiler alert… we'll learn shortly this self is the one that causes all your pain and suffering in life. Because it causes pain and suffering, and because there is a deeper self, many spiritual teachers call this top level self of the mind the false self. You might know the false self as the word ego. Some contemporary happiness teachers use the word self, with a lowercase s. What you need to know here is that regardless of what word we use, it's all the same thing. And if you've heard the word ego from other speakers/writers before, hopefully you'll understand the science behind this ego concept better than you ever have by the time we finish these next two chapters.

The second level of your self is the deeper and hidden level of self that all the world's leading luminaries spoke of in the previous chapter. This is the Self (capital S) you haven't yet discovered. We need to understand the first-level self before taking a crack at the second, so let's take a close look at your mind's false self so you can see where it comes from, and how and why it works to unnecessarily complicate your life.

Question: Why do we have a mind's false self in the first place?

Answer: Our brain actually requires it.

Let's look at your brain for a moment to understand how all our negative crap comes to be in our minds.

The brain in your head is friggin' amazing. How's that for nontechnical? It's a three-pound gelatinous mass of life that also happens to be the most complex system in the known universe. Inside your skull are a system of 85 billion neurons, each one with up to 10,000 connections to other individual neurons, all of which support a larger nervous system of communications and intelligence that exists throughout every part of your body. Neuroscientist David Eagleman says one square centimeter of your brain tissue has more connections than the number of stars in our entire galaxy. Expand out beyond that one square centimeter, and you've got a head full of galaxies. That's crazy to think about.

As complex as it is however, the human brain in your head is an organ. And like every other organ in your body, this specific organ has a very specific purpose. For instance, while the purpose of your lungs is to provide oxygen for your body, and the purpose of the liver is to help remove toxins from your body, the brain's main function is to assist you in surviving from one day to the next. Otherwise stated, your brain is your organ of survival. In fact, every function of your brain can be connected with self preserving or self sustaining activities. From a survival standpoint, your memory helps you remember where food and water is, your cognition helps you figure stuff out like how to build shelter, and your charm and humor can even help you coax other people into bed to make new humans, which perpetuates the human species. One brain system in particular, however, is specifically focused on this survival task. That is a section of the brain called the limbic system.

The Limbic System

The limbic system's job is to scan your thoughts and senses for potential threats. If your limbic system identifies a potential threat, it raises an alarm in the form an emotional response. When you see that coiled garden hose out of the corner of your eye and jump because you think it's a snake, that's your limbic system in action. When you hear about pending layoffs at work and start to get nervous about your job stability, that's your limbic system in action. It's there to identify potential threats, and urge us into action when it finds one. The limbic system works like this all day every day, even while we sleep, constantly watching what we see, hear, taste, smell, and feel in the world, asking itself with every thought, "Is [this] a threat?," "is [this] a threat?," "is [this] a threat?"

From the perspective of the limbic system in your head, it's here that an interesting second question must be asked, however. Because each and every time your limbic system looks at something like a garden hose and asks, "Is [this] a threat?," it needs another piece of information to make that determination. "A threat to what exactly?" What exactly is it that I'm supposed to be protecting? The reason this second question must be asked is because the limbic system must know exactly what it needs to protect, otherwise it could spend valuable energy resources urging you to run away from absolutely everything. That would then leave no energy for when you encountered an actual threat, like when those Jehovah's Witness boys on their bikes are making their way down your street, and everyone needs to get into the house and be very quiet for a while. Seriously, though, from a survival perspective, a leaf cutter ant is only a threat to things with leaves. But if your limbic system doesn't know you're not a plant, a leaf cutter ant could be a threat to you. It's only when the limbic system says, "That's a leaf cutter ant, but I'm not a plant, so that ant poses no threat" that the all-clear can be sounded about the ant. So the limbic system needs a definition of self to compare potential threats against. As a result, a **self** must be logically defined inside the brain so the limbic system can do its job. And thus, the mind's definition of self (aka top level self, aka ego, aka false self) is born as a basic physiological survival requirement.

So the mind starts to make a self map. It grabs a piece of paper and a pencil and says, "Okay, so let's map out all the things associated with **self** so we can then have a definition of what potentially threatens self, then the limbic system will know what to raise the alarm about, and what to ignore." Of course, the first thing the mind puts on that self map is our body. Our body is what we see when we look in the mirror, is what people point to when identifying us in photographs, so it certainly plays a big role in defining self in the mind. In addition, we know when the body quits, that is the termination point of our human existence, so it's clear the body must be defended against harm, lest we not survive into tomorrow.

Adding the body as a self item that needs protecting is where our fear of spiders and other creepy crawlies comes from. It's also where many of our unconscious reactions come from, like when we duck out of the way of a baseball flying toward our head. That's certainly a beneficial service of the limbic system to say the least. But the mind's self list doesn't end with just the body. The mind adds other things to our self map that extend into stuff not connected with the body, which then become things that must be protected as a result. Let's look at a couple of studies that prove this out.

An Amazing Discovery

Dr. James Coan, Director of the Virginia Affective Neuroscience Laboratory at the University of Virginia, has a very cool job. He gets to shock people with electrical current unexpectedly. If I had this job, I would probably not ever leave my office. I'd install a popcorn machine, set up a video camera for instant replay purposes, and sit around all day hunched over the magic red button that makes people jump out of their seat. I would probably giggle every time I pressed it, and I might consider selling the cable rights so everyone else could watch, too. But in his lab, Dr. Coan has a much better purpose for shocking people unexpectedly than mere entertainment. He actually does science while shocking people unexpectedly, specifically looking at the real time brain activity in his study participants before, while, and after shocking them. And it's because of this extra smart step that Dr. Coan provides us with an amazing piece to our self puzzle.

In 2013, Dr. Coan did this cool experiment: He invited some study participants into his lab to see what would happen in their brains when faced with a pending threat to self. Specifically, he was looking for how holding hands with someone might affect the study subjects' reactions. What they discovered came as a bit of a surprise. The experiment was set up like this: A study participant would lie down in an fMRI machine to watch their brain reactions in real time, while a signal was given to them that they might receive a small electrical shock to their ankle in the following moments. A short pause between the signal and the potential shock was inserted so the fMRI machine could measure the changes in the brain while waiting for the shock. Then the shock was either delivered or not delivered. All Dr. Coan really needed was the fear that a shock could be delivered, and it turns out you can get people nervous about being shocked if you actually shock them about 20 percent of the time. So to recap, the progression was; visual signal, pause, and then a shock or expected shock. So what happened in the subjects' brains?

After the study participants received the signal of the pending shock, in Dr. Coan's words "their brains lit up like a Christmas tree," and specifically in areas associated with self, emotion (fear in particular), and emotion regulation. And so in this first portion of the experiment where the study participants were alone, they got a reaction from the brain, and it was a reaction that brain scientists would completely expect. Someone was expecting to get zapped, and they freaked out a little as a result. Then Dr. Coan changed things up a bit.

After the original baseline was captured from the study participants, the researchers brought a stranger into the room and took the ankle zapper off the original study subject and hooked it to the stranger's ankle. They left the original subject in the fMRI with the visual signal. So in this second scenario the study subject lying in the fMRI had no potential to be zapped. They would see the signal for the pending shock, and the pause would occur, but if anyone was going to be shocked after that pause, it was **not** the study subject. It was the stranger at risk. So the researchers fired up the fMRI machine and watched the new process play out in the original subject's brain. The original study subject got the signal, the pause occurred to measure the brain, then the shock or no shock conclusion was delivered to someone they didn't know.

What they found this time was that the areas associated with emotion and self did not light up. It seemed there was no negative anticipation about the shock being delivered to the stranger. Although this was a different response than the first run, it wasn't really a surprising outcome. Fear and related emotions are pretty much universally defined as the reaction we have when there is a pending threat to self. A shock to a stranger's ankle isn't part of self, so it was no big surprise to see the subjects' brains not light up in response to a threat to something other than self. But it's then that things got **really** interesting.

After shocking the strangers, researchers then replaced those strangers with someone who was known and dear to each original study subject, such as a significant other, family member, or close friend. They then placed the ankle zapper on the person who was familiar to the subject, and initiated the same process as before; signal the original subject, pause to measure the brain, then a shock or no shock to someone the subject cared about. So what happened this time?

This time something unexpected happened. While many brain scientists might have previously guessed that the brain would react the same way it did with zapping the stranger (someone who was not self), instead the opposite happened. The signal was given, and in the moments before the potential shock to the loved one, the subject's brain lit up like a Christmas tree again. In fact the results of the fMRI scan were so similar between the scenario of the original subject being themselves zapped, and the loved one being zapped, that they couldn't tell the two scans apart. It seemed that the brain reacted like the self was completely at risk again when it was the loved one who was at risk. The brain reacted no differently when the loved one was under threat than it had when the subject's own body itself was under threat. This suggests that as far as the brain is concerned, people around us who we care about **can actually be added to our mind's definition of self and be considered a portion of self.** Dr. Coan confirmed this assumption with his own conclusions on his observations during a TED Talk he did in 2013. (You can find the video embedded at MindHackingHappiness.com.) During that talk, he said "And this is not only true in places [in the brain] that register alarm and danger. It's true in places that are associated in many studies with creating a neural representation of the self. And this includes readings in the brain that are associated with mapping the state of the physical body. So it looks for all the world like what happens with familiarity is that the person who has become familiar . . . becomes mapped onto the self."

Looking at the results of Dr. Coan's experiment, should this really be surprising to us? Frankly, no. It's somewhat common sense that we have emotional reactions to potential threats to those we care about, and sadly, no emotional reactions to threats against those we don't care about. That tendency seems to be an epidemic within the human race globally. But it is very interesting that Dr. Coan revealed that the reason we react this way is because the people who are dear to us become a portion of our very sense of self, thereby activating the brain circuits designed to protect and sustain self.

If you didn't already know it, this new science solves a huge riddle in psychology. We've known our brain is the organ of survival that protects our self. But until just very recently it's been a mystery why we have emotions about other people. **So this science explains why we have emotional reactions about other people.** They become a portion of our sense of self. But how far does this phenomenon go? Do we attach just our family, friends, and pets to our sense of self, or can other things become a portion of our sense of self also?

The Weird Stickiness of the Self

To answer that question, we look to a study co-authored by business school professor Tiffany Barnett White at the University of Illinois. Dr. White was curious about how people might react to positive or negative news connected with a brand they cared about. What she found was that when people have a strong connection to a particular brand (what they call Self Brand Connection, or SBC), they react to bad news about that brand just like they react to a personal failure. In other words, the failure of the brand was seen in their minds as a failure of self. In addition, the brand-loyal folks then wanted to ignore or discount the bad news about the brand, which is part of what psychology calls the self-delusion process, or sometimes denial. So it seems that not only other people can become attached to our self, but ideas of brand favoritism can become part of our self as well. And it's the word **ideas** that we need to pay attention to here.

What is a brand but an idea? It's an idea about a function or product or service. An idea about the value that a brand brings to our lives. Coca-Cola. Apple. Google. Ford. Those names mean something to us beyond just the name of the company with which we do business, and if those meanings become important to us, the brand itself can become a portion of our sense of self.

That said, brands aren't the only ideas to which we can become attached. We attach mentally to anything and everything. We attach to a particular religion and make that a portion of our sense of self. We attach to politics and make that a portion of our sense of self. We attach to our possessions and make the things we own a portion of our sense of self. Our jobs, our life stories, our ethnicity, our opinions on things, our likes and dislikes, our pets, our friends, and of course, our family all become a portion of our sense of self. They all get added to our mind's self map. In our minds, we just see these things as being who we are. They are simply what makes our life our life. But with every added item on the self map, the limbic system then works overtime to scan for threats to all the things we've allowed ourselves to become in our mind. And of course with more things on our self map, the more opportunity there is to have something in the world drop some bullshit on us.

If you become attached to a certain brand of politics, a perceived threat to those politics on Facebook, in the news, or in live conversation fires up your limbic system causing a negative reaction in your mind. If a religion (or non-religion) you identify with is attacked, your limbic system responds to that information as well. If someone insults one of your family members, or a friend, or your personal life story, or your job, or your opinion on something, your limbic system reacts to that insult generating a negative reaction in your mind.

Some Science

The results of a study published in 2016 at the University of Southern California by neuroscientist and author Sam Harris and psychologist Jonas Kaplan showed this model of understanding the mind to be exactly on point. Kaplan and crew did an experiment where they put study participants in an fMRI and challenged their strongly held political beliefs. The result was that the portions of the brain that illuminated under scans were the very sections associated with both self and negative emotion. From an article about the piece on Vox.com: "Partisan identities get tied up in our personal identities. Which would mean that an attack on our strongly held beliefs is an attack on the self. And the brain is built to protect the self." The article went on to mention, "The results also jibe with some of Kaplan and Harris's past works on religious beliefs. 'When we compared evaluating religious statements to nonreligious statements, we [found] some of the same brain regions that are active in the current study,' Kaplan said. Which makes sense, because our religious beliefs also factor into our identities.'"

Although the two studies by Kaplan and Harris just noted only cover politics and religion, our self isn't limited to making attachments to just politics and religion. It can attach to any idea we see as a portion of our sense of self, from our racial identity, our cultural heritage, and nationality, to things as simple our favorite beer, and our favorite color. Personally, I'm team Labatt Blue, and the color blue. No relation. Our mind's self can attach as easily to a treasured family heirloom that becomes a part of our identity as we can to the idea that we like the loose sheets of toilet paper to hang from over the top of the roll, and not from behind and under it (or vice versa). **So in reality, our self (aka top level self, aka ego, aka false self) is really more of a curly brackets {self}.** The brackets I place around the word are a mathematical sign I borrow from set theory. They signify that the whole of the thing within the brackets is a collection of all its different parts. It's just an easy way to remind us how to look at {self} from here forward; as a list or map of items that come together to create our mind's self. If you're listening to the audio book, just know every time I say the word "self," I'm talking about {self}, which is how the mind defines **us**. [Later in the book sometimes I put an {individual self item} in these brackets, too, signifying that whatever is in the brackets is considered a portion of {self} in the example being discussed.]

{self} Map

This is an important concept to grasp, not just how the {self} works in the mind, but that there's absolutely nothing that our {self} map doesn't touch in our minds. Your {self} is involved with every emotion you have ever and will ever experience, and it governs absolutely every decision and action you take from the moment you take your first breath, to the moment you take your last. **That's** how important the {self} is to your minds. Everything that makes up the mind's {self} map influences every moment of your life and every movement of your mind. Your mind's {self} governs absolutely everything connected with your personal emotional landscape, and it's the main villain in your personal happiness story. It's why everyone from Jesus and Muhammad to Einstein and Emerson told us that {self} holds the secrets to becoming a better and happier human being.

Next, we'll look at how to easily identify the mind's invented {self} and reduce the effect it has in creating our inner turmoil.

Chapter 4 Takeaways

1. The brain is our organ of survival.

2. The limbic system's job in the brain is to constantly scans for threats, but before identifying any threat must then must ask, "A threat to what, exactly?"

3. Our brain builds a definition of self because that definition is required to be an answer to the limbic system's question.

4. Science shows our brain's {self} is more than just the body, and includes other people and ideas that are favorable to us.

5. Our emotions are the result of the limbic system checking our senses for threats to this augmented {self} map.

Chapter 4 Reflection

1. What kind of things are on your self map?

2. What things do you think of when you think of what makes you **you**? These are the things that your brain is wired to defend.

5. So Who Are You? Scratching the Surface of Your{self}

There is nothing noble in being superior to your fellow men.

True nobility lies in being superior to your former self.

—Ernest Hemingway

As I swam the last few meters toward the end of the pool, my muscles burning and my heart pounding, I heard the whistle blow. "You guys are done. Get out of the pool, get your uniforms on, and head back to your barracks." The short, but muscular, Petty Officer in Navy athletic gear was looking at me and a handful of others who were still in the pool when time ran out on the SEAL entrance exam swim. "I'm done," the guy said who was just ahead of me, now climbing out at the end of the pool. "You weren't out of the pool. Almost... doesn't cut it here," replied the instructor. He added a very focused stare which reiterated to the recruit that he was done, just not in the way he thought he was. A small group of recruits who had made the swim in time were currently out of the pool doing sit-ups, pushups, and pull-ups for instructors who seemed to be giving them a hard time as well. "I already did the push-ups," a fellow recruit said." The instructor gave him a steely look. "Yeah? Well do another 25. I didn't like the first ones."

We were no strangers to being given a hard time. We were attending U.S. Navy Basic Training at the Great Lakes Naval Training Center outside Chicago. It was the Navy's job to give us a hard time during this phase of our service. But this wasn't just regular boot camp hazing. That night we had all made the trek through the cold winter winds across the frozen grounds of the base to the indoor pool, so we could try out for the Navy's elite special forces combat unit, which at the time was still cloaked in a great deal of secrecy. Even though many in the group seemed to be in great physical condition, it seemed most, if not all, of us would soon be making that same cold trek back to our boot camp barracks as SEAL rejects.

Today, while it's common knowledge that the U.S. Navy SEALs operate at a level of physical fitness that most other humans simply can't attain (including me), what is less widely known is the Navy SEALs also also strive to operate at high levels of mental and psychological fitness that exceeds typical human parameters as well. And though it isn't spoken of often, this too, is a qualifier and ongoing training requirement for membership in this most elite group of military operators.

Because the SEALs want sharp minds to go along with sharp bodies, they have an elite mind training facility right alongside the combat training facilities at their headquarters in Norfolk, VA. In this special mind gym, Navy SEALs work on brain wave entrainment, and heart rate control. They use EEG monitors, cardiac coherence devices, and sensory deprivation tanks. This mind training helps them focus better, and learn new tasks faster, reducing the time it takes to learn a foreign language from six months down to six weeks. Beyond that, the SEALs work on learning to intentionally enter a state of mind called **flow**, where the mind's {self} moves out of the way, and a perfect melding of awareness and action is attained. This allows them to more easily become one with their team during missions, and it helps them perform at a higher level than they normally could without experiencing flow.

Flow was a concept originally identified by psychologist Mihaly Csikszentmihalyi, who wrote a book about it in 1990. He explained how flow helps us achieve superhuman performance, writing, "the self expands through acts of self forgetfulness." Flow is the magical state of awareness where our {self} actually dissolves, being replaced by experience and action itself. The processing of the {self} cycles in the brain move out of the way to provide a more pure and integrated experience. Athletes call this being in the zone. It's where you can't miss, because you're not even thinking about it.

In Steven Kotler and Jamie Wheal's book Stealing Fire, which also tells of the Navy SEALs mind gym, they cite the science of how flow affects how well our brains operate:

> Being in the zone significantly boosts creativity. In a recent University of Sydney Study, researchers relied on transcranial magnetic stimulation to induce flow. Using a weak magnetic pulse to knock out the prefrontal cortex and create a 20-40 minute flow state, subjects were then given a classic test of creative problem solving, the nine dot problem; connect nine dots with four lines without lifting pencil from paper in ten minutes.
>
> Under normal circumstances, fewer than five percent of the population pulls it off. In the control group, no one did. In the flow induced group forty percent connected the dots in record time, eight times better than the norm. And this isn't a one-off

finding. When neuroscientists at DARPA in advanced brain monitoring used a different technique, neurofeedback, to prompt flow, they found that soldiers solved complex problems and mastered new skills up to 490% faster than normal.

Flow isn't just for athletes and Navy SEALs. It's also for business executives, parents of children, anyone who wants to get more done in a day, or people who just want to reduce the turbulence that attempts to interrupt the awesome ride of their life, like you and me. When you're in flow, whatever you're doing is just easier. More effortless. Even if that activity is just waiting for a stoplight.

Attaining flow has all to do with getting the {self} out of the way in your mind. But how do you do that if you don't know what your mind's {self} is? The short answer is, you can't, unless you're ready to wait around for flow to initiate spontaneously, in some magical moment of laser focus that only happens once in a blue moon. Waiting around is not your path. Your path is to take charge of the mind and get your mind's {self} out of the way of your peak performance and happiness at will.

But to get our {self} out of the way, we need a deeper understanding of our mind's {self}. This not only opens up the door to flow, but also gives us immediate access to the control room of our mind, and as a bonus, it's here we're introduced to that really cool brain wiring hack I promised to tell you about that can turn down your internal bullshit at will.

Identifying your mind's {self} is easy. Basically stated, your mind's {self} is every answer you could ever think of to the question who are you? Let's do a quick mind exercise for a moment to clarify this point.

If I were to ask you the question **who are you**, what would your answer be? Take a moment to actually think about what you would say if I were standing right in front of you asking you this question. "Hi, who are you?"

If you're like most people, when faced with the question who are you, you tend to answer it quickly by giving your name. "Hi, I'm Sean." I've said it thousands of times, usually holding out my hand for a requisite handshake. This is a normal answer and probably the one everybody expects when they actually ask us who we are. Our name is, after all, the name that our parents gave us so we could know when they were yelling at us and not someone else. But it's also the first identifier we typically go to when searching to answer questions of our identity. However, without hiding behind semantics, your name is not really an accurate answer to the "who are you" question.

When you first introduce yourself to someone by sharing your name, does that person really know anything about you besides the word people use when they point their finger at you? No. They don't know anything about your passions, your thoughts, or your feelings, where you've been, or where you plan to go. Your name says nothing about you. But your name is certainly something that lands firmly near the center of your mind's {self} map, which is why you go to it when your mind is questioned regarding your sense of {self}.

Expanding on this "who are you" idea, we could continue this exercise of asking the same question over and over again, digging deeper into the minutia of explaining how all our other standard answers are wrong. But hitting you with this question over and over will ultimately end up with you eventually telling me about the choices of mind you've made in your life that you believe make you **you**.

This is where you start sharing details about your life that your mind believes quantifies you. This is where a woman in Texas might tell us, "Well, I'm a thirty-five-year-old mother of two, I'm from Dallas, and I'm a Christian." But that's not who she is, that's how old her body is, her parental status, where she decided to live, and the religion she chose. Someone else might tell us, "I'm a student at XYZ University, I'm the President of the Young Turks Club on campus, and I plan to go to law school." That's not who she is either. That's where she's going to school, a club she's involved in, and a plan she has for her future. And it doesn't matter what details are given or ideas that are conveyed. "I'm a computer engineer at Google." That's someone's present job, which could change next week. "I'm a proud black man." Nope. That's just the attitude toward, and the race of, that person's body.

Similarly, who you are is not defined by your age, or your ethnicity, or your job, or your religion, or one of the roles in life that you fill for other people. You're not your gender, or sexual preference, or educational status. You are not your beliefs, or culture, or life traumas, or hobby participation. Your politics do not define you. Your life's story does not define you. None of that stuff defines you, because if all the other humans in the world disappeared tomorrow to where you couldn't tell your particular story or compare your{self} to others, none of anything you could have said would matter. But there, alone, as the last person in the world, with the bonobos feeding you grapes, and the dogs looking to you to throw the stick, you would still be who you are. And this is why whatever answer you try to give to the "who are you" question… is wrong.

Now… I know at this moment your mind is pushing back on this idea. Your mind is saying "Hey, wait a minute! Those things matter! Those things like religion, and politics, and family heritage, and life story make me who I am. I know who I am, and all those individual things that help define me may not completely define me individually, but when we pile them all up together, that pile of things, with nationality, and beliefs, and ethnicity, and sexual preference, and opinions, and my roles in life, and my likes and dislikes, and my interactions with other people . . . and all the rest . . . all that stuff together . . . is me."

And although that thought in your head right there is complete and utter bullshit… my friend, **I would like to take this moment to cordially introduce you to your mind's {self}.**

The thing that is in your head pushing back right now to defend it{self} with all its ideas about who and what you are, including all the labels and attachments your mind looks to when wanting to define you . . . that thing attached to your roles in life, your job, your possessions, your life story . . . that feeling within your mind that seems to be alive… that's your mind's {self}. That's your false {self}. That's your ego. It's your mind's flawed understanding of you which clings to people and ideas and memories to create a definition of what needs to be defended.

This false {self} is the thing that causes every bit of your life's pain and suffering. It's what causes every bit of your life's bullshit. It's the laundry list of things your brain creates and needs to protect in its defense of {self} charter. Learning exactly how it works to make all your pain and suffering happen will allow you to break that pain and suffering process and thus increase your happiness. It's then you'll be able to get your mind's {self} out of the way, so you can flow through life if you want to.

The fact is that the secret to our increased happiness is as much about who and what we **aren't** . . . as equally as it's about who and what we are. Who and what we aren't is everything our mind tries to attach to in defining its {self} and our existence, which then saps our happiness as it looks to defend that list. And some of the things it tries to attach to are just flippin' crazy, and that causes us nothing but pain and suffering as a result.

For instance, when we attach a temporary project at work to our sense of {self}, if something happens with that project we can have a meltdown **as a result of a project at work**. When we attach our {self} to getting to a destination on time, it can cause us to flip out **if we arrive late somewhere**. When we attach our sense of {self} to a preference of how we would like a family member to act, it can **sour a family relationship** when they don't act the way we wish them to. What we attach to our {self} runs our lives. Let me share with you a story about a weird attachment that my son's mind added to his {self} not long ago.

A Personal Story

My wife and I are licensed foster parents, so sometimes we find ourselves with extra kids staying in our home when their parents need to take a break to deal with some issues. As a result, about half of our house could pass for a playroom. Where other people might have a dining room table, we have a regulation air hockey table. Where other people might have pictures on the walls, we have framed toddler art and white board walls to draw on. One of the coolest things we had for a while was a play-table that I helped my wife build out of raw wood from Lowe's. It was a six-by-six table with a big hole in the middle so the kids playing there could be completely surrounded by trains or Legos or whatever, and be able to reach any and all the toys at once. But admittedly, that table was friggin' huge. Here's a picture of it:

When our son gave up toy trains for baseball, my wife and I decided it was time to get rid of the big table for a smaller one, so I put the table out in front of our house and listed it on Craigslist as a free item for anyone who wanted to come get it. Unfortunately, no one wanted it, so it then became my job to go outside and cut the table into smaller pieces that could fit into the garbage truck which was coming the next morning. My son followed me outside to watch. As I finished cutting up the table with my cordless circular saw, I noticed my son standing in our front yard with tears in his eyes, silently crying. He was sad to see the table being destroyed.

This confused me for a moment, because we had discussed giving the table away so other kids could enjoy it, and he seemed to be okay with not having the table anymore. But when the moment of truth came, he broke down in tears. As I reflected on the situation on my way over to give him a hug, I realized his reaction to the table's end totally made sense. Declan was attached to that table.

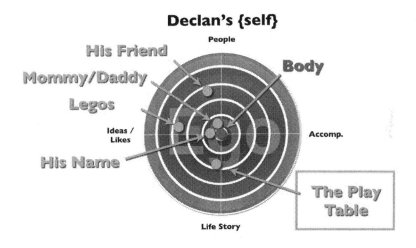

It had become a small portion of his sense of {self}, and thus an item on his mind's {self} map. That table had become a part of his history, a part of his daily existence, always there as a witness and supporting player to whatever fun was being had. There were always good feelings associated with being around that table. It was an awesome table to him. And now the world (in the form of daddy with a circular saw) was negatively affecting this small portion of his {self}. His limbic system was in overdrive.

Right along with our normal ideas of who we are, sometimes we don't realize all the things that can make up a portion of our mind's {self}. Further, we don't realize each and every one of these {self} items can affect us emotionally and create turbulence for us when something in the world affects that {self} item. Knowing what's written on your mind's {self} map is important for a few specific reasons. First, when you are able to know what's on your mind's {self} map, you can anticipate your negative reactions before they happen. Anticipating your negative reactions in turn reduces the severity of your negative reactions. I liken this to having an early warning about a big clap of thunder. I always get more startled when a bolt of lightning and booming thunder come simultaneously than when the lightning is farther away and I have a second or two to prepare for the expected big boom. With the delayed thunder, I know it's coming and can prepare for it. As a result, my body jumps a little less than when the thunder comes as an unexpected surprise.

Second, when you know the items that make up your mind's {self} map, you can actually start to witness the mind reacting in real time to the world around you. This insight does two cool things for you simultaneously. (1) When you are watching your mind react in real time, that looking into your own mind action throws you into meta-awareness, the control room of your minds. It's here that you have the option to grab a few control dials and adjust a few things to help your mind regain calm immediately. (2) When you completely understand an emotion in process, there's a magical hardwired function of the brain that physically turns down your negative reactions in real time, giving the negative crap a one-two punch that diminishes its influence on you dramatically.

Name-It-Tame-It

Matt Liebermann at UCLA was the first to discover this last benefit in the brain. The study he co-authored was so compelling that it spawned a whole group of associated studies in psychology called the Name-It-Tame-It studies. Here's why it was so compelling: A group of men and women were asked to lie in an fMRI machine while pictures of people expressing mostly negative emotions were shown to them. Participants had various tasks to complete while watching these images a number of times to create a baseline reading. The baseline showed that when people viewed the negatively skewed pictures, their brains showed reactivity in a portion of the limbic system responsible for generating some of our more powerful negative emotions called the amygdalae. The amygdalae are two almond sized areas known to be a catalyst for much of our inner turmoil, including fear and anger. After the baseline was captured, the participants were then asked to go view the images again, but this time the subjects were told to name the emotion that was appropriate to what the face on the picture was showing. What happened this time was that the amygdalae within the limbic system quieted immediately upon performing the emotion naming task.

This was a huge discovery, because a turned-down limbic system is a turned-down pain and suffering engine. It's a turned down inner bullshit engine. And what Liebermann found during that study was a way to turn down the limbic system at will. What he found was that when the brain thinks about and identifies an emotion being experienced, that emotional reaction subsides much faster that it normally would. In fact, researchers reported seeing the limbic output start to turn off almost immediately when study participants identified an emotion consciously.

I thought this was an amazing result to say the least, as did much of psychology, which rushed to test and expand on the discovery. What I later discovered however, was that this turning-down-of-negative-emotion effect could be strengthened with implementing a deeper understanding of the emotion within us being experienced. It turns out that looking at and understanding the moving parts within our mind that created an emotion creates a greatly enhanced name-it-tame-it effect. Thus, when we look at the process the {self} map feeds to create our negative emotions, those reactions can be turned down quickly to give us back immediate control of our minds (not to mention turn back on our thinking minds, which the limbic system shuts down when it starts firing). So not only does this give you a mechanism to turn down your negative inner bullshit in the heat of the moment, over time this has a neuroplastic effect of turning down your negative crap with less effort, and keeps your brain working in a less stressed and happier state.

Understanding what's on your {self} map and how those items play into your individual emotions is a powerful tool to take control of the negative emotions process. Let's discuss how to identify the things on your mind's {self} map, and in the next chapter I'll show you how all those individual items help create each individual emotion you have ever and will ever experience. In order to help you better understand your mind's {self}, let's look at how your {self} comes together from the time it's created. To do that we will need to turn back the clock and watch your mind's {self} being assembled from the time you were very young.

Your {self} from Day One

The day you were born, you came into this world with a ton of intelligence already operating within your body. We don't think about that very often, but even on day one, our baby bodies already know how to breathe, how to circulate oxygen everywhere, how to suckle on a nipple, how to turn the food we ingest into the energy we need to survive, and we even already know how to crawl up Mommy's tummy to get to the breast milk if she doesn't lift us up there herself. You can find videos of newborn babies who are only minutes old crawling their way up to mommy's breast on the Internet. So on day one, your immune system was functioning, your nervous system was primed and ready, and don't you dare believe you weren't also primed and ready to start stinking up some diapers starting with the remnants of your first meal. We take these natural abilities for granted, but every one of them is an amazingly complex process, and the reality is that there is a ton of intelligence within the body already at work the moment we take our first breath.

That said, while your body knew its internal environment well enough to operate independent of the umbilical cord in just nine months, you knew absolutely nothing about your external environment on day one. This is actually an awesome thing about us humans, because this environment we call Earth changes constantly, and if we came out of the womb ready for how things were yesterday, it might be bad news for us as a species if a comet has wiped out half the planet, taking much of yesterday's ecosystem with it. A human baby prewired for knowing how to avoid polar bears would be wasting a lot of their survival talents in a world where polar bears no longer existed. And thus on day one, your mind was fortunately a clean slate. You knew nothing of the world into which you were born, but you were ready to learn.

And so at that moment your brain kicked into high gear, becoming a sponge to absolutely everything going on around you. After all, your brain had an important job to do. As the organ of survival, your brain needed to learn about the things that might harm you, and it also needed to define what exactly it was that needed protecting, so it needed to create your mind's definition of {self} to know what to protect, and figure out what was and wasn't a threat to {self}.

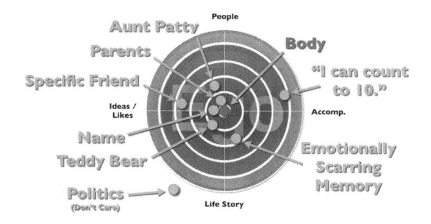

During our early moments in life, our {self} is defined by our bodily senses and our immediate surroundings. Science calls this the oceanic field. Life is pretty simple at this point. Our existence is defined by our direct experiences and our environment. When our experiences and environment are pleasing, we are pleased. We may even give out one of those amazingly awesome baby smiles. When our experiences and environment go negative with things like hunger, fatigue, diaper irritation, smelly strangers, loud noises, or cold milk, our emotional circuits then react and cause us to cry. But life doesn't stay this simple for long.

As we get past just eating, sleeping, and pooping, and we start getting into some playtime, we pick up extra information that comes when our parents or caregivers start to teach us the first portions of language through their interaction with us as a baby: "Hey, you! It's me. How are you? Are you ready for a bottle? Look, there's Daddy. Look, here comes Mommy. Look, there's Aunt Patty. See the doggie?" And what our parents are usually pointing at or looking at when they start teaching you the ideas of "you, me, Aunt Patty, and doggie," is your body, their body, Aunt Patty's body, and the doggie's body. So along with the nervous system being hardwired to protect our body, we also make the implied connection even as babies that the identity of something equals the body's form.

As we grow and continue to soak in everything we can, our brain starts to add things to our {self} map. Our memories get added to {self}. How we think about things gets added to {self}. What we think we know gets added. Over the years, we learn about our family's heritage, religion, and culture. We learn traditions, values, and morals. These all become a part of who we think we are. We learn about our nationality. We collect our likes and dislikes. We select favorite foods, favorite music, favorite people. We pick positions on social and political issues. Then as we get older and accumulate more experiences, our entire life story gets thrown into the mix of {self}. Our education. Our job. Our accomplishments. Our failures. Our missed opportunities. All along the way our possessions regularly fall in and out of our definition of {self}. Our clothes become a part of {self}, which feeds the individuality of our closets, and makes us feel weird when someone else shows up to a party wearing exactly what we are wearing.

The cycle never changes. We start with getting attached to our toys as kids, and abandon those toys for more meaningful toys and other material items that become a part of our life later. All of these things then become part of what we think creates our personal world. They become the very definition of our existence. And they are what the mind points to when looking for a definition, or quantification, of {self}.

During the course of our lives, our mind's {self} changes. It's a fluid definition. It changes with the changes in our body, including aging and weight fluctuations. It changes with our life's changes. Sometimes people enter and leave our lives. This changes {self}. Sometimes we change political affiliations, or religions, or beliefs. This changes {self}. Sometimes we like a certain brand, then later we switch brands. And as weird as it sounds, if we switch brands for a certain reason, being attached to that new reason and new brand means we've actually altered our mind's definition of {self}.

Our Ever-Expanding {self}

So although this is going to sound a bit crazy (it wouldn't be one of history's best kept secrets if it wasn't crazy), but basically your mind's {self} is everything your mind thinks about when you think about who you are. Everything you consider a part of your personal world, from your body and its characteristics and tendencies, to your name and ideas of who you are, to the people and items that belong around you, to your internal mental opinions about life, to whether you think the loose toilet paper should hang over the top of the roll or from behind and under it... all these things together make up your mind's sense of {self}. Unfortunately however, all the individual components that create this idea of {self} then become a rather long list of things that the brain checks against potential threats to {self}. So the more things that show up on your {self} map, the more shit in the world there is to get upset about.

Don't worry, this mind's {self} concept will become more and more clear as we move forward, but if you're still a little fuzzy on what exactly falls onto your mind's {self} map, we are building an online tool at MindHackingHappiness.com that might help identify some of your {self} items in the different categories of People, Accomplishments, Ideas/Likes/Dislikes, and Life Story. It's free to use if you would like to increase your mastery of understanding your mind's {self}.

In addition, you should pick up a physical copy of Soul Pancake by Rainn Wilson (he played Dwight Schrute on the American version of The Office). It's one of the most fun workbooks on exploring {self} I think I've ever seen. I suggest getting a physical copy, because you can write in it. It's full of activities like, "Carefully list 5 things you would literally chop off your little toe for." Then there's a space for the list. The book also asks questions like, "Does your family see the real you?" It's a great book that helps you explore the mind's {self} without actually telling you that's exactly what it's doing. I think it's one of the most underrated workbooks in modern history if you want to better understand the mind's {self}. Everything you write into that book will be a part of your mind's {self}. Truth. Get a copy.

In conclusion, any answer that your mind formulates to answer the question "who am I?" or "What makes me me?," or to borrow from Rainn again, "What are the 5 risks you haven't had the guts to take yet?" … all those answers… that is your mind's {self}. They are all ultimately answers to the question "who am I." Answer the "who am I" question differently a hundred times, and a hundred times you will reveal something that falls onto your mind's {self} map. And as I've noted, if you can name it, it ain't you. But if you can name it, it's on your mind's {self} map, and it affects the operations of your mind, and helps create your mind's bullshit.

So now you have a loose grasp on how the mind sees our {self}.

In the next chapter, I'll show exactly how all of our {self} items help create our individual emotions.

Chapter 5 Takeaways

The mind's {self} is absolutely any person, place, thing, or idea that the mind points to when answering the question, "Who am I?"

Chapter 5 Reflection

So who are you beyond your mind's idea of you? Are you just your mind's idea of you, or are you more than that?

6. Your Equation of Emotion

Where fear is, happiness is not.

—Lucius Annaeus Seneca

In opening this chapter, I would like to start with a confession. It's not something I'm overly proud of, but the fact is . . . I was kicked out of preschool. That might make me the only person you've ever encountered to have been expelled from school at the age of four, but I feel I should share the story because it's a great example of how {self} gets us into trouble, even at four years of age. The school in question was a Methodist Christian preschool in Elkhart, Indiana. It was nice. I liked it there for the whole two weeks I attended.

Although I have siblings, I was pretty much raised an only child. By the time I came around, almost everyone had moved out of my parents' home, so there weren't any other kids to play with when I was young. Beyond that, my mom never made the effort to socialize me with other kids, so preschool was the first time I was exposed to the discipline of sharing. In the solitude of my bedroom at home, although I didn't have a lot of toys, I never had to share any of the toys I had. So when faced with being put into a room with a bunch of other kids with a limited number of toys, it was a challenge for me. For all the first week, and most of the second, the Methodist nuns explained the concepts of sharing and taking turns to me multiple times, and finally after a number of days, I thought I pretty much had it nailed down. I remember the following events like they happened yesterday.

A Personal Story

It was a rainy day, so we were stuck inside all day playing with whatever toys were in the classroom. During morning playtime, I identified a little blue truck I wanted to play with. Another boy had it, so I walked over to the boy and asked if he would share playing with it. He declined. I re-asserted my wish to play with the truck and started to give a speech about sharing to the little boy, which was fresh in my mind thanks to how much it had been hammered into me over the last number of days. I'm sure I was probably having this conversation with a whiny little elevated voice little boys can have when they don't get their way, because we were interrupted by the younger of the two nuns who were supervising class that day. She crouched between us, and asked a few questions to better assess the situation, but in the end she explained that although it was great I asked the other boy to share, the fact was he also wanted to play with the truck during that particular playtime, and because he had it first, he could keep it. It was his turn. Although I didn't love the decision, I was surprisingly okay with the explanation, and I found something else to play with for the rest of the session. He was granted permission to play with the truck during the whole morning session. I figured maybe next playtime could be my turn.

At the end of morning playtime, I watched where the other boy placed the truck on the toy shelf. I thought if he had gotten to it first in the morning, and that granted permission to possess it for the whole morning playtime, I was going to get to it first in the afternoon so I could play with it the whole afternoon playtime. When afternoon playtime came around, I made a beeline for that little blue truck. And I got to it first. Yay! It was mine for the whole session! I started playing with it feeling proud my plan had worked, and I was really happy playing with the truck for the few minutes I got to play with it, driving it one time around the carpet of a planned many times around the carpet. But then a different boy came along and said he wanted to play with that same truck too. It was, after all, a cool truck. I declined, stating it was my turn to play with the truck and that he could play with it during the next playtime tomorrow morning. After all, this is exactly what had happened to me earlier that morning. He was unsatisfied with this response. As a result, he went and told the older and more stern of the two nuns that I would not share the truck. She approached with the little boy in tow.

I don't know if it was because of my pattern of having issues with sharing previously that caused her to make this call, or whether maybe she just didn't like me for whatever reason, but after I tried to explain that I had already shared the truck during morning playtime and that it was my turn to play with it (which to me satisfied both sides of the sharing/turns equation), to my four-year-old flabbergasted disbelief, without much explanation the older nun looked down and told me I needed to share the truck. It was then that she actually took the truck from my hands and handed it to the other boy, who ran off with it gleefully.

I was pissed and hurt to say the least. I started crying, screaming, and became inconsolable. I refused to play with any other toys or any other kids for the rest of the play session, and just sat in the back of the room screaming and crying loudly and refusing to talk to anyone. I was in complete meltdown. I felt violated. On this first day of finally understanding and being okay with the rules of sharing and taking turns, where I had quietly walked away from the truck in the morning and got to the truck first in the afternoon, only to have it ripped away a few minutes later, I was hurt, angry, and really confused. I felt like I was being punished for playing by the rules.

It was following our afternoon playtime that the incident occurred.

The hour after our afternoon playtime was particularly fun, because that was when we would get together as a group to sing songs and play various group games before our parents came to pick us up around 2:40 pm. The younger of the two nuns had taken me into the next room and got me psychologically reset for this last session, and I felt surprisingly even keel. She was good. I was ready for a new start and whatever was next. I think she even may have said something about it being unfair that I didn't get to play with the truck, but in all my crying and self pity, that part of the memory is a bit fuzzier. But I do remember that after all the toys were put away, I eagerly gathered and sat with the other kids on the carpet to see what our next activity would be. It was there that everything went south.

The older nun who had taken the truck from me was at the front of the room, and after getting everyone quiet, a little girl raised her hand and asked why I had been crying for playtime. The older nun asked me to stand up in place in the middle of the group. I did so. It was then that she tried to explain to the class why I was crying and screaming the entirety of our afternoon play session. I was okay with the first part of what she said. But at the end of that speech she made another point about how important it is to share, and that maybe I needed to learn that lesson.

Oh no she fucking didn't.

Now . . . it's here that you should know I did develop strong language skills at a very early age. I started talking at six months old, and was talking in short sentences before I could even walk. But that little talent meant at four years old, I was ready to have this conversation with this old lady who I still thought was in the wrong on this particular sharing issue. In short, I was about to unleash.

After her initial attempt to embarrass me in front of the group, I decided to push back a bit. From my perspective after being counseled on sharing for almost everyday for two weeks, I was

'Mr. Sharing' now. I had it down. I knew the rules of sharing better than any other kid in the room at this point. Yeah, you need advice on sharing? Go see that Sean kid. He's a sharing guru. I think he's the Dalai Lama's go-to guy on sharing or some shit. So seeing as I was an expert on sharing, I started to explain the details of the situation to her in front of the rest of the room, admonishing her for her decision to take the truck, stating I should have been able to play with it.

Not surprisingly, she did not take this direct feedback well. I don't remember exactly what she said, but I remember seeing her body language visibly change, and her tone also changed quite noticeably. She used some larger words I was unfamiliar with, but she was still talking about sharing. I remember she finished her mini-lecture with a question that was steeped in the attitude she had just won the argument. As I was standing there listening, she finished with a rather sassy, "So what do you think about that?" She even bobbed her head to the side for emphasis and raised her eyebrows at me, with an attitude reminiscent of early Queen Latifah, but not nearly as cool as Latifah.

I don't think I was completely sure what to say in response to that. Whenever women pull out the head bob, you know shit's gettin' serious. You can just feel it. But I knew I had to say something. And in my mind I knew I was in the right, so whatever she said with that crazy intimidating neck move thing, it didn't really matter to me. Because from my perspective, she was wrong, whatever it was. So as she stood at the front of the class waiting for me to sit down, instead I stood my ground. I looked her straight in the eye, put my hands on my hips, and replied with a single comment uttered loud enough for the whole class of preschoolers to hear very clearly. Out of my four-year-old mouth I replied, "I think that's a crock of shit."

When my mom arrived very soon after that to pick me up after being phoned by the younger nun, she blamed my profane response on my dad's potty mouth, but "crock of shit" was one of her favorite phrases. My dad favored the word bullshit over crock of shit any day, and if something really stuck out for not passing the sniff test, he pulled out the intentionally over-enunciated horse shit as a more emphatic response. I didn't know the difference as a kid, I'd never seen either cow shit or horse shit, but I was sure that horse shit was somehow worse, thanks to my Dad. But whomever I picked up crock of shit from, that was my last day at preschool. Ever.

The Mind's Defense of {self}

The reason I shared this story is to exemplify that every action and reaction we have as humans, regardless of age, is designed to defend or perpetuate {self}. Let's rewind to the afternoon play session to review how the rest of the day played out to see how every bit of it was a defense of {self} on everyone's part.

During that afternoon playtime that little blue truck became a portion of my sense of {self}. And it's not hard to see why. I had accomplished attaining that truck with my cunning plan to get to it first, which worked perfectly. I was proud of that. That was all me. Then that blue truck became an extension of my arm, and the complete focus of my attention, becoming a source of joy as I played with it. More sense of {self}. It was a part of my world that I favored at the moment. Although I had only played with it a few minutes, my mind had already laid claim to the rest of the playtime with that truck. For the next twenty minutes, that truck would be all mine, and no one else's. I had followed the rules of sharing and taking turns, so I deserved to play with that truck. I was proud of that also, because frankly I was tired of getting in trouble for being new to those rules. So when the older teacher came over to take the truck out of my hands to give to another boy, she was inadvertently attacking my sense of {self} on multiple levels, and in doing so was initiating a storm of automated processing in my toddler brain designed to defend {self}.

In the first moment I was Sean with command over a cool blue truck. In the second moment I was Sean being scolded with command over nothing. One moment I was a proud little boy who finally understood the fundamentals of sharing and taking turns, and was reaping those rewards. The next I was a confused little boy who was being told that he didn't understand sharing and taking turns. One moment I was a boy who had played by the rules and who deserved to play with the truck. The next moment I was a boy who was being told he had broken the rules, and did not deserve to play with the truck. Lastly, one moment I was a happy toddler with another twenty minutes left on the clock with the truck. The next moment I had 0 minutes left with that truck, and all future hope of joy was lost for the rest of all time. All these individual differences between one moment and the next were all attacks on my sense of {self} at that particular moment. The resulting emotions of sadness, anger, and confusion were a result of these shifts and were ruining my day.

To be fair, the older nun was also being driven by her sense of {self}. We can assume when she took the truck, she was defending the portion of her {self} connected to the idea that toddlers need to understand sharing and taking turns. And of course after playtime was over, her sense of {self} as an authority figure was certainly not going to allow it{self} to be challenged by a four-year-old disputing her actions. That provided the motivation for her to articulate her more aggressive follow up to my initial pushback. And it was of course my defense of {self} mechanism that prompted me to go scorched Earth and tell her she was full of shit, a personal attack which then prompted her to send this potty-mouthed child home forever.

We're All Cranky Toddlers Sometimes

Although this little story happened decades ago, we need look no further than social media to see the same pattern in play today with people we know personally. If you're like most of us, you won't have to scroll very far down your newsfeed comments to find someone who has posted a personal opinion about something, only to have someone else pop in with an opposing rebuttal comment. Then an argument ensues, and no one changes their opinions after the emotional exchange goes down. It seems we all, no matter our age, act like cranky toddlers sometimes.

The good news is that you don't have to be a slave to this process anymore. Because learning to see the process of your individual emotions coming to be in your mind gives you the freedom to influence that process in real time, and recover from your turbulent moments much faster than you normally would. If you remember cognitive neuroscientist Dr. Richard Davidson from Chapter 1, he states, "One of the key ingredients to happiness is being able to recover from adversity more quickly." And the name-it-tame-it studies show us that putting understanding to your negative emotions helps turn them down more quickly. So let's discuss how to do that by revealing how your personal {self} helps create the individual emotions you experience daily, which will throw you into the control room of meta-awareness and give you access to the controls that create your emotions in the first place. It's a pretty simple process to understand. It's based on the simplicity of how our nervous system works.

How Your Emotions Work

My friend Eiji Han Shimizu co-produced an independent film titled The Happy Movie, which discussed the basic science of happiness. Find it online and watch it. One of the guests interviewed for Eiji's film on happiness was Dr. Read Montague, who besides having one of the coolest names in the world, is a Professor of Neuroscience at Baylor College of Medicine. He summed up the nervous system, inclusive of the brain, in just a few words quite nicely. He said, "Your nervous system is a differential engine. It looks at differences. It looks at contrast. That's all it cares about. It integrates information by integrating a bunch of little differences in things." And in it's most elegant simplification, that is a completely accurate statement. When our nervous system tries to quantify anything, it first looks at something else to compare that new something to.

For instance, when your hand sends the message that something feels hot, it's because your hand was first **not-hot** which allowed it to make that calculation. Our hand isn't informing us about the actual definite temperature of something. Our hand doesn't say, this pot on the stove is 120°. It simply sends a message that the temperature of [whatever it's touching] is much higher than what the skin sensed just moments ago. This is why it's said that a live frog will not attempt to escape a pot of water that is brought to a boil very, very slowly. The frog's nervous system never creates the message about a substantial temperature increase, so it never takes action to save itself. This is the same reason that humans die of natural gas asphyxiation in their own homes. Someone wakes up in the middle of the night to smell natural gas leaking from somewhere, but after a few minutes they can't smell it anymore. Thinking it was a dream, or that the gas is now gone, they go back to sleep only to have the gas leak kill the whole family. It's a function of our nervous system to quit alerting us of the gas after about ten minutes. At that point, there isn't a difference in gas levels from one moment to the next. The gas smell went from low to high, which caused the initial olfactory alert which woke us, but now gas levels are just staying high. Nothing new to report. So we don't experience smelling the gas anymore even though it's still there. (By the way, if you smell gas anywhere at any time, get everyone outside into fresh air immediately and call the Fire Department. If you stay, your nose will normalize and ignore the smell even though the danger still exists.)

Our emotions are a product of our nervous system. So it should come as no surprise that your emotions are created through the process of your brain comparing two things against each other. And this is true regardless of what emotion you wind up experiencing. There are specific rules your mind follows to determine whether an emotion presents as happy, sad, fearful, angry, or one of the dozens of other variations, etc., which we will discuss later. Here we're just looking at the two variables your nervous system checks to see if an emotion should be generated.

The Two Variables Connected With Our Emotions

The two things in your mind that your brain compares to create every emotion you have are (1) your Expectation/Preference about [something], and (2) your Perception about that same [something]. Let's talk about how your mind creates these two basic variables for a moment.

Although our Expectation/Preference (EP) sounds like something we choose consciously, this is actually something our brain sets automatically based on its charter to protect {self}. The brain looks at our mind's {self} map and makes a rule that every individual {self} item must be held at status quo or increased in value. This need is actually driven by something in your body called homeostasis, but in its simplest form, this is how your brain sees its defense of {self} charter. If every individual item on your {self} map never takes a hit, then perpetuation of your {self} is assured, which is the brain's job. So this first EP variable, that everything within your mind's {self}… from your body, to your family and friends, to your politics, religion, and vocation... to your sports teams, hobbies, and possessions... to your aspirations, ideas, and opinions... all the way down to how you think the toilet paper should hang from the roll... your Expectation/Preference is set automatically for you based on the fact that your {self} stuff must always be protected from harm. Thus, the first variable is that every individual item on our {self} map must be affirmed or increase in value.

After setting the EPs that everything be okay with all the items on your mind's {self} map, the brain is then free to compare that list of EPs with the second variable, which is whatever is passing through your mind at the moment, otherwise known as your Perception (P). Our Perception is whatever we are noticing at the moment, including a quick appraisal process of whether what we notice might be positive or negative toward any of our {self} items. Perception is our brain's processing of reality, and/or the mis-processing of reality, to create a perceived reality that doesn't actually exist. The latter mis-processing of reality is the reason we can be scared of monsters under our beds as children, when the only thing really under there is a few dust bunnies. It also explains how emotions remain constant even in people with mental illness and cognitive disabilities. Screwed up perceptions still create real emotions. Our perceptions include our memories, thoughts, imagination, visceral reactions, etc., and our perceptions can even be subconscious sometimes. I'm sure we've all gotten that mysterious weird feeling about something we couldn't put our finger on. That's a subconscious perception.

At the point the brain has both your Expectation/Preference (EP) about {something} and a Perception (P) about that same {something}, it can then weigh those two variables against each other and decide if an emotion should be generated, and whether that emotion should be positive or negative. The brain's basic rule is this: If your Expectation/Preference (EP) matches your Perception (P), then a positive emotion is the result. If your

Expectation/Preference (EP) does not match your Perception (P), a negative emotion becomes the result. Lastly, and importantly, if one of the variables isn't present, the result is no emotion.

A Personal Example

Personally, I've been a fan of the Chicago Cubs baseball team since I started watching baseball in the late 70s and early 80s. My Cubs started with Dave Kingman, Bruce Sutter, Ron Cey, and Ryne Sandberg. Subsequently, the Cubs have had a spot on my mind's {self} map for quite a while. As a result, my brain looks at that {self} item of {the Cubs} and sets the Expectation/Preference that the team be held at status quo or better in all of my mind's interactions. So any time I see or hear something about {the Cubs}, like a score from a game, my Perception and appraisal process compares its assessment of that score with the EP they be held at status quo or increased in value. If the Cubs won the game, my mind's Perception of that outcome is seen as a valuation increase, which matches my EP, so a positive emotion becomes the result of the news."Cubs Win!" Yay! If the Cubs lose however, my appraisal process determines that information as a negative to {the Cubs}, and when my brain compares that Perception to my Expectation/Preference about {the Cubs}, they don't match very well. So a negative emotion associated with the loss is generated.

And we **do need both** an Expectation/Preference about {something}, and a Perception about that same {something} to compare, or no emotion will be generated. A great ancient master of mind, Sun Tsang, put it this way: "The great way is without difficulty, just cease having preferences. When the mind becomes so free that it is capable of letting go of preferences, the great way is no longer difficult." And true to his ancient wisdom, if I take {the Cubs} off my {self} map by deciding not to be a fan anymore, that changes things in my brain dramatically. Because at the moment I quit seeing the Cubs as an extension of my {self}, my brain doesn't take the time to create that Expectation/Preference about news about the Cubs. Now I can learn of a Cubs win or loss, but the Perception doesn't apply to anything on my {self} map, so no emotional reaction is the result. Similarly, if you were to tell me about some obscure high school team winning a state championship in lacrosse, there are multiple reasons why I don't care about that news. I'm not attached to the high school, I'm not attached to lacrosse, I'm not attached to any of the kids playing, and I wasn't following the championship race. So I have no emotional reaction to that news besides the fact I like to see people happy, and I'm sure the champions were, so yay for them. I'm happy that a team who worked hard to succeed won their championship and that no one got badly injured. Yay! But besides that, I don't give a shit.

This same thing works for the Perception side as well. Let's say I do decide to continue favoring {the Cubs} so they remain on my {self} map. If they play a game without me knowing who won, my Perception about the outcome of the game is blank. I have a {Cubs} Expectation/Preference, but don't yet have a Perception to compare it to. So I don't yet have an emotional reaction regarding their win or loss status for that game. Yes, it could bug me that I don't know who won the game yet, which may then prompt me to go check the score, but that's a different Expectation/Preference vs. Perception comparison in play; one where my Expectation/Preference is wanting to know the score of the game, measured against my Perception I don't yet know the score. And while that provides a separate equation to balance out, that's not the emotional reaction to the result of the game itself. I won't have an emotional reaction to the result of the game itself until I actually check the score. So the integrity of the rule is solid.

This simple nervous system comparison process works to explain absolutely every emotional response you have. Any time you experience an emotion, it is the result of your brain looking at something on your mind's {self} map, and comparing it to a Perception about that same {self} item. If the Perception is positive or negative, the resulting emotion will be too. Even if the perception is mistakenly positive or negative. And this is the basis of what makes you happy or unhappy about every little thing, every day of your life.

It's Fairly Simple

So it turns out that our individual emotions are actually pretty easy to understand. When my son brings home his report card, my Perception of his grades gets measured against my Expectation/Preference about those grades. The output of that subconscious comparison is how I wind up feeling about those grades. Pick anything from my {self} map and it works the exact same way. I teach happiness and brain hacking for increasing overall quality of life and attaining high performance in numerous fields. So my coaching method winds up on my mind's {self} map. Subsequently, when my books, podcasts, or mobile apps receive reviews online, my Perception of those reviews gets measured against my Expectation/Preference about those reviews, and that generates an emotional response about those reviews. (Thanks for the great reviews, by the way! You're spreading happiness by doing so. Keep them coming!)

From here, our emotions process can be simplified to a simple equation that becomes a super-useful tool for us.

The Equation of Emotion (EoE)

EP $\triangle$ P = ER

EP	$\triangle$	P	=	ER
(Expectation/Preference)	(Perception)			(Emotional Reaction)

(Note: The symbol $\triangle$ is used to represent set theory difference, not delta from calculus)

This Equation of Emotion tool is super-beneficial to us for six reasons I briefly touched on in earlier chapters.

Reason 1 the EoE is a Critical Tool: Increased Emotional Intelligence

Understanding your Equation of Emotion creates a direct path to understanding your individual emotions, which raises your emotional intelligence. There's a lot of science about emotional intelligence. Studies show that increases in emotional intelligence can raise your general IQ and make you smarter. In addition, higher emotional intelligence improves your cognitive functioning, increases your happiness levels, and reduces and/or eliminates anxiety, stress, and depression. Increased emotional intelligence results in improvements in your self awareness levels, self regulation levels, in empathy, and compassion. In students, higher emotional intelligence has been shown to increase verbal SAT scores, along with higher ACT and WAIS-III scores. In short, when you better understand our emotional landscape, it supercharges your brain to work better and increases the brain's efficiency and happiness output. In business studies, it's been shown that our mind's emotional competencies are twice as important to contributing to success as intelligence and expertise in a job role. Lemme say that again: In business, your mind's emotional competencies are twice as important as being smart and knowing your job. All the science behind how emotional intelligence helps the brain in business is what influenced the Harvard Business Review to call emotional intelligence "The Essential Ingredient to Success." Increasing emotional intelligence is a human life game changer. Understanding the Equation of Emotion helps us along this path.

Reason 2 the EoE is a Critical Tool: The Transition into Meta-Awareness

Any time you turn our mind inward to look at the two variables that create your emotions, you throw yourself into that space of meta-awareness, aka the control room of mind. This is the space where you make the transition from being on the leash of your emotions to having your emotions be on that leash. You make the transition from asking yourself how to serve and satisfy your emotions, to asking yourself how your emotions can better serve and satisfy you. It's in the space of meta-awareness you go from being a creature of emotions to being a creature with emotions. To make this shift consciously after or even during experiencing an emotion, simply reference the Equation of Emotion and ask yourself, "What was my Expectation/Preference of this situation?" Then follow that question with, "And what was my Perception that triggered this emotional reaction?" Those two simple questions turn your mind inward onto itself. That transports you immediately into the space of meta-awareness where you will then have the ability to answer those two questions and engage the third reason the EoE is such an awesome tool.

Reason 3 the EoE is a Critical Tool: Turning Down Your Inner Turmoil in Real Time

The simple act of identifying the two variables that created an emotional reaction in turn engages your "name-it-tame-it" brain circuits, which then physically turns down your brain's limbic system in real time. This is like pushing the off button on your inner BS engine. Understanding your emotions brings peace to the internal emotions process. This can be a critical tool, because we often make our biggest mistakes when under the influence of negative emotions. We often do the most damage to our personal and professional relationships when under the influence of our limbic system. Knowing where that OFF button is so you can repeatedly use it at will sure comes in handy during those times where your unexpected negative emotions may be inhibiting your best course of action. Anger blocks your forgiveness. Fear inhibits your courageousness. Sadness postpones your love and acceptance. Who wouldn't want to turn those inhibitors of happiness off quicker?

Reason 4 the EoE is a Critical Tool: Moving from Compulsion to Choice

Being able to view and understand your emotional process within gives you the freedom of choice. And you need that choice. Because having emotions isn't a bad thing. Your emotions are designed to serve and protect you. Do we want to eradicate your emotions? Absolutely not, and given the physiology of the nervous system, I'm not even sure that's possible. But that's not what we're talking about here. We're talking about going from compulsion to choice. We're talking about being able to make the decision of what emotions to use to our benefit, and what emotions to diffuse because they are mechanisms designed for a world in which we no longer live. Compulsion means you're forced to deal with and dig through the negative crap covering up your happiness. Choice means you can sweep that crap off the table and uncover your happiness at will. Knowing how your emotions work is your first step in transitioning from compulsion to choice.

Reason 5 the EoE is a Critical Tool: Accessing Our Mind's Control Knobs

Seeing the two variables that create your emotions gives you a better understanding of those variables and how you can hack them so as to take control of your entire emotional landscape at the level where your emotions are first catalyzed. You can now choose to alter the very building blocks of your emotions process, thereby changing that whole process for your benefit (and for the benefit of your brain). Psychology has been forever chasing the alteration of our Perceptions through almost every sub-discipline psychology utilizes. And how we see things does make a huge difference in how we react to them. But what you allow onto your mind's invented {self} map is where the real power resides. Because your {self} map creates half of your Equation of Emotion, and hacking your {self} map changes every moment of your life, and does so by using your existing brain wiring to assist with that change.

Reason 6 the EoE is a Critical Tool: Explaining All of Our Individual and Complex Emotions

How you decide to hack your mind becomes clear when we review exactly how the Equation of Emotion works its magic to create both your simple and complex emotions. In the next chapter, we're going to cover how our same elegant EoE explains your complex emotions as well. If you've always wondered what exactly causes you to become angry, or sad, or fearful, or jealous… or what causes you to mix your emotions into things like being happy and sad at the same time, you're gonna like the next few chapters where we lift the veil on that stuff. And of course later, we'll discuss the deepest secrets of self where all the world's wisdom traditions converge, and the whole picture really comes together to reveal your personal path to extended and effortless happiness.

Chapter 6 Takeaways

1. Our nervous system is a simple comparator, comparing one thing with another to create its output.

2. Our emotions are an output of our nervous system. Our brains are part of our nervous system.

3. The two variables your brain uses to create your emotions can be simplified to a simple equation that becomes a super useful tool. It's called this the Equation of Emotion (EoE). It's your Expectation/Preference (EP), as compared to your Perception (P), produces your Emotional Reaction (ER).

4. Your mind's {self} creates the EP side of the Equation of Emotion, which is that our {self} items must be held at status quo or increased in value. This is true for each {self} item.

5. Your mind's Perception and appraisal process creates the other side of the Equation of Emotion.

6. When the two variables balance, a positive emotion is the result.

7. When the two variables don't balance, a negative emotion is the result.

8. When one or the other variables is absent, no emotion is the result.

9. Knowing the Equation of Emotion is important for multiple reasons.

Chapter 6 Reflection

1. What are the things on your {self} map that automatically create your EPs for your Equation of Emotion?

2. Are your Perceptions of life events typically positively or negatively skewed? And how do you think this affects the output of your Equation of Emotion?

7. Our Complex Emotions Aren't That Complex

This chapter shows you how our one basic Equation of Emotion can explain not only all our individual emotions, but also our most complex emotions. We'll get into the details of our individual emotions in the next chapter, where we'll learn why your fear is fear, and why your anger is anger, etc. Let's look at the basic function of the Equation of Emotion (EoE) in your mind. We'll start with a very mundane everyday occurrence, because while the EoE can explain our reactions to the most moving stories of our lives, it's the everyday stuff that we deal with constantly.

A Personal Story

My son was standing too close to the swimming pool. That was definitely my fault. But in my defense, I wasn't expecting him to fall in. He knew the rules. No touching the water. He was really good at following the rules, but he was two-years-old at the time, and his coordination wasn't the best. We were standing next to the pool talking to a friend at an afternoon party. One moment I felt him touching my leg as he was bending over next to me, inspecting a bug on the poolside cement, the next moment I suddenly felt his hand falter and slip off my leg, then a small off-balance step forward, another stumble, then SPLASH.

Shit.

The split second after I realized my son had fallen into the pool, I didn't completely panic. That was partly because I knew my son wouldn't panic either. He was no stranger to being in the water. We had put him through an infant swim training program, and he not only knew how to hold his breath while submerged, he also knew how to float face up if no one could get to him right away. And I was standing right there next to him when it happened, so I knew it would be seconds before I had him out of the water and we would be changing him into dry clothes. But there was still the issue that my two-year-old son needed to be fished out of the pool, and that probably needed to be done rather quickly.

There was only one problem in that split second of reaction thinking. I had my cell phone in the deep pocket of my cargo pants. It was much too buried to try and pull it out before jumping into the pool after my son. And this was back when a quick dip under water meant the instant death of electronic devices. So no doubt about it... my next potential act of jumping into the pool to assist my son could potentially cost me about five hundred dollars. Ouch. Really? Could I take the few extra seconds to pull the phone out, throw it in the grass to save it from getting wet, and then jump in?

I really didn't entertain that thought before I was in motion. I hit the water even before the splash of Declan's initial entrance had completely erupted, and before he had popped back above the surface. My phone was still in deep in my pocket and now probably inoperative as I lifted him above the surface of the water. It maybe took a whole second-and-a-half between the time he had actually hit the water before I had him wrapped in my arms above the water safe and sound. He sputtered for a second and wiped the water from his eyes. I knew his reaction to this event would be influenced by my reaction to it, so I did my best to act normal, ignoring that we were both in the pool unexpectedly. I immediately engaged him in conversation to set the mood that he was safe and this was just a silly accident. I smiled and giggled as I looked him in the eye and playfully asked him, "Holy cow! Did you fall in the pool?" "Yeah," he said smiling as he wiped more water from his face. "Are you okay?" I asked. "Yeah," he replied again. This time he actually giggled. As he looked around while I moved toward the pool's steps, he seemed rather happy with this new experience, which was that of being in the pool while being still fully clothed, with Daddy holding him, who was also still fully clothed. It created a silly and fun experience for us both, although more for him than me.

The reason I share this everyday story is to show how our complex emotions work. I can use such a simple story because (1) our complex emotions can happen at any time during the day connected with almost any situation, and (2) it turns out even our most complex emotions actually aren't that complex. In the previous chapter, we talked about how our individual emotions are formed by explaining the Equation of Emotion and its two simple variables. But our complex emotions can't be as simple as that, can they? In a word, yes. Yes, they can. Our complex emotions are just as simple. Our mind forms them by taking multiple instances of our Equation of Emotion, and stacking them up simultaneously on top of each other.

If we rewind that one event, and take the emotions I experienced in slow motion, they appeared in quick order as surprise, fear, concern, disappointment, embarrassment, concern again, happiness, and finally joy. Let's quickly go through them so you can see how my complex emotional reaction was formed in split-seconds by simply piling up individual Equations of Emotion. This will give you insight into how your complex emotional reactions are formed the same way. Imagine if you will, that we are back at that pool before Declan fell in the water, and everything is happening in real time in slow motion.

Splash.

Surprise

First, let's talk about my surprise. When I was standing next to the pool with my son talking to my friend, I was engaged in the conversation, but I was also feeling for Declan's hand on my leg to ensure he didn't take another step toward the water, where he would then be at the very edge of the pool and primed to fall in. I thought he was safe where he stood, so when he actually stumbled and fell in, it came as a big surprise. Surprise is the emotion based on our Expectation of the following moment not matching our Perception of the following moment. Dr. David Eagleman explains this process exceptionally well in his book **Incognito: The Secret Lives of the Brain**, but when our Perception violates our Expectation, surprise occurs. This can happen with loud noises, when something touches us unexpectedly, and even with surprise parties, if they're done right. So when my Expectation that Declan would not fall into the pool was violated by my Perception of him going into the pool, that caused my surprise. And that was the first Equation of Emotion as it was played out.

Fear

The second Equation of Emotion came when Declan entered the water and became submerged. As a big part of my {self} map, my Expectation/Preference about Declan is that he be safe and sound at all times. But because I know humans aren't supposed to breathe water, my Perception that my son was now submerged didn't match my EP about him being safe. So that created a bit of fear that Declan might be in danger.

Concern

In the next split-second, the thoughts about me going into the pool after him entered my Perception. This gave rise to the memory of my cell phone being in my pocket. We don't need Dr. Jim Coan's fMRI machine at UVA to know our cell phones become a big extension of our {self}, so my EP about my phone is that it be protected from harm at all times. With the Perception of my phone being on the cusp of certain death, to include all my information and contacts going away, that caused my concern about my phone and the $500 it would take to replace it.

Disappointment

As I entered the water and felt the water soaking the pocket where I had the phone, my concern shifted to disappointment about my phone. That shift is a function of the individual rules governing our emotions, which we will speak about in the next chapter. But basically the EP about my phone was met with my Perception it was gone and no longer held any value for me. The phone was most certainly dead, and there was nothing I could do about it.

Embarrassment

At the moment I scooped Declan up out of the water, another Perception entered my mind. This Perception was one about me personally. I was now the daddy in the pool who let his 2-year-old son fall into the pool. Crap. Am I the type of father who doesn't watch his kids? Is my son in danger of falling into bodies of water frequently because I don't watch him well enough? These thoughts are how others might see me at this moment, which of course challenged my EP regarding my role of {father}. I am a father, which is an idea that winds up on my mind's {self} map, which then has a bunch of {ideas about fatherhood} connected to it, all of which must be protected. I don't want to be considered a bad father, and I don't want to be a bad father. This caused a flash of embarrassment in my mind about where I was and what I was doing.

Concern Again

But then came the moment of greatest importance. It was the moment of re-engaging with my son. In the last moments, Declan had taken an unexpected and possibly scary trip for him underwater. So I wanted to make sure he was okay both physically and psychologically, and I also wanted to ensure this experience didn't traumatize him to be afraid of being near water. So my EP that Declan be held safe and sound physically and psychologically was measured against my uncertain Perception that he would be. This caused concern for his future physical and psychological well-being. This is what prompted me to ask a question to get him talking so I could determine if he'd inhaled any water,and what prompted me to frame the question in a playful manner with a fun tone. If he was okay physically, who knows what was going on in my son's mind at that moment? I certainly knew his limbic system would be kicking in and creating surprise and fear of his own. I didn't want him being nervous about dad being angry because he had broken the rules about being close enough to the water to fall in. I certainly didn't want his memory circuits to paint this event as negative, which may later develop into an aversion to water. And so all these thoughts urged my playful questions to him about falling into the pool.

Happiness

After he answered in a clear voice, it entered my Perception that my son was okay, and his smile told me he thought the incident was just about as funny as I did. These Perceptions in my mind matched my EPs, both about Declan, and about his reaction to falling into the pool, so with multiple balanced Equations of Emotion, I started to experience happiness and relief on multiple levels.

Joy

Finally, the joy of being with my son, wherever we were, arose and flooded my being. Joy is the emotion we feel when we connect with something we hold dear. We can experience joy connecting with nature, connecting with great music, connecting with great food, or when reconnecting with old friends or family we haven't seen in a while. So when I reconnected with my son, I felt the joy of that moment. I didn't truly care we were standing in the pool together fully clothed. It didn't matter I was out the $500 it would cost to replace my phone. I didn't even care what others' opinions might be of my fatherhood as they watched the whole scene play out. My son was okay, and we were having fun together, so the surprise, concern, embarrassment, concern again, and whatever else I may have forgotten were all trumped by the happiness and joy that flooded the final moment.

We Assign Biological Value to {self} Items

As simple as it is, this mundane story actually carries two important lessons for us. The first lesson is that although we have tons of things that wind up on our {self} map, we don't attach to them all equally. Some {self} items we attach to more than others. For instance, I'm more attached to my son than I am my phone, obviously. That means when I'm faced with a decision about two different {self} items, such as my decision to delay jumping into the pool after my son, or take a moment and save my phone, the {self} item I'm more attached to will win the day every time.

The same is true for you. If you are more attached to one political candidate over the other, that's how you vote. If you are more attached to one restaurant over another, that's where you eat. If you are attached to one sports team over another, then that is the team you will secretly pull for over the other when they play each other. This goes all the way down to the point that if you have a horizontal toilet paper holder, and you are more attached to the position that the loose toilet paper is supposed to be hung over the top of the roll, where the end of the paper hangs out front, where it's easy to grab, that is how you will install the toilet paper when the old roll runs out.

This selection of the more important {self} items actually has a scientific explanation. It's based on something called biological value that USC Neuroscience Professor and consciousness researcher Dr. Antonio Damasio spoke about in his book Self Comes to Mind: Constructing the Conscious Brain. When it comes to making decisions, whatever means more to us is what gets protected when we reach a fork in the road that requires us to pick one or the other course. And this works in everyone the same way, because it's a simple comparison of the nervous system. And it doesn't even have to be a life or death situation for our {self} items to throw their weight around in this survival of the fittest fashion. This phenomenon follows us into the most mundane situations of our lives. In fact, every decision we make is governed by this phenomenon.

If we go out to buy a new [whatever], the [whatever] we choose is the one that aligns best with our sense of {self}. Buying a new car? Does better gas mileage, longer warranty, and free oil changes with the hybrid align better with our idea of {self}, or does the amazing acceleration of the V8 engine in that fancy sports car align better? And look, the V8 even comes in your favorite color! Do we appreciate all the signal inputs of that high-end flat screen TV, or do we appreciate the cheaper model that will still work with our wireless TV box and leaves enough money to buy a video game system as well? Hmm, do I save my son immediately, or is he good for an extra two seconds so I can save $500 by digging my phone out and tossing it in the grass? Believe it or not, some people would gamble with taking the phone out of their pockets first, and that's totally okay. Maybe their son is Michael Phelps and performs in the water as well as out. Whatever better serves and affirms our mind's {self} is the decision we make. 100 percent of the time. By the way, I'm proud to say that I share my reaction with Amy Poehler, who reported making the same decision about her child falling in the pool vs. saving her electronics in her book, Yes, Please! So at least I'm in good company. By the way, great job, Amy! I loved your book!

Equations of Emotion Are Additive

The second lesson of this kid-falls-in-the-pool story is, of course, how our one simple Equation of Emotion piles up multiple times, one by one, to create all our complex emotions as our Perception shifts to the various facets of whatever situation we're in. In about five seconds flat, with just one EP connected with my son, I experienced more than one emotion based on the Perceptions I was having about Declan. In addition, the one Perception I had that my son had fallen into the pool interacted with multiple EPs on my {self} map, including Declan, my phone, and even my image as a good Dad. So the one Equation of Emotion filled itself with numerous variables that then created a rather complex emotional situation. Take any complex emotion you've ever experienced, or study the next one you experience the future, and you'll see at its core will be a pile of individual Equations of Emotion that have all been processed in your subconscious mind one at a time. This understanding of how your emotions come to be isn't a nice-to-have when looking to up your happiness game, it's a must-have. Because although its a little weird to dig into your own emotions to see how they all come together, taking the actions to understand your emotions then kicks in all the brain benefits we spoke of at the end of the last chapter, including having your brain physically turn down the output of your inner bullshit engine in real time. It also illuminates what two variables you need to adjust that create all your emotions, so that you can begin to control what emotions get created for you in the future.

With this new knowledge about your emotions comes an amazing amount of additional power in life. Because not only does this allow you to see better into your own mind, it also allows you to see into the minds of other people as well.

Chapter 7 Takeaways

1. Your individual Equations of Emotion pile up on top of each other simultaneously to create our complex emotions.

2. One EP from an item on your {self} map can interact with multiple Perceptions, creating the opportunity for mixed emotions from any single event.

3. One Perception can interact with multiple EPs from your {self} map, creating the opportunity for mixed emotions from any single event.

Chapter 7 Reflection

1. What is a situation in your life that is complicated for you? Can you identify all the individual emotions of that complicated situation? Can you list out the individual Equations of Emotion which create this complicated situation in your mind?

8. Why You Feel the Way You Feel about Stuff

If your emotional abilities aren't in hand,

if you don't have self-awareness,

if you are not able to manage your distressing
emotions,

if you can't have empathy and have effective
relationships,

then no matter how smart you are,

you are not going to get very far.

—Daniel Goleman

This last step in explaining where our emotions come from is where the process starts to get really cool. Because now we can discuss the simple specifics of what makes you (and everyone around you) experience different emotions like fear, anger, sadness, worry, regret, etc. In doing so, we bring your emotional intelligence game to a whole new level, and we begin to unlock the secrets to your personal happiness. This is where your understanding of mind starts to open doors within you that you didn't even know existed, and your entry into the control room of your mind becomes more effortless.

It's also where you start to gain a crystal clarity on the activity within other people's minds as well. Not only will this help you calm the turbulence in your own mind, it will also help you understand how you might help reduce the turbulence in the minds of those you care about. This raises your emotional intelligence. And don't forget that studies show that higher emotional intelligence equates to higher IQ, increased focus, lower stress levels, improved health, higher levels of happiness and well-being, and according to the Harvard Business Review, even higher financial incomes, increased work productivity, and increased business success. Studies have shown that over 80 percent of the competencies that differentiate top performers from others are in the domain of emotional intelligence. Increases in EI have been shown to improve sales performance by almost 20 percent, increase work productivity by almost 20 percent, and improve employee selection success by 300 percent.

A study done at a Motorola manufacturing facility showed that training in stress reduction and EI provided a productivity increase in 93 percent of the participants who took the training. A review at Johnson & Johnson of 358 managers showed that high EI scores correlated with significantly higher performance. A study done at a multinational consulting firm showed that consultants who scored in the top half EI scores on tests brought in 71 percent of the company's revenue compared to just 29 percent from the bottom half of EI scoring consultants. A large beverage company hired executives based on emotional intelligence scores, and half the low EI execs were dumped for low performance within 2 years, compared to only 6 percent failure from high EI execs. A national insurance company found that their high EI sales folks sold almost exactly twice as much insurance as the low EI reps. American

Express trained existing executives in emotional intelligence and saw an 18.1 percent business growth from trained teams as compared to teams that were not trained. The big insurance company, Aetna, even found that providing training that delivered higher emotional intelligence and lowered stress in employees reduced their company healthcare costs by $2,000 per employee, and increased productivity by $3,000 per employee. EI science is why the cover of On Point magazine from Harvard Business Review called Emotional Intelligence "The Essential Ingredient to Success," not just for individuals, but for companies, too.

The reason EI helps businesses is because it helps the individuals running those businesses. It makes people better at everything they do because it reduces the mental noise that would otherwise get in the way of being superior at their chosen activities. We spend tons of resources trying to hire the best and brightest employees. We want to be the best and brightest leaders so the economy can reward us for that talent. In short, EI is the golden goose that ensures both. Because it supercharges our minds, it's the most effective way to allow a team to attain it's happiest, healthiest, and most productive state. When you supercharge your brain, you supercharge it for everything you do. And whether your personal increased mental capacity is used for the business of your chosen profession, or tending to the business of your everyday life, it doesn't matter. A supercharged brain is a supercharged brain. When people get their mind's {self} out of the way, amazing things happen.

As Meng Tan so eloquently reminds us in his book Joy on Demand, "when you can perceive mental processes in sufficiently high resolution, you may find that the mind continuously creates a sense of {self} in reaction to sensory input and thoughts that arise. When the mind is so calm it doesn't react to sense input, nor does it generate any thoughts, there may be moments when the sense of {self} does not arise." When {self} arises less in the mind, so do our negative thoughts, emotions, and reactions because {self} is one half of that process. So it's here that we'll take the one last step of giving you the details of how your mind generates fear, anger, sadness, etc., so that you can learn to see it happening in real time in your own mind, and get your {self} out of your own way. Understanding these last particulars will give you a better understanding of your subconscious mind (not to mention a better understanding of the subconscious minds around you), and it will also give you a quicker and more firm control of your own mind when you need it.

The Caveats for This Chapter

Before we discuss the individual emotions, there are a couple quick caveats: First, what I'm going to provide here is a simplification of the rules the mind uses for the different emotions into terms we can all easily understand. That said, please know there are some rather technical explanations behind these broad brush definitions, even though I don't present those technical specifics here. What I present here is what you can remember easily so you can use this information to up your happiness game every day from this day forward.

Still, you should know the depths of this science will indeed be what gives artificial personalities real human emotions in the next few years. So don't be surprised when Siri and Alexa start being able to talk about your mom with you. But as a warning, service providers will also be able to track and predict your emotional responses to content you haven't even consumed yet without laying a single eye or ear on you, so don't freak out when your online interactions start responding to your emotional reactions, even though they're not measuring your facial expression, heart rate, respiration, skin conductivity, jaw muscle tension, etc., all of which are currently required to determine your human emotions after they've left the barn. If you're a little worried about service providers being able to predict your emotions, don't fret. This book is your Kryptonite, and will ensure that no one can emotionally manipulate you without your permission. You reading this book is like getting to see all the secrets behind all the magician's tricks before he or she even performs them. You won't be fooled moving forward.

So let's get to explaining your individual emotions.

We've already discussed how your internal Equation of Emotion fires off the process of creating all your emotions. And we discussed that if your Equation of Emotion is balanced, you will experience a positive emotion, and if it's unbalanced you'll experience a negative one. But what determines if an emotional reaction shows up as fear, or anger, or sadness, or other emotion in your mind, and what determines if it's a powerful emotion or a weak emotion? Well, there are some simple rules your mind follows to create your various individual emotions. Let's discuss some of those now.

The Variation of Your Individual Emotions

The first step in understanding why particular emotions come to be is to understand that all your individual emotions come in differing levels of severity. You've experienced this before. I'm sure there have been many times in your life where a low level of anger arose about something that you were simply able to let go of quickly. You saw or heard something that upset you a bit, but you decided, "I'm not even going to waste my time responding to that." But there have been other times in your life that something pissed you off so much that you couldn't help yourself but to speak up and say something about it, or maybe even take physical action. Maybe this stronger anger reaction started an argument, or put a stop to someone doing something offensive or mean. These were simply two different levels of anger that surfaced in two different life situations.

Sometimes, we give these different severities of emotions different names entirely, even though they come from the base emotion they're related to. For instance, fear at a low level is something we call concern or sometimes nervousness. While fear at a high level, we often call panic or terror. Anger at it's lowest level can be called annoyance, while anger at a higher level can be classified as rage. Sadness at a low level can be considered disappointment, while sadness at a high level is typically called despair. Every unique emotion group has these subjective levels of severity, and frankly the words we use are completely subjective. I typically look to split each emotion group into five different severities, but that said... I also humbly acknowledge that due to the subjective nature of naming / grouping emotions, science will eventually probably refine these a bit. Maybe we'll learn there are actually 20 levels of anger, not five. Who knows? But what really is the difference between being flustered and being shaken anyway? Is there one? Or are they just two different words for the same state of mind?

Coincidentally, right before this book went out to editing, world famous researcher on emotions Dr. Paul Ekman, along with his daughter Dr. Eve Ekman put out a visual Atlas of Emotions at paulekman.com. The Atlas of Emotions breaks down emotions in a very similar fashion to what is presented here. When I first published these groupings five years ago in my first book, How Emotions Work in Humans and Computers, I had no idea that the leading lifelong researchers in the space of emotions were headed in the same exact direction. The parallels of these two independently derived sources will gain some profound gravity in Volume II when we discuss how I discovered the truth versus the decades-of-research process now just starting to be published.

All that said, the words we use don't really matter to our mind. Our mind simply creates our basic emotions at different power levels that we then name as different emotions. The rules about your emotion power levels apply to all your emotion groups equally, so we'll discuss what in your mind selects emotion severity first, then we'll discuss the simple rules your mind uses to create your individual emotions themselves.

The Rules of Your Emotion's Severity

The rules that determine how severe an emotion winds up being in your mind (i.e. the difference in anger from being annoyed to enraged, or the difference in sadness from being disappointed to in despair) are super-easy to understand, and even easier to explain. Here's the rule:

The severity of any emotion you experience is determined by the importance of the Expectation/Preference, and seriousness of Perception, combined.

That's the official definition, but frankly we already know this basic truth about our emotions. In our Equation of Emotion, we know our Expectations/Preferences are created automatically for every idea on our {self} map. And it's no secret we care about some things more than others, so not all things on our {self} map are created equal. Some things are more important to us. For instance, we saw earlier in the book how I bricked my phone by jumping into the pool after my son when he fell in unexpectedly. Both {my son} and {my phone} are firmly attached to my {self} map, but my son falls closer to the center of my map, so when it came time to choose, the more powerful emotion about my son won out over the weaker emotion about my phone, and into the pool I went, phone and all.

You attach to different {self} items unequally as well. You feel this when you want to give preference to one thing over another, or one person over another. For instance, you might be more connected to your mom in your family than one of those distant cousins you've never met. So when your mom calls to borrow your last $5 at the same moment you get that unexpected email from one of those anonymous cousins asking the same favor, if mom is in good standing, she gets your last five bucks, not your anonymous cousin.

Attachment level differences even happen with our material possessions. Maybe you have a favorite pair of shoes or boots you like more than your other ones, that if I grabbed from your closet to donate to Goodwill, you'd immediately grab them back from me and suggest, "yeah, I'm all for donating shoes, but let's donate a different pair instead of these."

Well, in short, these degrees of importance on your {self} map are partly what help make your emotions more or less powerful depending on how attached you are to the {self} item creating the Expectation/Preference in play. If the {self idea} is more important to you, and lands closer to the center of our {self} map, then the resulting emotion associated with that idea has the potential to be more powerful than if the {self} item is out toward the edge of your map where you don't care about those things as much.

Let's imagine an Equation of Emotion where we grab a static Perception and compare two different EPs for an example. Let's say the Perception is that someone has gotten the flu. If it's your grandma who got the flu, you might be more concerned or worried than if say, your local television news broadcaster got the flu. Both exist in your world, and you care about both, but grandma is closer to the center of your {self} map than the news anchor, so the severity of worry is higher with grandma.

In my mind's eye, I see {my son} as much closer to the center of my {self} map than say . . . my appreciation for {the Chicago

Cubs}. So in my mind, {my son} has a much higher power level on the {self} map than {the Cubs} do. This means my emotional reactions to my son will be more powerful than my reactions to news about the Cubs, or my politics, or my favorite brand of cell phone, or anything that lies farther from the center of my map.

This power level of the {self} item is one-half of the emotion severity puzzle. Of course, this passes our common sense sniff test because you already know that the things you care more about are the things you have the strongest emotional reactions to. But it helps to look at it doesn't it? You feel you know your emotions a little better even at this very moment, don't you? Get used to looking at your emotions in this way. When you focus your mind on the power levels of items on your {self} map, you're in the control room of the mind called meta-awareness. In your control room, you are powerful.

The other half of the emotions severity puzzle is just as simple. It has to do with the power level of the other half of the Equation of Emotion, our Perception. As an example, we can agree that {my son} is close to the center of my {self} map. But admittedly, I will have two differing levels of emotional response regarding {my son} if two different Perceptions arise in similar situations. For instance, if I witness a family member in a bear costume running across the lawn toward {my son}, that presents a low level threat to {my son}, limited only to the possibility that Uncle Craig in the bear suit might trip and fall on him at the last second, or maybe just really scare {my son} because he doesn't know it's Uncle Craig inside the costume. So this first Perception of the Uncle Craig bear carries a low threat level, which makes the fear response low as well. However, if I saw an actual wild bear running across the lawn toward {my son}, that second scenario with the real bear is a powerful Perception of danger toward {my son}. This second scenario is that a wild animal known to sometimes kill people is moving aggressively toward {self}. While the first Uncle Craig–filled bear might cause me mild concern, just enough to watch my son's reaction to the bear suit itself through the window, the second real bear gets me immediately moving toward the door and thinking about how I'm gonna kill a bear with my bare hands. Badum-tish! (Sorry, I had to throw one dad joke into this book; feel free to chastise me through the contact form at the website.)

But you get the point. The power levels of the EP and P from the Equation of Emotion determine the power level of the pending emotion that's about to be generated. The mind first figures out "how serious of a situation is this?" Subsequently, it knows whether **concern** or **panic** should be presented if the fear group is selected, or if **annoyance** or **rage** should be selected if it's the anger group. And it works the same way for happiness, sadness, and all other emotion groups with their individual emotion severities.

If our grandmother gets a cold, we care more about that than if our local TV news broadcaster gets the cold, because they hold different power levels on our {self} map. If our local TV news broadcaster has a stroke and winds up in the hospital, we care more about that than if they've simply contracted a cold, because our Perception of the stroke is much more powerful than someone having a simple cold. And when it's our grandmother who is the one who is in the hospital, that's when our limbic system really kicks into overdrive and we experience the highest levels of worry possible because both the {self} map power level and Perception power level are both high.

Easy peezy, right? Right. So let's now take a quick moment to see how the mind chooses between fear, or anger, or sadness, or other emotions.

A Few of Our Most Basic Emotions

To save time and space, we'll discuss a few of our most common emotion groups. Again, other emotion groups are available on the website. We have a Mind Hacking Happiness mobile app planned, as well as a weekly podcast, and some online courses for those looking for true mastery. But here we'll take a quick look at our most common emotion groups, including fear, anger, sadness, worry, regret, and couple others.

The Emotion of Fear

> Nothing in life is to be feared,
>
> it is only to be understood.
>
> Now is the time to understand more,
>
> so that we may fear less.
>
> —Marie Curie

It's time to learn about how your fear works. We've used fear in more than a few examples in our previous chapters, so it's no surprise for us to learn that the definition of fear is as follows:

Your fear is the emotional response that occurs when your mind perceives a threat to {self}.

A bear walks out of the woods twenty feet in front of you. Your lungs inflate. Your irises contract. Your conscious attention is acutely focused. Adrenaline starts to spill into your blood stream. Maybe you poop in our pants a little bit. And as your body is prepped for a fight-or-flight response, your waking consciousness is also urged into a similar path; defend or get the hell out of there... and maybe go find some toilet paper. This type of subconscious reaction is classified by psychology and neurobiology as the genetic affect of "preparedness." It is thought to have been bred into physiology through natural selection, since it is presumed organisms with better fear response probably survived longer and went on to mate.

Fear can typically be separated into five levels of severity:

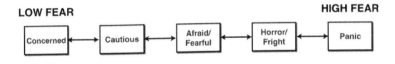

Please note: There's a version of fear that goes beyond panic, which I personally call "spiders." Spider-level fear has no equal.

The process of fear generation as seen from 50,000 feet occurs just as we explained it in the previous chapters: The limbic system constantly scans and analyzes our environment through our senses for things that do not meet the mind's expectation or preference of that environment, and when something is identified outside of expectation or preference, and is perceived as a threat to {self}, fear is generated. This isn't a new idea. The understanding of this process is accepted science, and the definition of fear proves to be accurate in anecdotal and study examples pretty much 100 percent of the time in a healthy mind. If you would like to better understand this Expectation vs Perception process, again, pick up Dr. David Eagleman's book Incognito: The Secret Lives of the Brain. He explains it rather elegantly.

Where science falls behind a bit in understanding fear (and our other emotions) is where all the world's spiritual and scientific luminaries have told us to look for all the answers we seek; and that place falls solidly within the walls of {self}. Remember that our {self} contains all the things your mind points to when defining your existence, thereby creating the map of what needs to be defended in the brain's charter to perpetuate {self}. This means everything on your {self} map has an opportunity to create fear within you if a Perception floats through your mind that any one of those individual ideas may be under threat. Sure, you can be afraid of losing your life, but you can also be afraid of losing your job, losing your money, losing your family, losing your prized possessions, losing your memories and identity, and of course, spiders. Show me someone who isn't afraid of spiders, and I will show you a sick mind! Blech!

Understanding {self} in this new way allows us to understand every fear we have in life. Take for instance, the Top 5 Human Fears as reported by some anonymous list maker on the Internet. They listed humans as being afraid of the dark, being afraid of heights, commitments in relationships, speaking in public, and of course spiders. Who could forget spiders on a Top 5 List of Fears? It's indeed why I went with this particular list. A list without spiders on it can't be very scientific.

Getting back to our point, though, it's not that we're afraid of the dark itself, we're afraid of what is out there in the dark that could pose a threat to {self}. It's not that we're afraid of heights or flying in a plane, we're afraid of what could happen if we fell from that great height and had to deal with the sudden extreme stop at the bottom of the ride. We're not afraid of committing to a romantic relationship, we're afraid of having our {self} take a hit when we truly open up to someone and get rejected. We're not afraid of speaking in public, we're afraid of how {self} is going be seen when we look like a blithering idiot in front of an auditorium full of people. And of course it's not that we're afraid of spiders because they are big enough to eat us. We're afraid of them because . . . what kind of God-awful ugly predator can hang from a string it pulls from its butt, can jump multiple body lengths with eight hairy legs, and can literally look at you from any direction it's facing because it has eight shiny black orbs of soul sucking emptiness to stare at you with? Are you friggin' kidding me? Of course we're afraid of spiders!

Seriously though, this way of understanding fear corrects a rather large misconception in psychology that fear is a learned emotion (psychology used to espouse this, and some psychologists still do). The science suggests its actually hardwired into us. It's not fear itself that's learned. What is learned from our parents and our environment is what kind of things pose a threat to {self}, and also what items should be added to the {self} map that can be threatened. The fear itself is a hard-wired mechanism. And as beneficial as fear can be in helping protect us from harm, fear can also be a crippling emotion when it spins out of control. So while we discuss this more serious topic, I will temporarily suspend my attempts at humor, if only for the rest of this chapter.

A Personal Story About Fear

In the tech sector crash of the early 2000s, my friend Mark (not his real name) and I were sales reps for a large international data center company. If you don't already know, data centers are those big refrigerated clean rooms you see on TV and in movies full of rows and rows of vertical racks of computer servers mounted on raised floor tiles with all the wires neatly organized into big bundles and zip tied every six inches. We had learned through the grapevine that the company executives had figured out the company could be profitable and sustain itself without any further funding if it literally chopped off the entire sales division from the SVP of Sales on down, including the positions Mark and I currently held. Cutting those jobs and related costs would allow the company to make payroll and pay infrastructure costs indefinitely if they didn't lose too many existing customers. But it was a big gamble, a drastic move, and they weren't sure if they were going to pull that particular trigger. After all, who would get them new customers to replace any that left or went out of business themselves, and how would they grow the company without any sales folks?

In the limbo phase of not knowing our future, Mark and I responded very differently to the news that our jobs might be eliminated. Admittedly, we were in different life situations, so our {self} maps looked pretty different. I was a single guy approaching my thirty-second birthday, had a low mortgage payment, and had a good enough reputation in the industry not to have gone a single day without employment since I entered the tech sector. Mark was younger, just out of college, married, had just bought a nice new house, his wife was expecting their first baby, and because Mark's wife had quit her job to become a mother, their only health insurance was tied to the very job that was now in jeopardy.

For me, the pending layoff situation posed a threat to a few things on my {self} map. My expected income was being threatened. This was something to which I was mentally attached as a portion of {self}. If I got laid off, I would no longer have a steady paycheck coming in, which was a negative shift to {self}. Next, many of us get a large portion of our sense of {self} from the jobs or titles we hold, so losing my job meant a negative shift for {self}. Being unemployed has social implications that often worry us, so I was preparing to add a big ugly "unemployed" sticker over the top of my {self} map. That sucked. Lastly, the industry I was tied to was now in turmoil, so I wasn't sure about my job prospects at other companies. Many companies were laying off or closing their doors altogether. So having my {self} attached to {tech} was not exactly a positive thing at the moment. My only saving graces were that I had a bit of money saved up, and I had a lot of friends in the industry, so I didn't completely expect to be without a paycheck longer than I could afford it.

Mark's position was a bit different, however. Thanks to having just made a down payment on a house, Mark really needed his regular paycheck to pay the monthly bills. So his ability to {put a roof over his family} and {put food on the table} was being threatened. Both these ideas were connected with the idea of {being a good husband and father} to his wife and unborn child. These were a big part of Mark's {self} identity, as they were instilled within him by his father, so the threat to these particular {self} items freaked Mark out a bit to say the least. If that weren't enough, he was also facing the payment of some rather large hospital bills in a few months with his wife being due to give birth, not to mention that preparing to bring a new baby home isn't exactly cheap either, with all its required purchases of crib, baby monitors, strollers, swings, bottles, diapers, formula, etc. All those purchases were still looming. In addition, the pending layoff would require Mark and his wife to cut many items from their monthly household budget. So no more cable TV, dinners out on Friday night, or going to the movies on Sunday afternoons. All these were a part of Mark's Expectations/Preferences about how his life had been lived until the moment we heard the layoff rumors. Furthermore, possibly not being able to pay for the elective doctor visits and tests could put the baby at greater risk. And then there was the uncertainty about getting another job to replace this one at a time where everyone in the tech sector was laying people off, not hiring.

It's easy to see how Mark's fear reaction to the potential layoffs was much stronger than mine. He had much more on his {self} map under threat than I did. Additionally, his Perceptions about losing our current positions were more dramatic. Mark was young and inexperienced, he had been with the company for less than a year, his sales numbers were average at best, and he didn't have many friends in the industry, so his future job prospects were worse than normal. This more powerful Perception added power level to his fear responses.

As we sat one day in my office discussing the pending situation, the differences in our fear levels became very evident. Mark broke down in tears. He told me that he and his wife had a huge argument the night before, that his marriage was on the line, and that he literally didn't know what he was going to do to help support his family if he lost his job. And he wasn't exaggerating at all. He literally did not know what to do in the next five minutes, five hours, or five days. I didn't realize this at the time, but it's obvious to see now that his limbic system was in overdrive, and true to form, his negative emotions had substantially shut down his higher thinking brain. He couldn't think of even one thing to do in response to his current situation. His fear had him literally psychologically paralyzed.

Thankfully, although I was also nervous about the future, my situation was different, so my fear levels hadn't gotten to the point of shutting off my prefrontal cortex. Subsequently, I was a little more clear-headed than Mark was, so in response I said this to him: "Mark, here's what you're going to do. You're going to call your wife and take her to lunch today. You're going to be honest and tell her you're not completely sure how you're going to resolve this situation yet, but that you are going to resolve it, and that everything is going to be okay. Let's reduce the amount of worry your wife is experiencing while she's pregnant with your first child, and get you guys on the same team to come up with a solution. Next, take all the time you would have spent looking for customers this afternoon and polish your resume. Start making calls to everyone you know letting them know you're available because of pending layoffs. Then tonight from home, read up on COBRA insurance, which will be available to you after the company insurance drops you, call your family and ask them if they have any rainy day funds you might be able to borrow from for a short time if there's a lapse in employment for a few months, and cut off any elective expenditures in order to conserve cash." I could almost see the fog in Mark's expression dissipate before my eyes. "Yeah" was all he said. Being a man of action no longer frozen, he took out his phone, called his wife to invite her to lunch, and walked out of my office.

The next morning Mark was a new man. Where just the day before his Perceptions had him paralyzed with fear, now his Perceptions had changed, and with them, true to form, the output of his individual Equations of Emotion had changed as well. It turned out that his parents had about $20,000 he could borrow, which reduced the threat to his {self} items of {providing food and housing for his family} and {being a good husband and expectant father}. One of his contacts was going to set up an interview for him at a different company, which reduced the threat to the {self} items of {being a tech salesperson} and {being gainfully employed}. And over their shared lunch, the rift between he and his wife had been almost completely repaired, so there was a greatly reduced threat to his marriage. They were now on the same team, and his wife had even secured her old job back. I could tell Mark's thinking brain had been re-engaged, and his attitude about the future was much more optimistic.

In the end, everything turned out fine. Mark decided to start a business to solve his employment problems and did well. Our company did decide to eliminate the sales division and survived long enough to be purchased less than a year later. The layoffs cut hundreds of jobs, but they also saved hundreds of others from unemployment by not shuttering the company altogether. I was hired into the executive ranks of a Fortune Global 100. So it turns out none of us needed to fear anything in that horrible situation. But for a time, faced with this particularly challenging situation, everyone froze, even the company executives. And none of that emotional strife was either constructive or necessary.

What I wish I had been able to tell Mark at the time was that if he looked into his mind at his fear from that internal space of awareness and understanding called meta-awareness, seeing exactly how and why his emotions were coming to be, that might have rebooted his thinking brain without the need for another person to be in the room. That might have headed off the big blow-up with his wife that had added stress to their acute situation. Furthermore, an ability to see a bit into his wife's potential fears may have given him the insight necessary to generate more empathy and compassion for his wife, who was dealing with this same exact situation he was, with the added joy of the pregnancy hormones.

When we are gripped by fear about losing our job, or losing anything else of great importance to us, it throws our mind into a tizzy of activity that millions of years of intelligence has developed into a superb system for defending against physical threats. But that same fear reaction may not serve us as well as it once did, now that we need to think our way out of numerous fearful issues. So why shouldn't we grab our fear volume knob and crank it down? Answer: We should.

The Emotion of Anger

Anger dwells in the bosom of fools.

—Albert Einstein

First, let's look at the anger group, which covers the severity levels of this emotion.

LOW ANGER   **HIGH ANGER**

Annoyed ←→ Frustrated ←→ Angry ←→ Fury ←→ Rage

The ancient philosopher of mind, the Gautama Buddha, once said, "In a controversy, the instant we feel anger we have already ceased striving for truth, and have begun striving for ourselves." Say what you want about the Buddha, but the dude knew the human mind better than most people ever will. Without psychological science, without Western philosophy and rhetoric, and without the ability to measure the brain electronically, 2,500 years ago the Buddha simply knew that anger was all about the {self}.

Anger is a very similar, but separate, emotion from fear. While the two may not necessarily be direct blood relation, to lift a phrase from internal mind spelunker and comedian Joe Rogan, "they're definitely neighbors, and they frequently borrow cups of sugar from each other." A couple pages ago, we defined fear as the emotion caused when the mind perceives a potential threat to {self}. Anger changes only one word to find its definition, and that word isn't {self}. Here is the definition of anger:

Your anger is the emotional reaction that occurs when your mind perceives an attack on {self}.

After hearing that definition, your first question might be, "So, what's the difference between a threat to {self} and an attack on {self}. Aren't those two things the same?" No, they are not the same. The difference is found in the Perception side of the Equation of Emotion. In the computing world, the difference between determining fear and anger is complicated, but from our mind's perspective it's easy: Fear occurs when you believe the perceived threat is real and comes from your own internal appraisal of a situation. Anger occurs when you want to call bullshit on the perception and want to resist the validity of the threat.

So anger differs from fear in the one regard that when you experience fear, it's our own mind creating the Perception and believing that a threat to {self} is valid. It's our own appraisal of the situation. You truly think you're about to take a hit. When you're out in the woods and find a bear, if you become afraid, there's very little question about your mind's belief the threat is real and probably out of our control. Time to run. That's your own assessment. But when anger is your resulting emotion, it's because your mind is resisting that a devaluation of {self} is deserved or should be accepted.

Otherwise stated, your fear is the response to your mind saying, "oh shit, this may actually happen," while anger is the reaction when your mind says, "nuh-uh, that ain't happening, in fact we're gonna stop it from happening."

The Blown Call

In our communications technology society, there aren't many things that can get a large group of people immediately and collectively angrier than a blown officiating call in a major televised sporting event, which then changes the outcome of the game. And we don't really even need to be sports fans to understand this truth. In Game 6 of the 1985 World Series, the first base umpire made what might be one of the worst calls in pro sports history. With the St. Louis Cardinals leading the series 3-2, and looking to win the championship in game 6, having produced a lead of 1–0 into the last inning of the game, Kansas City Royals player Jorge Orta was called safe at first base on a play where Orta was clearly beaten to the bag by the ball, and should have been sent to the Royals' bench. After the botched call, which created an undeserved base runner, the Royals then rallied in the last inning to win the game by a single run. The Royals then went on to win the World Series itself in game 7, when the Cardinals might possibly have ended the series in game 6 without the umpire's blown call. For the Cardinals fans and players who lived through this situation, it's a perfect example of an attack on {self} that the mind feels it should defend against.

In a sporting event, virtually every play of that event becomes an Equation of Emotion to be calculated. For instance, in baseball, if a player hits a ground ball into the infield, a race is then initiated to end that play. Either the batter makes it to first base to end the play, or the ball does. In the event the batter makes it first before the ball, the players, coaches, and fans from the batter's team experience a balanced Equation of Emotion. Their EP that the batter make it to the base before the ball does is balanced with their Perception that the batter actually did get there before the ball. As a result, those who identify with the batter's team are pleased with the outcome of the play, so YAY! Base hit! In the event the ball gets to the bag before the batter however, then the Equation of Emotion for the players, coaches, and fans of the batter's team is now unbalanced, and they feel disappointment as the result of the play.

But when the Perception of the threat can be challenged by the mind, anger arises to fight against the devaluation to {self}. The fact of this 1985 World Series situation was that Orta was not quick enough to get to first base before the ball. So the outcome of the play should have been a negative for the Royals (with an offensive player being retired), and a positive for the Cardinals (them gaining one of the three outs they needed to win the World Series that very night). But what happened instead was that an umpire inserted his Perception that the opposite was true. And everyone watching lost their friggin' minds.

Just like fear, anger gets its foundations from the brain's survival mechanism. After all, if more people think like you, then you are in the bigger tribe, and are safer when dealing with others who think differently than you do. So when you encounter others who think differently, especially when they think differently about something solidly attached to your {self}, anger arises to help you defend those {ideas} that are dear to you. This of course started with control of the water hole or that especially awesome cave thousands of years ago, but then it grew into fights on Facebook about politics, or reasons to fire missiles at each other because of differences in ideas about our {religions} or {forms of government}. From your brain's perspective, it's a survival thing. If we have more people on your team or in our tribe, we are safer and more likely to survive and perpetuate {self}. Anger is the subconscious mechanism which aids that survival function when we feel a devaluation of {self} should not be accepted.

Let's look at some quick examples of anger, keeping in mind that an individual's Perception plays a key role in any emotional reaction. If we do not perceive an attack, due to cognitive disability or mental illness, or maybe just a different perspective on life, the resulting emotion group or severity level may be reduced dramatically.

Anger Situation Examples

Anger Situation 1: Someone cuts you off in traffic.

The act of someone cutting you off in traffic can be seen by your minds as an insult. When someone cuts you off, your mind can see it as that driver saying, "I'm more important than you are," or "where I'm going is of higher importance than where you are going," or "you don't matter in my decision to take your lane. I am more powerful than you." So the action of cutting you off becomes an attack on {self} that you don't agree with, which can initiate the anger family of emotions. Of course, if you were to adjust your Expectation/Preference of the situation to expect idiots to cut you off from time to time, that would lessen your anger reaction when it happens. Maybe you could wind up being simply annoyed as you tap our brakes, instead of freaking out and flipping them the bird.

Anger Situation 2: Someone insults your religion or non-religious status.

It depends on the attachment level you have to your {religious position}, but many people include their religion (or lack thereof) as a large part of their sense of {self}. Sam Harris even proved this in a study mentioned earlier in the book. So a verbal attack, if the Perception of that attack holds any weight in the mind at all, will activate some level of anger. Physical attacks on our {religious position} raise our ire even more, as physical attacks connected with anything should.

This same exact pattern of anger plays out with attacks on {politics}, {nationality}, {race}, {sexual orientation}, or any other attachment which people include within the walls of {self}. And so now you understand every argument that has ever surfaced on social media. Congratulations!

Anger Situation 3: Chronic Anger - We're just angry overall in life lately.

I have a friend from high school who's Facebook posts I used to see all the time before I silenced them. I silenced them because it seemed like every post he made was one he was making in anger. Everything in the entire world pissed this guy off daily. Subsequently, almost everything he posted wound up being a long argument with someone. I even had a mild disagreement with him one time after suggesting he look into a stress reduction program like MBSR (Mindfulness Based Stress Reduction), so he wouldn't have to deal with being angry so much. I said it might reduce the negative effects it was having on his health, which he posted about frequently. I referenced numerous studies, including one in 2001 that looked at 13,000 people, which showed high levels of anger created a 200 percent the risk of developing coronary artery disease and 300 percent the risk for early heart attack. I told him his anger was slowly killing him, and he would potentially leave his kids without a father too early in their lives. And of course, true to form, my comments angered him.

He said his constant anger was an asset, and that it gave him the drive to protect what was important to him. His anger helped him defend his religion and his family, and fight against the idealistic attacks on the things he held dear. His anger provided his kids the proper motivation to do their schoolwork and stay out of trouble so as to not make Dad angry. His anger made sure his wife knew when she was meeting his expectations of how he thought she should keep their home and provide caregiving to the children. It seemed his patterns of being an angry guy had become a very portion of his {self} map. He was actually proud to be an angry guy. So when I suggested that being angry about so many things may not be the best course of action, **of course** he saw that as an attack on {self}, which then got added to the pile of things that pissed him off that day. You may know someone with these tendencies. We often call them grumpy.

In other chronic anger instances, sometimes an extended Equation of Emotion situation could be at fault. If your general Perception of our overall life situation doesn't match your Expectation/Preference of our overall life situation, the anger group can remain activated constantly without any other acute triggers. "I hate living in this ratty house." "I hate this piece-of-shit car." "I hate this horrible job and wish I could quit." "I'm not getting paid enough money compared to what I'm worth." All these and other similar thoughts can be Perceptions that attack your EP in the Equation of Emotion every time you are presented with that Perception. Note that our Expectations/Preferences or Perceptions do not in any way need to be reasonable. They just need to exist within our minds, and the world needs to not be meeting them. If our life doesn't meet our Expectations as a chronic Equation of Emotion imbalance, we can walk around our entire life angry for seemingly no reason at all. This type of long-tail Equation of Emotion explains why certain people blow up in anger at the smallest things. This explains how someone can be harboring a deep-seated anger about a portion of their life that goes unresolved, which then later manifests as an out-of-proportion explosive anger to the smallest of anger triggers.

Anger Is the Same Process Every Time

Admittedly, we've gone a little out of our way with a few extra examples to support the definition of anger presented here.

Why did we do that?

It's because, believe it or not, according to some in the psychological sciences community, an official definition of anger has not been agreed upon even as I write these words. That doesn't make sense to me, because it was Aristotle over 2,000 years ago—who invented the very word "pathos", which became the foundation for psychology's entire idea of emotional suffering—who first offered up a pretty accurate definition for anger right from the very beginning. Aristotle said, "Anger may be defined as an impulse, accompanied by pain, to a conspicuous revenge for a conspicuous slight directed without justification towards what concerns oneself or towards what concerns one's friends." To paraphrase that pile of thoroughness, anger is the impulse to defend against a slight directed toward what concerns oneself or one's friends. We already discussed how Jim Coan's work at UVA shows on fMRI how our friends get integrated onto our {self} maps. Tiffany Barnett White at UIUC showed us how ideas themselves can become a portion of {self}. So it seems Aristotle was really the first person in recorded history to suggest anger is the reaction you have to an attack against things on our {self} map (or to paraphrase Aristotle's words, the stuff that concerns oneself or the stuff that concerns one's friends).

While psychological scientists may have forgotten that we already had definition of anger from over two millennia ago, they may have also missed the recent research that proves that ancient definition is accurate. One of the world's advanced researchers in anger, award-winning psychologist Dr. Dolf Zillmann, started research on emotions and human communication in the 1960s. He worked for decades digging into the science of anger and aggression. His conclusion was the same as Aristotle's; "anger occurs when someone feels they are being endangered psychologically or physically." Furthermore, while science previously thought anger worked differently across different groups of people and different cultures, the most recent science shows anger is pretty much the same worldwide. The only real exception being Polynesia.

As a weird false-exception to everything we've discussed about anger thus far, the indigenous people of Polynesia don't experience anger as much as people in other areas around the world do. Their culture seems to have weeded anger out of their existence quite a bit. Researchers agree that they've done so because Polynesians see the emotion of anger as a childish reaction, and not becoming of an adult. So any Polynesian adult reacting in anger to something is seen as having a childish immature tantrum. When we review this truth with our handy Equation of Emotion, it actually makes sense that they experience less anger than everyone else. Because the resulting emotion of anger they may have normally generated without their culture's influence, winds up creating a negative Perception about {their Polynesian self}. So their minds preempt the whole anger process and avoid it because that anger would then create a second Equation of Emotion, which would make them look immature. This in turn may be what reduces their anger output overall as a {self} defense mechanism. Although we should note here that Polynesians also have different ideas about {self} than much of the rest of the world, which also plays into lower levels of anger. We'll discuss what alterations in {self} can do to our emotions later, but for now, just know that your angry reactions are simply you're mind saying, "nuh-uh" to attacks to stuff on your mind's {self} map.

The Emotion of Sadness

It's sad when our daddies die.

It makes us one less person inside.

—Pamela Ribon, Author

We've all experienced sadness. We know what it feels like. The tightness of the chest. The weakness and shivering in the belly. The virtual but almost real hole in our existence that leaves us feeling incomplete and can seemingly only be filled and repaired with the sands of time. Sadness sucks. But the fact is it doesn't have to suck as much as it does. Understanding why sadness arises within us provides a way for us to adjust the knobs on sadness itself if we choose to. First, let's review our official definition of sadness:

Your sadness is the emotional reaction that occurs when your mind perceives a loss of {self}.

Here again is a definition of an emotion that simply astounds the mind by how much it simply restates what we already know. We know sadness arises when we experience loss. That's not really a huge revelation. It's how sadness arises for all our individual {self} items that is somewhat of a revelation.

The severity levels of sadness are as follows:

LOW SADNESS   **HIGH SADNESS**

Sadness is a very simple, but powerful, emotion. And in the grand scheme, it may also be one of the most destructive emotions to human health and well-being. This is because sadness is one of the easiest emotions to cause its own degenerative loop. By that I mean that the reaction of sadness from any Equation of Emotion can then actually loop back around and become a Perception of sadness itself, which then feeds right back into another Equation of Emotion. This then creates even more sadness as a result. And so on. And so on. Through this process, sadness can snowball out of control easily sometimes, and even land us in depression.

While fear is your reaction to a potential credible threat to {self}, and anger is your reaction to an attack on {self} that we wish to dispute, sadness is the emotion you experience when the mind believes the {self} has actually taken a hit or is experiencing a loss of some sort. In layman's terms, when you experience or maintain a state of loss in your mind, sadness is the result.

Let's look at some quick examples to see the mind creating sadness in action. We'll start with the mildest forms of sadness first, then talk about a more profound loss.

Sadness Examples

Sadness Situation 1: Our favorite sports team lost the big game. We are a Superfan of our team.

We live, breathe, and bleed the colors of our team, and they just lost the big game. In this case, our team is substantially attached to our sense of {self}, so a high power EP is generated. The Perception of the loss is pretty solid, because the game is over, and maybe now we even perceive that the entire season has been ruined. These two powerful variables together combine to create a reaction ranging from high disappointment up through utter despair, depending on how far reaching the loss is in our minds, and the extent to which the team has taken over our sense of {self}. A quick web search will uncover pictures of people crying in despair over a sports team's loss. Google "fans crying" when you get a second if you'd like a visual representation.

Sadness Situation 2: A sports team we kinda like lost the big game.

So our team lost the big game, but this time our team isn't a substantial portion of our {self} map. So a lower power EP is generated. Because there's a lower power attachment to the team, this in turn reduces the amount of sadness we feel as a result of the loss. So we feel a low level disappointment in this situation, compared to when our favorite sports team created more of our identity in the last example. True to form, our reaction to this team's loss will be less severe than someone else's who is very attached to this team.

Sadness Situation 3: We are overweight, which is subconsciously making us sad.

There are many people who do not see their weight as a problem, and consider themselves big and beautiful. This is a Perception about weight that meets with their Expectation/Preference about their weight, so they are genuinely happy with their weight. Leave them alone.

But for those of us who do not want to see ourselves as overweight, or for those of us who do not wish to be overweight, every time we look in the mirror, we are faced with in imbalanced Equation of Emotion. And the Perception doesn't have to come from the mirror. It can come when we are reminded about our weight/size while shopping for clothes, or while speaking with our doctor, or while being rejected by a potential romantic partner, or while noticing the pain we are experiencing in our joints as we move around, etc. Any time we are presented with a Perception about our body weight or shape that does not meet with our Expectation/Preference, some level of sadness will be the result. And this type of imbalanced Equation of Emotion, like chronic anger, can be a chronic sadness about our weight or shape as it happens over and over again with every window we pass on the sidewalk. Since our Perception in question is a devaluation of {self}, some level of sadness occurs until the weight problem (or the Perception problem) is addressed. By the way, I'm not passing any judgments here, just explaining the phenomena. I've addressed my own weight issues in the past when I let it get out of control because I absolutely love food.

As a side note, if you are sad about some extra weight on your body, the fact is that somewhere in your mind you've accepted the extra weight as a realized devaluation or loss. If you want to transition into a mindset that may be more conducive to dumping some extra weight, try letting the idea that your thinner {self} is in there looking to get out, and that you'd like to dispute that the extra weight should be there. This will help you shift from sadness (which saps your energy) to a healthy level of anger (a motivating emotion) which can help you take the actions you need to achieve the results you want.

Moving into the Profound Depths of Sadness

Situation: Our internal biochemical pharmacy is creating chemicals that are pushing us into sadness or depression.

Although the creation of all acute emotions, including sadness, has a lot to do with cognitive Perceptions in our mind, genetics and the chemistry of the brain can also help create negative Perceptions that feed our sadness engines. I remember a couple days where I woke up and just felt down for absolutely no reason whatsoever. Millions of people deal with that kind of chemical malfunction every day. Thankfully, for me it only took a couple days of taking brisk walks out in the fresh air (which have been scientifically proven to reduce depression) to subdue the sad feelings I was experiencing. But the fact is that our internal chemicals can and do help create negative Perceptions that can cause us pain and suffering.

Scientists generally accept the definition of depression as a sadness that lasts more than two weeks, although more solid measurement lines are being developed around certain chemical levels within the body. Many in the medical community believe that depression is a physical problem only, determined by genetics and the chemical composition of the brain. However, the medical facts about depression seem to eliminate most of the logic behind this argument. For instance, people born after 1945 are ten times as likely to suffer from depression than those born before 1945. Did we go through some sort of major genetic evolution in 1945? Some scientist would argue the reason for this outcome is that people now go to the doctor more and are getting diagnosed with depression more often. But this reasoning was refuted within the very study that exposed the depression phenomenon to begin with. The study adjusted for the shift in our doctor visits.

That said, our internal chemistry can and does become an issue for our emotional processing. However, the real question here is what comes first, the chicken or the egg? Is it the chemistry that creates negative thought which feeds the Perception side of our Equation of Emotion sending us into a tailspin? Or is it the negative thoughts that get the chemistry rolling, which then adds to our depressive state? Frankly, we don't know yet. I personally believe it may be a mix of the two, with the initial catalyst being the negative Perception in the mind that gets the ball rolling. This idea is actually catching momentum in cutting-edge pockets within neurobiology.

Currently, science suggests both chemistry and mindset help contribute to depression. A National Institutes of Health study showed how diet soda was clearly linked with depression, which would certainly score a point for the chemical side of the argument. But on the cognitive side, studies show overly positive {self} assessment also leads to depression. And we can easily see how unrealistic Expectations/Preferences connected with overly positive {self} assessments could be upset when we're handed real world Perceptions that suggest "we're not all that". And of course, there's the argument that if depression was caused by our physiology alone, then things based in the mind, like meditation and emotional intelligence training, should have no effect. But studies show that both emotional intelligence training and meditation have higher success rates than antidepressants for reducing sadness and depression. So the science itself suggests it's a mix, and regardless of how that mix was first caused, the fact is that sadness and depression can be reduced by work done within the mind. Here we are reminded of Dr. Richard Davidson's statement from Chapter 1, "It turns out that there is no more effective way to produce localized and specific changes in the brain than behavioral or mental interventions." So maybe our answer to depression isn't found just in our antidepressant medications. Maybe it's found in altering the mind to the point it quits generating the internal chemicals that can add to sadness and depression. We'll discuss this more in the following chapters and present the science that supports this conclusion.

A Last Sadness Example: We just got the phone call informing us that someone we dearly love has died. We were very close to that person.

I realize it's a bit cavalier to attempt to fully explain the loss we experience when we lose someone we love. It almost seems unacceptable to talk about a very personal loss in this cold and logical way. The reason we don't like to discuss how our mind sees losing someone we deeply care about is because there's a bit of our inner illusionist that doesn't like having its tricks revealed to the crowd. The truth is that the false {self} within us secretly knows its a fraud. And what fraud likes to be exposed as a fraud? This is the space from which Spinoza said, "When the mind imagines its own lack of power, it is saddened by it." It is also why Paul Valery warned us, "To enter one's own mind, you must go armed to the teeth." Our minds can sometimes fight back when we look to expose its deepest secrets.

But in order to clearly see how the mind's {self} isn't really our true Self, we need to trod through this muddy water. Because it's only in viewing how our minds see those we love as ideas on some {self} map, that we can fully start to comprehend how our mind's understanding of {self} is utterly ridiculous. This is part of the secret the world's historic luminaries wanted us to know. The way our minds see {self} isn't the reality of Self. And so as we go through this last example of sadness, know that any weirdness we feel is directly connected with the fact that we may be catching a glimpse of the fact we've been duped by our mind's definition of {self} our whole lives.

A Personal Story

One of my most profound losses in life came when my grandmother passed away. My grandmother was a huge portion of my life, and subsequently made up a large portion of my sense of {self}. She had been an AT&T telephone operator from back in the days when operators wore headsets and pulled physical wires on the switchboard and plugged them into connecting circuits, and she was as caring as anyone I ever met. Except when it came to getting me up at 6 a.m. on Saturday to go yard sales.

She took me to yard sales in and around Berrien Springs, Michigan, at insanely early hours of the morning, because, Grandma told me, "the best antiques are gone in the first hour of the sale." She was a smart woman who knew her antiques. She could buy an antique doll, or ornamental plate, or piece of carnival glass for a few dollars, knowing it was worth over twenty times what she paid. The meager contents of Grandma's two-bedroom house at 1203 Sycamore Street sold for almost a quarter million dollars after she died.

One of the coolest memories from those weekly yard sales was where I was introduced to the first black man I ever met. His name was Muhammad Ali. Yes, that Muhammad Ali. The Heavyweight Boxing Champion of the world. It was 1975, I was six, and was not yet fully awake when we got out of the car at our first yard sale on that very early Saturday morning. I was still wiping the sleep from my eyes, not paying attention to anything but how tired I was, when Grandma tapped me on my shoulder and asked me if I wanted to meet someone famous. "Who?" I asked, looking around. She pointed to a tall black man leaning against a table talking to someone standing next to him. He was wearing tan pants and a white dress shirt, and had really weird hair. I wasn't keen on the idea. She had to literally pull me over to him.

The conversation I had with the Champ was short. He crouched down to my level next to me, put his right hand on my back and asked, "Who are you?" I'm not sure I had ever met a stranger who wasn't a family member or neighbor, let alone a stranger with dark skin and weird hair. And no one had ever dropped down to my level to speak to me. This guy seemed larger than life. I was afraid to respond, so I looked to my Grandma for help. "Tell him your name," my Grandma said with a big smile and a nod toward Ali. I told him my name barely loud enough for him to hear. "Hi Sean. It's nice to meet you," Ali said. "Do you know who I am?" At the time, I had no clue who Muhammad Ali was. I didn't even know what boxing was. I had no idea I was speaking with one of the most famous men in the world at the time, and one of the greatest athletes to ever live. I noticed he was attracting the attention of the other yard sale attendees, and everyone was smiling at him, and listening to our conversation. But that's all I knew. So I slowly shook my head. This is when Ali went into his famous public character for a second, probably for the benefit of the people watching. "What?" he said incredulously. He balled up his left fist which was opposite of me and shook it slowly but non-menacingly. His fist looked as big as my head. "Boy, you better find out who I am," he said with the frowning sideways glance Ali was famous for. Everyone laughed except me. I looked up at my Grandma again. She told me his name. I looked at him. He looked at my face looking for some recognition. In a kinder, softer tone, half in character and half out, he raised his eyebrows and asked, "You don't know who Muhammad Ali is?" I shook my head. "That's okay," he said reassuringly. "Sometimes I don't either."

His tone softened from that point forward, putting me more at ease. "It doesn't matter. Are you in school?" I nodded. "What grade are you in?" We talked for maybe a minute, with him pulling nods and single word answers out of me like he was pulling teeth. He closed our conversation kindly, telling me, "Listen, you make sure you study hard in school. Can I shake your hand?" I didn't know what shaking hands was. I'd never done it before. When he held out his hand and told me to put my hand against his, my whole hand with outstretched fingers didn't even cover the soft center of the enormity of Ali's hand. He closed his hand slightly around mine and we shook. It would be only later that I would learn how earnest Ali was when he was telling me to study hard. He was a big fan of kids getting a good education. I would later learn about how much money he gave to the area schools, and that one of the baseball fields I played on was actually built by Muhammad Ali.

I'd only learn that fact when I was sitting across from that field at the restaurant where my aunt would hand me a check from my

Grandma's estate and asked if I remembered meeting Ali. My Grandma lived independently in her home until she was 95. I was devastated when I got the news she had died.

When we lose someone we love, the closer they are to us, the harder it is to process. In my case, my grandma was the person I was closest to in the world. It was my grandmother's influence and love which helped me transition from the troubled youth I was becoming into being a more confident well adjusted kid. I loved my grandmother dearly, and saw her on a daily basis for a while, even spending my high school lunch hours at her house having the most amazing food with my friend, Craig, who came along because Grandma's cooking was far superior to our high school cafeteria food.

Obviously, during my young lifetime, my grandmother became a large portion of my mind's sense of {self}. And this is where we start to see how our mind's idea of {self} is so flawed, and actually deserves the moniker of false self. It's weird to think of the people we know as our mind's {self} items, but science proves that's exactly how the brain sees them. But the truth of the people around us goes much deeper.

When I learned that my grandmother had passed away, it literally felt like a large portion of me had been ripped out from the inside. The intense sadness came immediately and set up camp in my heart. Of course, what I felt in my body at the time was an accurate representation of what was happening in my subconscious mind. My grandmother had indeed become a large portion of {self} in my mind, and so when she died, a number of things were being forcibly and unexpectedly ripped from my {self} map. When we lose someone dear to us, we also lose everything associated with that person. When I lost my grandmother, I didn't lose just Grandma. I also lost all the future hugs we would share. I lost all the future talks. All the future pieces of advice. I lost all the future moments of laughter and love we would share. I lost the joyful looks she would have on her face whenever I experienced triumph. I lost her future words of wisdom. When my grandmother went on to whatever is next in this universe, so did her sense of humor. So did her warm smile. So did her great cooking. So did the house that had always proved to be a safe haven for me in times of trouble. That was sold to someone else. It didn't seem right. All of these things were ideas associated with my grandma that had become a portion of my {self} map. And so when she died, many, many things died along with her, and were violently yanked from my mind's {self} map. So the sense of loss for me was huge.

Every individual Perception of loss I recognized created an individual instance of another Equation of Emotion which then just piled up the sadness. And every time those same thoughts came into my Perception, they would process through yet another Equation of Emotion causing the piled up sadness to persist. After a short while, the sadness itself became a Perception in my mind which spotlighted how bad I was feeling overall. As I reflected on my sadness itself, this in turn made me feel even worse. This was my sadness turning around and becoming a Perception which then filled up the Equation of Emotion again, resulting in even more sadness. And every time I looked at it, putting the ever growing sadness itself into the Perception slot, I would feel even worse. I was looking at my now somewhat empty {self} map, and wasn't at all happy with it.

The sadness process works the same way in absolutely everyone's mind. If something on your {self} map takes a valuation decrease or is removed for any reason, some severity of sadness will occur. When we lose something which previously helped define us in our mind's eye, sadness arises within us. When we lose someone we love, we get sad. When we lose one of our pets, we get sad. When we lose something of importance, such as a family heirloom or prized possession, we get sad. When we lose a contest, or drop an ice cream cone on the ground, or see little dogs being carried around in purses while wearing funny little hats, we get sad. When we lose our job, we get sad, unless of course we hated our job, at which point, losing something negative from our {self} maps turns into a big positive, which means we're having margaritas at five o'clock. Don't be late.

Sorry. I'm not wired to dwell on sadness. You get the point, so we're moving on.

From here, we're going to race through some additional emotion groups just so you can understand the basic rules the mind uses to create all our specific emotions. As you better understand how {self} feeds into every emotion you experience, that knowledge will open some pretty amazing doors for you moving into the future, the least of which is the ability to reduce the grip your negative emotions have on you, which will increase your happiness levels dramatically.

So let's now take a quick peek at some of the other emotions with a paragraph or two explaining how they connect with {self} before we move into what you can do with all the information you are learning about your mind.

Worry

The emotion of worry is simply just another instance of fear, except that resolution of the pending devaluation of {self} is expected at some time in the future. So worry is simply fear with an extended time component. Fear happens when you see the bear walks out of the woods near where you are standing. Worry is the fear a bear may walk out of the woods near you, but hasn't yet. Fear is what you feel the moment you hear job lay-offs may be coming. Worry is your reaction to the thought of how you are going to pay the bills if those layoffs come to be. So the worry group of emotions has the same exact rule as fear, with the exception the pending devaluation is not immediate, and in fact may never come to pass. It was the ancient philosopher Seneca who said, "The mind that is anxious about future events is miserable." Don't be of that mind. Worry is a {self}ish emotion. Worry group severities include distressed, nervous, worried, distraught, and dread.

Regret

Like worry, regret is also closely related to one of the three emotions we've already covered in this chapter. At its most elementary level, the emotion of regret is simply a sadness that has resolved at some time in the past. Subsequently, regret has the same exact rule as sadness, with the exception the {self} hit occurred in the past and is no longer being processed as active sadness. You can regret things like past mistakes in your life, those mistakes being a perceived devaluation of {self}. You can regret past events which occurred that were out of your control, but which delivered you a sad chapter to your {self} story. Some of the severity levels of regret don't even have different words assigned to them. The severities of regret include mild regret, regret, lament, deplore.

Pride

Pride arises within us when we bring to our Perception the high valuation of something on our {self} map. So pride is our reaction to reflecting on, and thus making a Perception of, the high valuation itself connected with something on our {self} map. For instance, if our child gets good grades in school, that {self} item (our child) has a perceived valuation increase, which reflects as an internal valuation increase of our {self}. This, of course, makes us happy, as the EP and the P balance regarding the grades, but if we then reflect on the high valuation itself, even subconsciously, pride also occurs. A parent can be proud of a child who has brought home good grades. An athlete can be proud of a championship trophy. A business person or artist can be proud of their last successful project or body of work.

Pride is often listed as a positive emotion because of the positive valuation associated with whatever {self} item we are currently proud of. But pride is also listed as one of the seven deadly sins because of its vanity of being a reaction to an inflated {self} worth, whether it is deserved or not. Drawing attention to high value {self} items is called bragging, which is a behavior birthed of pride. So while the mind may want to argue that pride in our children is okay to have, and pride in our country is a good thing to have, in reality this emotion of pride moves to isolate us from others through the Trojan horse of good feelings. Pride is an emotion that is completely {self}ish.

Pride group emotion variations include gratification, pride, conceit, and vanity.

Shame

Shame is just the opposite of pride. When the Perception side of the Equation of Emotion is filled with the low valuation of something on the {self} map, then shame is the resulting emotion.

For instance, if you see that you've made a mistake, you may feel ashamed of that mistake because that action is attached to your {self} map. In that instance, you're looking at the valuation of the mistake itself as a Perception, and feeling the shame as a result.

And it's always our personal Perception that creates this emotion. I had a gay friend in high school who was ashamed he was gay because of the value judgments he had inherited from his parents that made homosexuality a bad thing. Thankfully, he learned otherwise soon after. Contrarily, I also knew a kid who was the son of a member of the KKK, who was not ashamed of his affiliation with the group because he didn't see racism as a bad thing. If we are in denial of the lower valuation of something on our {self} map, we will feel no shame even if we deserve to.

But if our own mind perceives the negative valuation of something on our {self} map, our shame will be the result. Right or wrong. Associated group emotions include contrition, guilt, shame, and remorse.

Embarrassment, Envy, Disgust, Boredom, Curiosity, Confusion

See the website.

Stress

There is much ado about stress in today's world, mainly because stress is one of the main causes of illness and disease in the human body. Understanding stress is simple.

Stress is the resulting emotional state of mind and body that occurs when an Equation of Emotion goes unresolved for an extended length of time. When a person's anger situation goes unresolved, it causes stress. When a person's fear or worry situation goes unresolved, it causes stress. When a person's sadness situation goes unresolved, it can cause both stress and depression. When ANY Equation of Emotion goes unresolved, stress is the result.

Stress in the mind causes stress in the body. Stress in the body causes stress in the mind. And thanks to the mind-body connection, stress can be held in the body, thus creating opportunities for tension, illness, and disease.

In the case of cellular stress, where a system within the body is not in good health, and it is causing stress to the greater organism, the EP of the body's cells is that a good health status be the active state of the body (called homeostasis); thus, when an alternative Perception is presented, when health difficulties are occurring, additional stress within the body is the result.

There's a really weird thing about stress however, which shows the power our Perceptions have over us: Studies have conclusively shown that although death rates are 43 percent higher in people who experience high stress, those same studies show **the death rates are the lowest in people who experience high stress, if they believe their stress helps them**. So their belief changes the entire medical outcome right over the top of the bell curve and skews it to the other side based on what we believe.

Relief

Relief is simply the equalization and rebalance of any Equation of Emotion. We can be relieved of anger, fear, sadness, stress, etc.

Note: Some level of happiness can also be an added result of the resolution of an Equation of Emotion, due to the Perception about the change to a previously imbalanced Equation of Emotion that has fallen into balance.

Hate

Your very existence insults my {self}. We could write a whole book on hate, but I think this one statement sums up hate pretty well, from the hate racists have for their targeted victims, through the hate religious zealots have for their targets of hatred, down to the hate some Boston Red Sox fans have for the New York Yankees. Hate is simply the manifestation of the thought that your very existence insults my existence. This is hate from its most basic definition. Award-winning writer and journalist Ta-Nehisi Coates once pointed out, "Hate gives identity. We name the hated strangers and are thus confirmed in the tribe."

Love

Love is a tricky word because sometimes we call an internal process or feeling the word "love", when in reality that feeling is simply our Equation of Emotion responding to affirmations of {self} without having any components of altruistic or unconditional love, which is what I personally classify as love.

But true to form, opposite of hate, love can generally be considered, "Your very existence is wonderful, and I appreciate it greatly." Think about this one when you have some time and review the people in your life from this lens.

We will discuss unconditional love in Volume II.

Happiness

There is a whole chapter on the emotion of happiness in the

follow-up to this book, but so as to cover it in this chapter on emotion definitions, consider that happiness is the result of experiencing a Perception that balances with the Expectation/Preference regarding a {self} item or overall {self}. When our Perception of the world is meeting or exceeding our Expectation /Preference, happiness is the result. And yes, it's that simple.

Again, we will discuss some science on happiness in much greater detail later in the book, and we'll discuss how to hack our happiness later, but I include it here just to exhibit that our positive emotions come in severities also.

LOW HAPPINESS   **HIGH HAPPINESS**

Satisfied ⟷ Pleased ⟷ Happy ⟷ Elated ⟷ Ecstatic

Moving On

There are other emotion groups, and a lot of complexity within emotions we have not discussed here. But frankly, you have attained the level of understanding you need to change your life dramatically and get you back control of your mind from the automated subconscious processes that have created every bit of your pain and suffering from the moment you took your first breath until this very moment. You needed to understand how every one of your emotions is connected with your mind's {self}. Now let's look at what we can do with all this cool and interesting knowledge.

Chapter 8 Takeaways

1. Science proves that increasing your Emotional Intelligence is one of the best things you can do for your brain.

2. Your individual emotions fall into groups of severity. Your basic emotions like anger, fear, sadness, all have differing levels of severity which then create the myriad of your various unique emotions.

3. Your emotion severity, regardless of the basic emotion group, is selected by the power level of the {self} item creating the EP in the Equation of Emotion, and the power level of the Perception in the Equation of Emotion, combined.

4. The emotion group, which along with emotional severity determines the individual emotion we experience, is selected based on a number of specific rules in the mind. See each emotion group for those rules.

5. Understanding the whole emotion creation process in your mind can be an amazing tool of understanding, both in ourselves and others.

Chapter 8 Reflection

1. Can you see how your individual emotions map onto the definitions of emotion for fear, anger, and sadness?

2. Do you see how your individual emotions come as a result of your individual {self} items being effected by your Perceptions?

3. Do you see how reviewing your individual emotions might give you some relief from troubling thoughts and emotions in the future?

9. Well, That Explains Everything

It is our mind, and that alone,

that chains us or sets us free.

—Dilgo Khyentse Rinpoche

In the beginning of the book, I promised you this was a different type of book on happiness than any other book you've ever read. I also promised you that I was going to show you how deep the rabbit hole goes on {self}, both in this book and in the second book which discusses the deeper Self. I'm about to deliver on those two promises in this chapter.

In this chapter, which is the last chapter before we move into the practical applications of how to take advantage of what you've learned about your mind to improve your life, we're going to take a turn into the philosophical to discuss just how deep the rabbit hole of our mind's {self} goes, and just how much it negatively affects our lives individually, and especially collectively as a civilization and species.

As you've seen thus far, when we open and educate our conscious mind to the understanding of how our mind works, that allows you to do some pretty amazing things, including six awesome things in particular. First, it allows you to identify the variables that create all your personal pain and suffering in life, which opens the door for you to play with those variables and adjust your entire emotional landscape as a result. Second, knowing those same variables gives you a specific target within the mind at which you can point your conscious attention. This, by default, deposits you firmly into the space of meta-awareness, the control room of your mind. Third, it gives you a tool to turn down a negative emotional reaction in the heat of the moment and turn back on your thinking brain when you need it the most. You do this by focusing on and thinking about the emotion itself, not the situation that caused it. This alters your Perception in your Equation of Emotion, and allows the name-it-tame-it circuits to be engaged in your brain. Fourth, as we practice the first three amazing things, as a result of being more peaceful and relaxed, your brain can then become supercharged in a long list of areas. When the brain's processing connected with {self} becomes quiet, that allows for higher levels of concentration, higher levels of creativity, and allows you to fall into the state of flow. Fifth, it gives you the insight you need to better understand the people around you and how you might be able to increase your empathy and compassion. Both empathy and compassion for others have been shown in studies to have positive personal health and well-being results in the compassioneer. So when you become a more compassionate person, you become more healthy as a result. And finally, it provides all of us an amazing tool to understand how and why the train of humanity has run off the rails a bit to create every one of our social illnesses.

I'd like to quickly discuss this last benefit, so as to understand the bigger picture we are facing as humans en masse. Because it's by understanding the bigger picture we become motivated to make a positive change for ourselves personally, which in turn makes the world a better place. We're never going to be able to make ourselves and our world happier without completely understanding the challenge before us, and understanding how deeply our mind's {self} affects us collectively as well as individually. So let's review what we've already discussed about {self}, and see how that same mind thing which causes our personal pain and suffering also creates all the pain and suffering in our greater world. We'll start with looking at how we as a society actually revere the people who ignore the influences of the {self}:

Our Actions Speak

Timothy Stackpole is a hero. In 1998, as a member of the New York Fire Department, he and two other firemen ran into a burning building to rescue a woman trapped amid the four-alarm blaze the firemen had been called to. While inside searching for the woman, the floor beneath the three firemen collapsed, trapping them within the inferno. Stackpole and his colleagues, Lieutenant James Blackmore and Captain Scott LaPiedra, were trapped in the building for nearly a half-hour before they could be rescued. Lt. Blackmore died on the scene. LaPiedra and Stackpole were carried away in ambulances with severe burns.

"My whole body was trapped up to my neck," Stackpole would later recall in a PSA video made to support the burn unit that saved his life. "The fire was still roaring all around us ... I remember the excruciating pain in my ankles, burned to the bone. And I remember just praying to God: Just let me die bravely." He then added, "I had this tremendous sadness that I wasn't going to see my children again, growing up, walking my daughter down the aisle."

Although he survived the fire, with severe burns to 30 percent of his body, it was not likely that Stackpole would survive the next week in the hospital. He did. His wife didn't think he'd ever walk again. He did. He was told that after his twenty-one years of faithful service, he should retire from firefighting and take a pension. He didn't. He stayed on with the NYFD and within half a year fought his way back onto the active duty roster. Three years later, just one day after he was promoted to the rank of Captain on September 10, Timothy Stackpole would be one of the first firemen to arrive at Ground Zero on September 11, 2001. He led his team into 2 World Trade Center before the twin towers collapsed, killing Timothy and 342 of his heroic colleagues. Ten thousand people came out for Timothy Stackpole's funeral, including New York mayor Rudolph Giuliani, who said Captain Stackpole was "one of the most exceptional human beings I've ever met."

Why do we consider Timothy Stackpole a hero? We all do, right? He's a firefighter who literally ran into a burning building with hundreds of other first responders who wound up giving their lives that day in the process of trying to save others. Why do we hold that action in such high regard? It's because Timothy Stackpole and others like him literally put all of their attachments of {self} aside, save just one, to put the {selves} of other people first. To be candid, Timothy Stackpole's mind would not have allowed him to run into that burning building unless he had a very strong mental attachment to the idea of {being a fireman}, and being {someone who helped others at all costs}. Those were his attachments of mind. That's the {self} Timothy Stackpole was defending that day when he ran into the Twin Towers and not away from them. If you want to call that {self}ish, be my guest. Personally, I'm not going there. Because the fact is that Timothy Stackpole suspended all his other hardwired attachments of mind to be able to run into that building. He suspended his attachment to {his wife} and what it would mean for her if he died. He suspended his attachment to {his kids}, and what it would mean to them to be left without a father for the rest of their lives. He suspended his attachment to all his future joys and life experiences, including walking his daughter down the isle at her wedding, which he could have done, had he only run the other way that morning. But he rose above all that mental noise to assist thousands of others whose {selves} were also at risk.

We consider the most {self}less people in the world our heroes. They are the people who, regardless of what it costs them, choose to put the benefit of others before their {self}. We hold our firemen and police officers in high regard because of this perceived {self}lessness. We appreciate and have holidays for our soldiers for this same reason. Being {self}less is an admired trait in humans. And it doesn't have to be life or death stakes for {self}lessness to be appreciated. Hundreds of thousands of people daily choose to use their time or income generously to help others they don't know. We feed the hungry. We build houses for the poor. We give money to charities to help people we'll probably never meet, and who will never be able to thank us personally. We consider these anonymous and generous people heroes, too. We appreciate all these {self}less acts because {self}lessness is so rare in comparison to all the behaviors we humans have that are considered {self}ish. Unfortunately, there are too many {self}ish behaviors to even mention. What should no longer go unmentioned however, is how much our defense of {self} mechanism, when left unchecked, helps create every major societal ill we face as a species globally. And that not only ruins our happiness, it ruins everybody's happiness. When we are ignorant of {self}, we do some pretty stupid and mean shit, and maybe it's time to thrust that process into the spotlight.

A Note from the Author

I realize this whole book classifies as a note from the author, but this particular note deserves special attention. In the last chapter we reviewed how the mind's malfunction of {self} causes all of your personal turmoil. Some of that was a bit uncomfortable to look at, especially when we looked at how we allow our minds to reduce other people to be items on a {self} map. As a warning, we're about to discuss how the mind's {self} causes almost every blight on humanity for the very same reason. We need to look at this last bit with open eyes so we can understand what we as a species are doing unintentionally to cause pain and suffering for others around the world. Consider this a slight tangent from our primary purpose of making your life more awesome and amazing and giving you the tools to be happier regardless of your life circumstances. But consider it an important and relevant one.

Besides, a wider review of the {self}'s role in the global picture allows a leap in understanding the first half of the secret about {self} that Jesus, Muhammad, the Buddha, Laozi, and many of the world's historic thinkers and scientists wanted us to know. It is only in seeing our egregious errors against humanity itself that are caused by our internal wiring that we can then address those errors. That said, because of how our brains are wired to defend {self}, we should expect that our minds might resist the idea that we humans are responsible for a lot of evil in the world. In his famous book Ethics, Dutch philosopher Spinoza reminds us, "When the mind imagines its own lack of power, it is saddened by it." True to what we've discussed in the last few chapters, our {self} doesn't like to be connected with negative stuff. So as we go through the rest of this chapter, your mind may want to push back and say, "Hey, {self} isn't a bad thing (even though all the evidence speaks to the contrary)." Or your mind might say, "Yeah, {self} creates the evil in the world, but not **my {self}**." If that comes up for you, just realize that when we talk about {self} here, we are talking about **we humans as a species**, not you specifically. The troubles of the world are not your fault. It's a bit of an ugly truth to face, but we need to acknowledge this ugliness in our{selves} if we ever hope to create real, long-lasting, beneficial change in our{selves} and in the world.

—-

The Root of All Evil

> In battling evil, excess is good;
> for he who is moderate in announcing the truth is
> presenting half-truth. He conceals the other half
> out of fear of the people's wrath.
>
> —Kahlil Gibran

When we think of all the types of things that generally classify as being evil, including conflict (with or without violence), deception, thievery, bigotry, greed, oppression, murder, genocide, war, poverty and hunger, just to name a few, most if not all of those evil things seem to classify as blights against humanity itself. Let's discuss each of them quickly in regard to how they are all firmly connected with the human mind's {self}.

Argument and Conflict

Every human argument and conflict that ever was, or ever will be, is caused by the existence of the {self} within the mind. Why do people argue and fight? Because the two-or-more sides to any conflict have behind them humans who are hard-wired to defend their different mental attachments of {self}. Anger arises because each side perceives that the other groups' mental position attacks their own. This triggers the limbic system's fight reaction, which simultaneously reduces our intelligence by shutting down the prefrontal cortex, thereby reducing the chance for wisdom and compassion to win the day. And so the fight is on.

And whether it's two or more governments jockeying for a superior trade position, two or more political parties battling for control of a country's government, two or more armed groups of fighters out on a battle field somewhere, a husband and wife arguing about whether to leave the toilet seat up or down in the bathroom, or my six-year-old son arguing with me about wanting more iPad time, it's all the same thing, and it's all created by the same process within the mind. It's a battle of {selves}. A battle to defend the attachments of {self} on the mental maps of the individuals involved in the conflict. And so arguments and conflicts ensue.

Without the existence of the {self} we would not have conflict globally, and the fewer things we keep at the center of our mind's {self} maps, the fewer conflicts we will have in the future.

Murder

Murder is the ultimate escalation of a conflict. Whether murder is premeditated, passion driven, or spawned by a spur of the moment catalyst of reaction, all murder is caused by the defense of {self} mechanism, even if that {self} is simply filled with a mentally unstable murderous rage. In its simplest form, murder is the {self}'s removal of someone else who stands in the way of an increase in valuation of {self}. In any murder trial, one of the requirements to convict someone of the crime is to prove they had motive to do the crime. If said motive doesn't track back to some sort of benefit to {self}, it doesn't qualify as motive. So here even our courts acknowledge the reason for murder connects back to {self}.

Deception

In 2016, TED.com published an amazing TED talk by Dr. Kang

Lee, a University Distinguished Professor at the University of Toronto, and Associate Editor for the scientific journal Developmental Science. In his talk, Dr. Lee spilled the beans on the science of children and lying. He shared a story of an experiment where children were asked to play a game and guess the numbers written on some slips of paper lying face down on the table in front of the child and researcher. The kids were told if they won the game, they would receive a big prize. But at some time in the middle of the game, after the kids had made a few wrong guesses, the researcher would then be called out of the room for some reason, leaving the slips of paper on the table and alone with the child. The kids were of course told not to peek at the papers while the researcher was gone. So what happened? Well, over 90 percent of the kids peeked as soon as the researcher left the room.

What was interesting however was what happened when the researcher came back into the room and asked the child if they had peeked at the papers. Dr. Kang Lee showed us the results of those answers: "We found that regardless of gender, country, and religion, at two years of age, 30 percent lie. ... At 3 years of age, 50 percent lie . . . At four years of age, more than 80 percent lie. And after four years of age, most children lie. So as you can see, lying is really a typical part of development, and some children begin to tell lies as early as two years of age."

So in summation, 90 percent of the kids cheat at the game presumably so they can win, and then when asked about it, more than 80 percent of the cheaters lie about their cheating. These kids' actions are clearly connected with wanting to win a game and get a prize, which adds to the child's {self} (as well as covers up actions to hide the fact they cheated, which of course avoids a hit to {self}). While this study didn't research the reasons why the children lied, the latest science from Dr. Charles Ford at the University of Alabama, Birmingham outlined the thirteen main reasons all humans lie. And they all track back to reducing taking hits to {self}, and/or creating positive perceptions about {self}. You can find his work at UAB.edu.

Bigotry

Bigotry is the reaction we have to the thought, "your very existence threatens my ideas of {self}." Bigotry is defined as "prejudice and intolerance: intolerance toward people who hold different views, especially on matters of politics, religion, or ethnicity." So we don't even need to go past the basic definition of bigotry to learn that bigotry is defined by an intolerance toward people who have different {self} maps than the bigot does. Bigotry is the reason that racism exists. Bigotry is the reason that genocide exists. Bigotry is the reason religious extremism exists. Whether it's ethnocentricity, theocentricity, or politicocentricity (which are are the fancy words to describe the thoughts "my race is better than yours," "my God is better than yours," and "my way of governing people is better than yours"), it's the process of a person's {self} attempting to uphold its own attachments to race, religion, or ethnicity that causes bigotry to exist. I think it's important to note that it's only within the weakest and insecure human minds where bigotry arises. No individual who is completely confident in their personal existence can be threatened by the presence of someone who is different than they are. So bigots are among the weakest minded and insecure individuals in the world. I love science.

Greed

Contrary to popular belief, money is not the root of all evil. And before you say it, the love of money is not the root of all evil either. Not directly, anyway. Money and the love of it are only symptoms of the deeper entity from which the striving for money emanates. For the {self}, money can mean power. It can mean freedom. It can mean a more comfortable lifestyle which makes it easier for the {self} and all its attachments to survive into tomorrow, which we are reminded is the brain's entire charter, and the reason for the brain's existence. Money can mean a higher score on the leaderboard of capitalism within a monetarily driven society. How nice is your car? How big is your boat? How is the view from the balcony of your mansion? How well did your last business transaction go? All things we consider greedy map directly back onto all things {self}. The {self}'s need of money or financial gain, or political power, or extravagant or one of a kind things . . . or even at the lowest end of the spectrum, where attaining money can mean simply having the next meal for you or your family without even knowing where the meal after that is coming from... money and the mental need for it is a {self} motivated endeavor.

Us vs. Them

When people with similar attachments of {self} gather together with other people with similar attachments of {self}, an {us} can be formed. {Us}es come about due to the {self}'s need to validate its existence, and from a survival mechanism standpoint, there's strength in numbers. If a person can find other people who agree with ideas on their {self} maps, or who have similar {self} attachments, that's powerful. Formation of an {us} comforts the mind, and we often seek them out.

A person can belong to many individual {us}es that don't necessarily relate to one another. For example, Joe from Boston can belong to the {us} of being from Boston, while he also can belong to the {us} of being a New England Patriots fan, while also belonging to the {us} of the Democratic party, while also belonging to the {us} of a worker's union, while also belonging to the {us} of the Catholic religion, while also belonging to the {us} of being a billiards player, etc. "I like you, if you're like me," the {self} says.

{Us}es are destructive in nature, because for every {us} which gets created, another group gets automatically created . . . the infamous {them}. Naturally, everyone not classified within the {us} is classified as a {them}, and the {them}s automatically become potentially evil because anyone who is attached to ideas that are not {us} are rival {selves} with attachments that threaten our own attachments. It's because of this perceived attack of simply being different that fear and anger can emanate from simply knowing of an existence of a {them}.

The {us} and {them} paradigm is the most useful tool wielded by people in power. And they use it for good reason. The {us} and {them} narrative plays on the hard-wired nature of the human brain to defend {self}. In elections and during political campaigns, it is critical for the politician or party to create an {us} that is strong enough to prompt its members to go to the polls on election day to vote for the {us} candidate. In wars, it is critical for nations to create an {us} strong enough for people to risk their lives to defend their leaders' ideas. Even in religious organizations, religious leaders improperly utilize the {us} vs. {them} model to discourage people from leaving the flock, and keep the money rolling in to build a larger organization to create a larger {us}. They think they are doing God's work by utilizing this process. But we shouldn't forget it was the founders of the religions themselves who warned us away from this path by preaching about knowing the secrets of the {self}. Therefore, any religious leader who warns anyone away from spiritual exploration may be the proverbial blind leading the blind, working against their founder's very teachings.

Moving forward, one of your most important uses of meta-awareness will be to ensure if you ever decide to join an {us}, that you do it consciously, with open eyes, open ears, and an open heart, so that you may ensure that particular {us} serves the greater good of all of humanity, not just the desires of a select few. Or even in the case where you decide to join the {us} cause for an oppressed select few, at least hold the mind's attachment to that {us} at arms' length, so setbacks to that {us} don't reduce your effectiveness.

Genocide

It's in the intention to not belabor the point into monotony that I think we can skip an in depth analysis of genocide. By now, you can see how {self} plays into this horrible human sourced phenomena. I won't insult your intelligence further by pointing out the obvious.

War

War is the ultimate derivative of the {us} vs. {them} phenomenon taken to the extreme. War is all about getting people riled up in defense of {self} and convincing them to kill each other. Plato said, "Only dead men have seen the end of war." But I don't believe that statement to be true. I believe our human minds are ready for a change from the animalistic behavior of the past that has been driven by uncontrolled, misunderstood, and manipulated fear and anger. I believe the human race is ready to take control of it's collective minds and understand and diffuse the drivers that influence us to kill each other over attachments to ideas. I believe the future will show that only cowards send men off to war. The real heroes will be the ones who sit across the table of diplomacy in the presence of people who want to defend entirely binary attachments of {self}. The truly courageous will be the negotiators who look to avoid the virtual landmines over the physical ones. Killing people over differences in attachments of our minds is the move of the weak minded coward who is not prepared to follow the ultimately courageous position of non-violent resolution.

Poverty and Hunger

In today's developed world, poverty exists because we don't share wealth often enough. Hunger exists because we don't share food often enough. Both are exacerbated because we don't share technology with impoverished populations often enough. We, as the lucky ones who live in an environment that provides the luxury to do things like write and read books on happiness, think we need to take care of {our own} first and foremost before helping others. So our {self} gets in the way a bit. And people starve and die from contaminated water as a result.

But Wait, There's More . . .

As awful as the negative global symptoms of our internal {selves} are, the wider scope of effects on our individual lives are just as bad. Potential devaluation of {self} is the reason our kids don't ask questions in school, which then becomes an obstacle to their learning and thriving. It's better to not ask the question than to look stupid by asking it. Beyond that, negative {self} image is what starts kids down the path of developing body image issues, with some studies showing boys as young as 10 years old vomiting in an attempt to lose weight, and some girls as young as 8 using mascara and lipstick so they can look more attractive. Potential negative shifts to {self} are what causes kids to remain silent about abuse or neglect occurring in their homes. Kids can't tell anyone about their problems at home, because that might get Mommy or Daddy in trouble, and within the mind, that means their augmented {self} is getting in trouble.

This {self} process is a problem in the human psyche we need to acknowledge and control. The {self} is what causes our world leaders to be corrupted by money, sex, and power, ultimately harming innocent people through the results of poverty, starvation, maiming and death as the unacceptable side effects of war profiteering. And just when we start looking at the {selves} of others as a problem, our own {self} sneaks up on us and sucks the happiness from our lives while we're focused on the other guy. To increase happiness in ourselves and in the world, we need to fix all this.

Yeah, This Sucks

Hey there! How you doin'? It's the guy who wanted to increase your happiness. Remember me? I just wanted to check in with you for a second. I know talking about all this source of evil stuff is a bit weird, and it may even be getting you down a bit. If you'd like to skip forward to Chapter 10 and refocus on how to increase your happiness, go ahead and do that now. But if you'd like the rest of the story on creation of evil, there's just a bit more to end this chapter.

I see the rest of this chapter like this: I'm a mechanic for your mind, and you brought your mind into my shop to ask me about a funny noise it's been making around town. You weren't sure if it was a big deal, so you just wanted to get a professional opinion. But now I'm telling you that it's not a harmless little noise, it's actually a big problem that will cause all sorts of additional issues if you don't address it. Trust that we're through most of the bad news. There's just a little more to cover before we wrap this chapter up and move on.

Scapegoating Evil

In reviewing how {self} is clearly attached to the numerous blights on humanity discussed above, one could try to argue that these blights of our behavior are not the evil itself, but that these are simply the symptoms of the bigger evil force that causes these evil things to exist. And while we just hammered out the extremely solid argument that {self} is the cause of everything evil, the persistent problem we face is that our {self} doesn't like to be connected with negative shit. That's a hard-wired phenomenon. It rejects the idea we create evil. So someone else has to be at fault in the creation of evil. We can't be the ones responsible for evil. That would just suck. If we as humans were responsible for evil, we'd be forced to take responsibility, and be obliged to look at changing our behavior. Who wants that? So there has to be an outside force. And of course here is where many people look to religious lore for an outside scapegoat at which to point fingers. And we need to address this topic in this book, because a great number of us consider ourselves religious or spiritual, and ignoring the topic in a book on happiness which discusses the source of evil would be irresponsible, at the very least.

First, let me plainly state I'm not against the idea of God or world religions (in fact, there's an amazing discussion where science may **prove** the existence of God in Volume II), but I do think religion can over-reach at times to save us from our own culpability of creating evil. Culturally, when we look at the causes of evil, we are taught to invoke names like the Devil, Satan, Lucifer, or one of its dozens of other aliases that attempt to name a fallen angel (or Jinn if you're favorable to the Islamic faith) to explain why bad things happen. Wait . . . did you here the latest? Evil isn't our fault. Just say, "The Devil made me do it," and your {self} won't be responsible for whatever it is you've done. Phew, that was a close one. But the simple common sense, and now even scientifically supported fact, is that the influence that leads us away from being more Holy (aka more aligned with God), and which causes evil to be committed, doesn't exist on some other ethereal plane. As much as religion might be a great path toward what some people call God, I think religion has it completely wrong when it comes to the source of evil, or at the very least, where the proverbial Devil may take up daily residence.

In the early 2000s, the late British journalist and literary critic Christopher Hitchens got off the intellectual bus one stop too early in his popular book called "God Is Not Great", in which he extolled the reasons that, in his opinion, "religion poisons everything." Though Mr. Hitchens is a much more eloquent writer than I am, and artfully used a number of wonderfully entertaining analyses, analogies, and anecdotes, the conclusions of his observations in his book could not be more wrong. It is not religion that "poisons everything." The real spoiler exists at the level of the mind's {self} that attaches to a religious dogma so firmly that it drives its victim to harm God's other children to defend the dogma. Rather than religion being the offense to intellectualism, which Mr. Hitchens proficiently defends, I believe it is the existence of the top level {self} (aka the false self, aka the ego) which creates attachments to all things, including religious dogma, that becomes the cause of every transgression of reason that Mr. Hitchens outlines in his book. Yes, people kill other people to defend their attachment to a particular religion. But so do people kill other people to defend their attachment to particular sports teams. People have died in sports arenas in the United States for wearing the wrong team's logo. People have suffered permanent brain damage from the beatings they've received at sporting events for loving the wrong team. The European readers of this book are jumping out of their seats wanting me to mention soccer (which the rest of the world calls football). Fan-on-fan violence has become so prevalent in soccer, it caused an Italian official to state that fan deaths are now simply a part of the sport. That is lunacy. It's not religion or any other singular or group of attachments to {self}. It's the whole {self} and defense of {self} mechanism that creates evil.

Humanity's evil influence isn't external. It exists within our own consciousness. Who knows, it may metaphorically be that our false {self} is that very Satan in the ancient story; that evil force which tempts us with the need to be special, which then separates man from good. And if we're talking about religion for a moment, removal of the influence of {self} certainly fits the teachings of Jesus throughout the New Testament of the Bible. Anyone within Christianity would be hard-pressed to suggest the Son of God wouldn't know how the human mind works. The reduction and removal of the {self} certainly fits the teachings of the Prophet Muhammad. Would the Prophet Muhammad not know the workings of the mind of man? And of course the Buddha, who was certainly one of history's greatest master of mind, simply told us: "It is a man's own mind, not his enemy or foe, that lures him to evil ways." Only a hundred years ago the great psychologist Carl Jung reminded us; "Man must recognize his complicity in the act of evil."

Knowing how our brains work, it now seems to be a simple fact that everything we consider an evil act is all our fault. Furthermore, it's certainly a travesty when we are unconscious of it, because that very ignorance is what perpetuates that same evil. We don't like to see evil as our own fault because our mind goes into denial when it perceives being attached to negative things. That's just the way our brains are wired. So maybe we need to change that and see what it ultimately does to happiness levels around the globe.

As a cool side effect, taking responsibility for evil does solve one of the oldest philosophical arguments against the existence of God, called the Epicurean Paradox. It goes as follows:

If God is willing to prevent evil but is not able to

Then He is not omnipotent.

If He is able but not willing

Then He is malevolent.

If He is both able and willing

Then whence cometh evil?

If He is neither able nor willing

Then why call him God?

If evil is an invention within the mind of man, the Epicurean Paradox becomes flawed within its very precepts. Fun stuff, solving ancient Greek paradoxes. ;-)

So . . . Getting Back to Your Personal Happiness

So in summation… yeah… you got fix that little rattle in your mind or your fucking house is going to blow up, taking the whole block with it. Sorry for the bad news.

But now that we've seen the depths of the effects of the {self} in the mind, let's get back to your personal happiness. Our tangent into the topic of evil is actually a useful tool, because when we're talking about our propensity to create evil by not paying attention to our minds, we're also talking about inadvertently creating evil at work. That makes work more difficult for us and for those around us. We're talking about inadvertently creating evil in our relationships. That makes our relationships harder for us and those around us. We're talking about inadvertently creating evil in our thoughts and inner monologue, which creates pain and suffering for ourselves and for those around us. So when we take the slight tangent of discussing the philosophical topic of evil and how our minds cause it, we're hitting at the very core of the problem of mind that ties up our mind with non-productive things, and activities that inhibit our overall happiness in life.

If you remember, I did promise you that this book was going to deliver more than just some weak-sauce of tips and tricks to marginally make your life better. With this topic, we're talking about stamping out evil and negativity from your inner existence altogether. In the process of removing the negative influence from your mind, you make your work life, your interpersonal life, and your private internal life awesome while we work on that bigger project of improving the world around us. You can indeed change how your mind works. And taking that control does allow your brain to work more efficiently, and allows you to increase your happiness at will whenever you wish to do so.

So How Do We Stop the Madness?

It's clear we have this hard-wired characteristic that comes with being human, which creates our individual pain and suffering within, and which also creates our collective pain and suffering around the world. And you've seen how it's possible to better understand and take control of this process to change how your mind works, to improve your work lives, your relationships, and even the internal operations of your brain. The question that remains is what are some practical methods you can use to change your situation on a day-to-day basis to best serve your personal existence, and the existences of everyone around you? What can you do so you no longer have to be plagued by this negative influence which emanates from within? That very question is what Section II is all about. So let's now move into some practical methods of how you can hack your mind to create a better daily life for you and those around you.

Chapter 9 Takeaways

1. The neural and mind phenomena of {self} is connected with everything in humanity we consider destructive or harmful to ourselves and others.

2. Being conscious of {self} helps you be less destructive to yourself and others.

Chapter 9 Reflection

1. Is your mind fighting back against the thought of the {self} being the root of all evil?

2. If so, what attachment of {self} is your mind trying to defend with that resistance?

Section II

Mind Hacking 101

10. The Quick Mind Hacks

> Dig within.
>
> There lies the well-spring of good:
>
> ever dig and it will ever flow.
>
> —Marcus Aurelius

In Section I, we spent time and energy to understand the basics of how our minds work, including the detailed process that creates our personal and collective pain and suffering. But the question remains, "What can I do with this stuff?" Well, in short, you can do a lot with this stuff. First, knowing how your minds work gives you some amazing control knobs to play with in your mind's control room. Now you can fine-tune how your mind works, and employ some mind hacks that improve your everyday life from here forward. Second, your new understanding of your mind gives you the power to understand the people around you, so you can accomplish some amazing things in your personal and professional relationships, and even on a grander scale, within society as a whole.

Let's get into some very empowering mind hacks that can change how your mind works overall. There are some quick mind hacks we've known about for a while, and some brand-new mind hacks that our new science of emotions enables. Let's review the familiar ones first so we can better understand why these tried and true methods work, then we'll check out the new ones.

The Tried and True Mind Hacks

The quickest old school hacks you can perform in your mind to change your emotional landscape are connected with the two variables that feed your Equations of Emotion, your Expectation/Preference, and our Perception. Those two variables are the ingredients that create your mind's stew of activity.

Consciously Altering Your Expectations

"I'm just trying to set expectations, Focker." Gaylord Focker was a character Ben Stiller played in the Meet the Parents movies, and it was the name my past Sales Manager Brian Higgins used with me when we worked together. He'd often shout from his office down the hall, "Focker, get in here please," when he wanted to discuss my sales funnel. Brian's three favorite subjects were tennis, absolutely anything to do with the rock band U2, and the topic of properly setting expectations in a business environment.

"It works like this," he said. "If you properly set expectations up the chain about our current sales funnel, then any news, good or bad, won't come as a surprise to Bob, and that makes life easier for both of us." Bob was our SVP of Sales, who kept a tight grasp on the projected sales numbers out of Atlanta, one of the company's flagship offices. "If you tell them a deal is falling apart before it falls apart," he continued, "they can't hammer you too hard when it does, and those times when you deliver on what you promise, or pull an extra deal out of the fire that was previously reported as a low probability, it builds credibility and trust, and you become the hero they count on to produce revenue." At the time that Brian shared this bit of wisdom, neither of us knew that the method we were using to manage expectations with our corporate overlords could be used to quell the inner turmoil created within our own minds as well.

While it's true that your Expectation/Preference is primarily set automatically in relation to things on your {self} map, you can step in and purposefully adjust your expectations if you need to. This loosens the effect a negative event may have on you when something does eventually go wrong. Take for instance a situation where you've decided to put up a website or blog about something that interests you, and you've developed that blog into a small bit of revenue for yourself by adding advertising or product sales to the site. Your website is something you care about. Thus, it becomes something that gets included on your mind's {self} map. Thanks to homeostasis, your website and revenue automatically gets an EP that it be held status quo or increase in value. So you never want to see the site go down, or be hacked, or defaced, or anything else that could happen to interrupt your message, be a discomfort to your community of readers, or interrupt the flow of revenue.

But we all know technology sometimes breaks. Even back when I managed hardened data centers, where we had backup generators, multiple Internet connections, and redundant failsafes to critical systems so that customer equipment would not experience outages . . . we still had outages. Outages just happen with technology. So it's not a matter of if something goes down for your website, it's simply a matter of when. But by knowing this, you can now adjust your expectation about your website being down or getting hacked and defaced at some point. Because if you expect something to eventually go wrong, even if it doesn't go wrong today, you'll be better prepared for when something does go awry. And so at the moment you get the news our website is down or has been hacked, while your hard-wired EP is that nothing bad happen (which will certainly then bring up the feeling of concern about the website being down), your conscious Expectation that something was eventually going to go wrong now somewhat balances with your Perception that something has gone wrong. This balance reduces the emotional fall-out of the website having issues at the moment. You knew this would happen. Maybe you even planned for it by having regular back-ups completed for the site, so that when something did happen, it wouldn't affect the site for too long before you'd be up and running again. As a result, your brain doesn't fire up your limbic system as much, and your thinking brain doesn't get shut down as much, so this adjusting-your-expectations move allows you to more quickly jump into action with your thinking brain on how to address this issue in the quickest way possible, thus possibly saving you more downtime for your site, and more revenue for your bank account.

Pat Flynn experienced such an issue with his website, Smart Passive Income. If you don't know Pat, he helps people navigate the world of online brand building and online small business development, and he's super popular in that space. At the time of this book's publication, the Smart Passive Income Podcast, which is simply Pat and a guest sharing some topical wisdom, was listed in the Top 20 of all business podcasts on iTunes, but it also regularly appears in the Top 10 along the likes of the TED Talks Business and Bloomberg News' Master in Business. I was honored to be a guest during one of his episodes in which we addressed how taking control of the mind can benefit business owners. It was during that episode that Pat shared his experience with a hacking event that took his website down for an entire week.

"It screwed up a lot of stuff," Pat said to me. "A lot of people perceived my reaction to it and said, 'Well, you're pretty calm.' But in my head I was just kind of livid. I wanted to scream and I wanted to throw my computer on the floor because I knew that every minute that my site was not up, those were minutes where people were trying to visit my site, and people would go there… income lost, opportunities to build relationships with people just lost, and it was just an overall negative sort of experience for my brand as a whole."

So let's break Pat's situation down for a second. I'm not sharing anything I haven't already shared with Pat, so I'm sure he won't mind we do a little analysis here for our collective benefit. Because of Pat's business model, his website means a great deal to his business, and his business of course means quite a bit to Pat. It's how he feeds his insufferably adorable kids. So his website fills a decent sized chunk of Pat's {self} map. Because Pat had not altered his expectation that his site might eventually go down at some point, his emotional reaction to the incident was much more severe than it might have been had he altered his expectation that things might go horribly wrong at some point. In addition, his non-adjusted EP may have affected his ability to think during the flurry of emotional activity going on in his head. "At first, I didn't even know what to do," he told me. As a result of the various challenges, they got the site back up within a week, which is forever in Internet time. Pat lost thousands of dollars in revenue because of the one event. But now Pat has altered his expectations and disaster planning so the next issue doesn't take so long to address, and so there are zero moments of paralyzation before action is taken to rectify whatever has come up. So he's altered both his expectations and his disaster planning, which will ensure his continued success. You can check out Pat's website and free podcasts at smartpassiveincome.com. I get nothing for that reference. I just think Pat's that good if you're looking to build an online revenue stream. He's a bundle of positive effectiveness on wheels.

Setting your own expectations and setting expectations within others around you can be a very effective way to reduce the emotional fallout of future negative events. I've even used this practice with my son in preparation for a long car ride to go see his grandparents. "It's gonna be a really long time in the car, buddy," I would say. "What things do you want to take with you to help pass the time?" Setting the expectation in my son's head that boredom or frustration may occur goes miles (literally) in reducing the probability that either boredom or frustration arise during the trip. I don't think the child has uttered, "are we there yet" even once in his life because of his mom and I taking the extra time to set (and then meet) his expectations about whatever we're doing that day. A long expected car ride, or dutiful trips to the store, or an extended adult [anything] result in him having a more balanced Equation of Emotion when his EP is consciously adjusted beforehand.

To reduce your inner turmoil regarding any upcoming situation, be it a special family event, a business meeting, or a regular life activity, simply ask yourself, "what is my expectation or preference about [whatever it is]?" Then ask yourself if that EP is reasonable, or if other outcomes may be possible. Review those potential outcomes, and how you might handle them in the moment. Adjust your expectations away from things going perfectly, if necessary. This can help you plan to react accordingly.

Setting expectations within yourself adjusts fully one half of our Equation of Emotion, which proactively reduces your negative reactions before they happen. I taught this strategy to a woman named Barbara, who's a rather short-tempered controller at a very small southern company. You'd love her if you met her. She has a good sense of humor, but she is definitely **no bullshit**. I saw her recently and she told me how she was altering her expectations; "Now I just expect people to do stupid shit. It makes it completely bearable when they do." And while that's pretty funny, it's really true. Setting expectations in yourself really works.

Beyond just setting your own expectations, setting expectations in others and meeting them can drastically reduce others' emotional fallout as well. This smooths our path quite substantially when dealing with other people, not to mention reducing their pain and suffering as a bonus. Review your expectations regularly, take a moment to set expectations for those around you, and then simply take every life moment as it comes, ready for anything. If you do that, you'll be as prepared as you'll ever need to be if something doesn't go as well as you wanted it to. And you'll spend less time dealing with any negative emotional fallout before taking your next effective action as a result.

Consciously Altering Our Perceptions

When we adjust the Expectations side of the Equation of Emotion, it can certainly alter your emotional output. But just as effective sometimes is altering the other side of the Equation of Emotion, which of course holds our Perceptions.

This practice is taken right out of psychology's basic playbook, and can be experienced through things like Cognitive Behavioral Therapy and similar approaches, such as Reappraisal. An example of altering your perceptions could be that when you get cut off in traffic by someone, instead of taking it as an affront to your personal existence or importance or safety, which could trigger an anger response, you alter the perception a bit to say, "maybe that person is in a hurry and just not paying attention," "maybe they are on their way to the hospital to see a loved one who fell ill," or "maybe they're on their way to an important meeting that will gain them the income to not have to drive like an asshole tomorrow."

It's easy to let your mind run away with creating negative Perceptions for you to deal with regarding events that happen. It's easy for you to feel like the driver who just cut you off did it on purpose because of some derisive thought they had against you personally. However, it's just as easy with practice to repaint those Perceptions in more positive colors that are more agreeable to your mind's eye. It's a great exercise to practice thinking about how you might see events in the world differently than how we first appraise them. More than being just a feel good Band-Aid to a potential slight against you, thanks to the science of plasticity, this exercise builds your optimism and the empathy muscles in your brain. Sometimes I even make a game of doing this with the family. "Why do you think that guy cut us off?" "Maybe he just wasn't paying attention?" When we do this, my wife and son can share in the reappraisal process and get practice with repainting our minds in a more positive light for when we run into daily challenges.

How we see the world and the things that happen around us creates fully one half of our Equation of Emotion. Mindfully looking at our Perceptions can have dramatic effects on our minute-to-minute and day-to-day emotional landscape, reducing the things that steal our happiness.

Some Crazy Science on Perceptions

The crazy fact about your mind is that to a large extent, your beliefs make your personal world. For instance, one recent study showed that if people believed they slept better than they actually did (as measured electronically by REM sleep monitors), they actually performed better on cognitive tests than they should have, given the amount of actual REM sleep they experienced. So the altered Perception made a physiological difference in the body, including how well their thinking brain worked. So we must be careful with how we see and think about things that happen around us. Learning to change your Perceptions is a powerful tool that can have dramatic effects on both your mind and body. When you change your Perceptions, it changes the output of your Equation of Emotion. If you change this in a positive way, good feelings can activate your vagus nerve, which connects the brain with the heart. When the vagus nerve is firing, the heart relaxes and feels like the heart is opening because of what biologists call our neuro-cardiac coupling. In Joy on Demand, Meng Tan explains how frequent activation of the vagus nerve turns out to be very good for our physical health. He wrote,

> If you often have thoughts of kindness, and altruistic joy, you activate the vagus nerve a lot. And after a while, your vagal tone improves. High vagal tone is correlated with a healthy heart, while low vagal tone predicts heart failure, and mortality after heart attacks. High vagal tone increases resilience to stress and the likelihood of positive emotional experiences, such as joy, interest, serenity, and hope. It also shows up socially. People with strong vagal tone develop richer relationships, and fascinating, are more likely to be trusted by other people. Somehow we know to trust people with strong vagal tone. As if all that is not good enough, people with high vagal tone also demonstrate superior cognitive flexibility, including better working memory, and directed attention. They also show fewer negative responses to environmental stressors, and show greater self regulatory capacity.

So as Meng points out, repainting your Perceptions not only makes you feel better, it makes you a healthier human being with a better brain, who gets along better with your fellow human beings, and who lives a bit longer than all the negative nellies do. Vietnamese Buddhist Monk and inner peace master Thich Nhat Hanh tells us, "Nirvana is the removal of wrong perceptions. When you remove wrong perceptions, you remove suffering."

So take time to notice when your Perceptions match your Expectation/Preference. Appreciate those moments. When your

Perceptions do not match your Expectations/Preferences, ask your{self} if there is an alternative Perception you could apply which might reduce any negative rumination and clear your mind of a negative reaction. With practice, you will begin to see events without judgement of good or bad, which will remove many of the challenges your mind creates for you, and reveal your best course of action in calmly and clearly dealing with the challenges which require your attention.

Affirm What Matters

Okay, just so you know, people have told you wrong on affirmations, so listen up. Affirmations are good, but not all affirmations are good, and some are even bad for you.

Affirmations are a great way to introduce Perceptions into your mind that in turn create positive emotional output for you. More than being merely hippie bullshit, the latest science suggests that utilizing affirmations can help a chronically stressed individual perform at the same levels of problem solving capability as their lower stressed counterparts. This is huge, because studies have also shown stress can inhibit your problem solving abilities by almost half. That's the difference between receiving an A, the highest letter grade available in most American schools, or an F, the lowest, and non-passing, grade. So extrapolated, utilizing affirmations could be the difference in you performing at the top of your game, or failing miserably at whatever you're trying to do.

Different than standing in front of the mirror and pumping yourself up, the best affirmations are simply bringing to mind the things that are most important to you and letting those thoughts soak through you. For instance, whenever my mind has taken a left turn and gets overwhelmed about all the number of things I have to do in a day, I stop and picture getting a hug from my wife, and/or son, and/or any of our foster kids. I think of how much joy my efforts at completing my work will bring them in the future. Those thoughts give me the renewed focus to organize and prioritize and knock things out one at a time, even if I have way too many things to do, which is usually the case.

That said, affirmations can indeed come in the form of statements said in front of a mirror. But you must be very careful about the language you use, because the words you select can make the difference between an affirmation working for you, or an affirmation working against you. A great observation of this truth came when Guy Kawasaki sent me an advanced copy of his book Enchantment, where he extolled the benefits of bringing about voluntary, enduring, and delightful changes in other people. In Enchantment, Guy astutely touched on the phenomenon that we often are influenced by the labels that wind up getting attached to our {self} map, which is what we're trying to do when we use affirmations. Being the smart guy Guy is, he leaned on some science to support his observations. In Enchantment, he wrote:

> "The concept behind labeling is that people will fulfill the prophecy of the labels applied to them. For example, in 1975, Richard L. Miller, Phillip Brickman, and Diana Boland divided students into three groups. And the student's teachers provided three different kinds of feedback. Attribution: "You know the material well." "You work really hard." "You're trying hard, keep at it." Persuasion: "You should do well." "You should be doing better." Reinforcement: "I [the teacher] am proud of your work." "I am pleased with your progress." "You're doing excellent." "The persuasion group showed the worst results. The persuasion group was the least persuaded. The reinforcement group was second. The attribution group, that is, the kids who were labeled as knowledgeable and hard working, did the best."

From our perspective, it's not hard to see why the persuasion group failed in that study. Because the affirmations given to that group of children basically qualified as negative statements against their {self} map. The word should suggests to the human mind that there's something lacking on the {self} map that should be there, but isn't. So when the teachers said, "you should do well," or "you should be doing better," what they were actually saying was, 'The items {do well} and {doing better} are not yet on your {self} map. You should have them, but you don't.' And so the kids in that group did the worst because the teacher was in effect saying, 'you're not good enough yet'. But when the attribution group kids were given affirming labels, their results were entirely different. When their teachers said, "You know the material well," "you work really hard," and "you're trying hard, keep at it," what those teachers were doing was attaching positive labels to the child's {self}, but most importantly they were attaching motivating labels. The labels {know the material well}, {work really hard}, and {trying hard, keep at it} became positive labels that directly followed the word "you", which then became mental attachments to {self} for the kids. This caused the kids to put out the effort to perform the work that would be most defensive of those new labels they had just been given. Their minds liked the attachment to the idea {I'm a hard worker}, and so then they did what they perceived a hard worker does.

So if you stand in front of a mirror and tell yourself, "You're a good person," or "You are successful," or even "You have the talents to be a success," those types of statements have little chance of doing you any good. Sure, they sound nice, but in reality they are non-motivating statements that attempt to award labels you have not yet earned for the day. They're not motivating labels. It is better for you to use affirmations that are similar to the ones the teachers used with the attribution kids in our 1975 study. Rather than say, "I am a kind person," say, "I can be a kind person to everyone I meet today." Rather than say, "I am good at my job," say "I can be great at my job today." Rather than say, "I am a confident, smart, effective person," say "I can be a confident, smart, and effective person for the rest of the day." Apologies to Senator Al Franken, but the SNL character Stuart Smalley's affirmation "I'm good enough, I'm smart enough, and doggone it, people like me," actually kinda sucks. Maybe that indeed was the whole joke. ;-)

The difference between a good affirmation and bad one lies in the label or idea you are attaching to {self} in making each of those statements. So while it may seem like a small difference between the two statements, "I am a confident, smart, effective person," and "I can be a confident, smart, and effective person today," the difference is actually huge in your subconscious mind. The first allows you to sit on your laurels and pat yourself on the back for being a confident, smart, and effective person, the second keeps your focus on the actions you need to take to be a confident, smart, effective person by the end of the day.

So as a good rule of thumb, if you like verbal affirmations, start your affirmations with "I can" before adding the details to create your personal affirmation. The simple statement "I can" is a pretty powerful statement by itself, and adding it to any affirmation will add that power to your customized thought. In addition, you might also consider adding the idea or word today to the end of all your affirmations as well. Because the fact is that no matter who you were yesterday, you can always take special effort to be the person you want to be today. So it doesn't matter if you were an asshat yesterday, or someone holier than the Pope yesterday. Today is your focus, and today's actions make up your life.

Being Thankful

The last old school mind hack that introduces a Perception which can generate positive responses in your mind and body is the time honored practice of being thankful. And the cool thing is that you can do this at almost any moment of the day. I love to start the day with the thought, "Well, at least I woke up again." Yeah, I'm weird.

Although that's an easy one to grab on those mornings where your brain isn't exactly engaged yet, you don't need to be thankful you're not dead. You can be thankful about how awesome the shower feels, or how good breakfast tastes. You can be thankful the people you love are safe. Or later in the day, you can be always just be thankful for your present moment.

We often forget to be thankful for the fact that we get to live a life on this massive moving object called Earth out here in the suburbs of our galaxy. But we should take time to be thankful for that. Because the fact is that the math of the whole thing is way against us even being here. From my perspective, we're super lucky. We live in a world that typically doesn't kill us too often, and the suffering we experience is almost entirely internally generated, with us having the ability to turn it off if we learn how. That's pretty damn awesome. If you ask me, this place called Earth is amazing, and the fact that we get to experience it is a gift.

But not everyone feels the same way all the time, so if you need something to be thankful about, just think about the simple math of your personal existence. You came about because you were partly the winner of a race with 100 million other entrants (which were the competing sperm racing to the egg), and the other half of you was the recipient of that one smartest, fastest, most deserving swimmer. Beyond that amazing math, you also wouldn't be here if any of your countless number of ancestors had died from sickness, or war, or getting eaten by a bear that walked out of the woods. So absolutely everyone of your upstream family tree members defied the odds to make it to procreation as well. So you, the person reading this book, are a friggin' miracle of existence. The geeky mathematicians of the world have estimated that you are the winner in a one in four trillion odds game called your life. Own that. In your times of suffering, find some thankfulness, and it will change your Perception, and because you're altering half of the Equation of Emotion, it will alter your emotional output every time you do it.

The New Mind Hacks

So now that we've covered the most obvious mind hacks that others before us have identified and studied, let's now discuss a few new ones based on this emerging science. These are the unique tools now available to you exclusively because you are a happiness hacker.

Entering Meta-Awareness at Will with the EoE Review

The first new mind hack is connected with the recent name-it-tame-it neuroscience discovered at UCLA we spoke about shortly ago. It's called the Equation of Emotion (EOE) Review. This new mind hack isn't as obvious as the old mind hacks, but it's just as effective as they are, if not more so.

This mind hack is based on the two variables connected with the Equation of Emotion, the EP and the P, which makes it simple for you to remember and use. This hack has to do with consciously identifying the two variables connected with any individual emotion you experience. Consciously identifying the EP and the P from any emotional reaction drops you into the control room of the mind called meta-awareness, and it gives you a better understanding of what arose within your mind to generate the emotion you are experiencing. This understanding turns the volume down on the limbic system in real time. You can use this mind hack both with negative emotions you've experienced in the past, and/or even in the heat of the moment when a negative emotion is trying to shut down your thinking brain.

When you have an emotional response catalyzed by the Equation of Emotion, there will always be an Expectation/Preference associated with a {self} item, and a Perception regarding that {self} item. And one of the most powerful tools you have to understand and process this emotion is to look at the two components that your subconscious mind compared to create the emotion in the first place. Dutch Philosopher Baruch Spinoza suggested this to us in his book Ethics. In the eighteenth century, he wrote, "Emotion, which is suffering, ceases to be suffering as soon as we form a clear and precise picture of it." Matthieu Ricard, a French-born Buddhist monk whom the press named the Happiest Man on Earth, even suggests looking at your negative emotions in his best-selling book Happiness. He wrote, "When anger arises, focus your attention on the anger itself, instead of on its object. Don't unite with the anger, but look on it as a separate phenomenon. As you keep on observing the anger, it will eventually evaporate under your gaze."

And so when reviewing any particular emotion, you ask yourself two simple questions from the space of meta-awareness to create a higher understanding for yourself. "What is the Perception that triggered the emotion I am experiencing?" Some folks simply call this the trigger of the emotion. But it's a quick way to ask, "What just happened in my mind that set off the emotion that I just experienced, or that I'm experiencing now?" Or if you'd prefer, you can start with the other side of the Equation of Emotion. Instead, ask yourself, "What is the {self} idea in my mind that is being attacked, threatened or devalued in some way?" Another way to ask is, "What about who I am is in play here?" The answer will always be an idea attached to your {self} map.

Focusing your mind on the variables of the emotion itself takes your mind off the Perception which caused the emotion in the first place, and replaces it with the process of looking at the emotion itself. This is precisely what Matthieu Ricard told us to do, which brings understanding to that emotion, which is what Spinoza told us will end the suffering of the emotion.

When you can say to yourself, "That headline I just read made me angry because it attacked my political stance, so my Perception is obviously that the headline is offensive and hurtful to me," we gain a crystal clarity over what upset us about the headline we just read. You may find that level of conscious understanding reduces the negative reaction much more quickly than if you didn't take a moment to look back in at your mind to what caused your reaction. Additionally, now you can alter your Perception to calm your turbulence. "Well, everyone has an opinion, and they all can't be the same," you could think.

We don't know why understanding your emotions is the secret sauce to help you process them quickly and move on, we just know it is. One of the potential weird explanations for it however, may be the requirement that your mind wishes to be heard and understood, and so when your emotions are, they calm down. More than being a crazy theory, this pattern spills over into almost every facet of our lives. Numerous studies show that when we feel heard, a ton of great things happen within the body connected with stress reduction and happiness levels. And it turns out this being heard thing is also the single required component for a happy marriage.

If you want to have a better relationship with your significant other, listen up.

Dr. John Medina wrote an amazing book called Brain Rules in which he discusses numerous facets of how our brains work. In it, he shared the work of Dr. John Gottman at the University of

Washington, whose work gives a hint about the power of being heard. Dr. Medina introduced Dr. Gottman in this paragraph:

"Famed marriage researcher John Gottman can predict the future of a relationship within three minutes of interacting with a couple. His ability to accurately forecast marital success or failure is close to 90 percent. His track record is confirmed by peer-reviewed publications. He may very well hold the future of the American education and business sectors in his hands."

I was impressed when I read that opening paragraph. And I was even more impressed when I read more about Gottman's work in his famous Love Lab studies. But it wasn't until I listened to John Medina's Author's Talk at Google in 2008 (on YouTube) that I heard him sum up Gottman's one determining factor that can predict the success or failure of a marriage to 90 percent. In that talk, he said this about Gottman's work:

He [Gottman] said . . . "you know, I've coded these behaviors, they are algorithms . . . could I dig in there… could I find a statistical correlation… could I find an independent variable that always predicted the number… a true independent variable such that if a behavior… was always present the marriage made it, and if the behavior was always absent the marriage failed?" And then in a big booming voice, Medina exclaimed, "HE FOUND ONE! Which is why he's world famous." Medina then explained the discovery itself. "If the woman feels like she is being heard by the man, in such fashion he begins to accept her good influence on his behavior (guys this does not look good) the marriage makes it."

Medina is amazing to listen to. I can't do his verbal delivery justice. Go find the video on YouTube and watch it. He's an entertaining scientist to say the least. Setting the compliments aside, what he pointed out from Gottman's work in that talk is telling. When the wife feels heard in a way that she can actually see (through the man's behavior) she's been heard, the marriage makes it. Period. End of story, statistically speaking. At least in the thousands of folks studied by Gottman.

This science makes it not so unreasonable to say the reason your emotions calm down once you acknowledge them is because they feel heard and understood. They are, after all, an output from a high level of subconsciousness in your mind. This may sound crazy, but this is what scientists see in live fMRI scans during emotions science experiments. They see that when the limbic system gets messages back from the emotional regulation portions of the brain, the limbic system turns down its output. Could this be the limbic system becoming satisfied with the fact it's been heard? Seems reasonable to me. Almost every other scientific study on the topic of being heard shows that nothing but good things happen in the body and brain when we connect to others in a way in which we feel heard and understood. Our overall human behavior is sourced from our cellular behavior, so that process has to come from somewhere. So it seems the same being heard phenomenon exists within our cells themselves.

To enable this new mind hack, when a troubling emotion arises, if you have a moment to pause, remember to think about just two things when reviewing how that emotion came to be in your mind and body. First, what on your {self} map was impacted by a Perception in your mind? Second, what was the Perception that triggered the emotion? It's in this moment of reflection, you will have entered meta-awareness intentionally, using your awareness to look back into the process within your mind itself. It's here that your emotional output may start to down regulate, if for no other reason than you sent the message to the limbic system that it's been heard and that you understand the emotion in play.

As a last quick question, can this technique work even in the heat of the moment? Personally, I think in the heat of the moment, especially for newbies, such as in the middle of an argument, is the perfect time to engage in this mental exercise. Many of our mistakes in life are caused by reacting too quickly to things and acting in {self} defense whether it is warranted or not. Think of the last time you did some damage to a personal or professional relationship. Could that damage have been avoided had you taken an extra moment to reflect on what was going on in your mind rather than react defensively or aggressively? Thinking back over my lifetime, my answer is "yes" to that question most of the time, and most people I talk to agree they may have been wiser to take a moment in critical instances as well. As long as it's not a life threatening moment, give your mind something proactive rather than reactive for a moment, and you'll reduce your mind's negative reaction, and regain some much needed {self} control. There's an ancient Chinese Proverb that states, "If you are patient in one moment of anger, you will escape a hundred days of sorrow."

As a footnote, as you practice this method more and more, you may find it gets easier to do every time you do it. And you also may find you'll get much faster at it over time as well. This is neuroplasticity at work. Similar to getting better and faster at working crossword puzzles over time, the mind also gets faster at understanding and processing emotions over time, and eventually many emotional reactions can even become **optional** for you. This is a step on the road to mind mastery. More on this in Mind Hacking Happiness Volume II.

Being in the Moment

Another amazing quick mind hack at your disposal is what you do with your thoughts and attention during the moments your mind isn't churning on immediately pressing matters. Whatever you are thinking about in every moment creates your Perception, which is one half of your Equation of Emotion. So if you do have a potentially negative situation to deal with at the moment, that's fine. But in your downtime, allowing your mind to churn on negative stuff from the past, or worry about things that may or may never happen in the future, really does you more harm than good.

Negative rumination, a.k.a. thinking about negative stuff that has happened in your past, has been shown to have tons of negative physical and emotional health implications, including landing people into depression. The act of negative rumination can be seen as allowing your mind to time travel to moments other than what is happening at this very moment around you. Whenever you think about past negative events, whether they happened five minutes, five hours, or five years ago, you're taking up a present moment by recalling a moment that is now gone. It's in the past. You're stealing a present moment to think about some other moment and reintroduce some past Perception. This Perception then runs through your Equation of Emotion again, thereby creating negative reactions in your present moment from things that happened in the past. In doing this, you're basically allowing a past moment to ruin **this** moment. And sometimes you do this over and over again, ruining numerous present moments with negative Perceptions about moments that no longer exist.

Similarly, although it's okay to take a moment to review and set your expectations about a future moment to reduce your potential negative reactions, when you focus too much worrying about the future, you burn present moments imagining future scenarios that may never be. When you engage in excessive worrying, you ruin present moments for yourself with an imaginary moment that doesn't yet, and may never, exist. Elkhart Tolle wrote a wonderful book called "The Power of Now", in which he eloquently pointed out the moments of peacefulness that can arise when we keep our mind and attention focused on the present moment, and nowhere else. He wrote, "Realize deeply that the present moment is all you have. Make the NOW the primary focus of your life." "Time isn't precious at all, because it is an illusion. What you perceive as precious is not time but the one point that is out of time: the Now.

That is precious indeed. The more you are focused on time—past and future—the more you miss the Now, the most precious thing there is."

When you find yourself thinking about negative aspects of past or future, this is your moment to act. Because by simply taking notice that you're thinking of past or future, you have entered the space of meta-awareness. Your awareness is looking in on your own mind. And this is when you can consciously change what your mind is doing. Do not waste this precious opportunity. Stop. Take a breath. Focus on your immediate environment and what is going on all around you at the moment. Notice what is, rather than what your mind is doing **which is what isn't**. Take note of what is coming through your senses. Sight. Sound. Smell. Touch. Is there a taste? Try to witness everything happening without judgment. Just observe what is in this very moment, ignoring the nagging influence of your mind wanting to reintroduce what you were thinking about moments before. It loves trying to distract you. It loves trying to be {self} important. Don't let it. This is the moment Horace spoke of when he said, "Rule your mind, or it will rule you."

One of my favorite stories in this vein is about the great master of mind Rinzai. It is said he once stood in front of a temple of Zen Monks to give what was expected to be a long talk. But when he stood in front of them, he simply raised one finger and asked only one question, after which he left the room, ending the talk. He simply asked, "What, in this moment, is lacking?" It was an amazing lesson for the monks who then could then ask themselves that very question at that moment. Because every answer they could formulate to that question would then betray where their thoughts were beyond experiencing and appreciating that very moment, and what they were wanting to be that wasn't being. This dropped them into meta-awareness, where they could clear their minds of any further yearning.

Of course, admittedly, if I was in that room, after Master Rinzai asked, "what, in this moment, is lacking," I would have probably gotten in trouble by answering from the back of the class, "I could use a beer." But that's just {me}.

And speaking of me, or more accurately, your {me}, I would like to share with you one last quick mind hack that may be one of the simplest and most powerful quick mind hacks ever invented in the history of man. Okay, maybe that's overstating things a bit, but if you try this next hack, it will probably prove super-useful for you, and it will certainly show you how powerful a change in perspective within your mind can be at any given moment.

THE Me

This new hack has to do with yanking yourself away from the false {self} of your mind, and toward your deeper, truer Self, in an instant. It's one of the most effective tools you'll ever have to separate from your mind's {self}, and it's also the most popular video I've ever put out on YouTube. It has to do with adding one word to our self narratives in a very particular place. The word is the word **"the"**, and the place to put that word is directly before any time you use the word **"me."**

So what's this exercise all about?

As we discussed in the previous chapters, because most of the movement in your mind is connected with defending, or promoting, or perpetuating {self}, after a while you start to believe that you actually **are** that false {self} within your mind. You actually believe you **are** your ego. You think you **are** the stories from your past. You think you **are** those ideas of {self} which get planted onto your mind's {self} map. You think you **are** what your body exhibits back to you in the mirror. But the biggest secret in the universe we discussed in Chapter 3, supported by the comments of history's leading luminaries, is that your mind's {self} is not who or what you really are. And that there's a deeper more profound truth about Self (notice the absence of brackets) hidden within you. Well, no single exercise I've found can more effectively remove us from being on the leash of our own minds than the exercise I call "THE me." Here's how it works:

Any time you want to use the word **"me"**, put the word **"the"** in front of it. That's it. That's all you need to do. Put the word **"the"** in front of the word **"me"**.

I know this sounds a bit silly, and it certainly isn't going to sound right in your mind when you say it, but that's actually part of its magic. The bad grammar makes you take notice. When you put the word 'the' before any instance of 'me', statements like, "that makes me angry," get transformed into, "that makes THE me angry." Or, a statement like, "it made me sad when she broke up with me," gets transformed into, "it made THE me sad when she broke up with THE me." Or even, "if there's a carnival barker of inner peace, it's me," gets transformed into "if there's a carnival barker of inner peace, it's THE me." True statement.

THE me is the false identity in your head that causes all the turmoil in your life, creates negative emotions and stress for you to deal with, and urges you into things like engaging in negative rumination. Your "me" is the false {self} within which drives all your negative crap, so much, that your false identity of {self} within you seems to take on a life of its own. That's why numerous wisdom teachers globally call it the false {self}, or sometimes "ego." This is the secret the world luminaries were trying to tell you about when people like Jesus said—I'm paraphrasing here—those of you who do not know your{selves} live in poverty and are the poverty, or when Einstein basically said that the true value of a human being can be found in how much they have attained liberation from {self}.

Why This Hack Works

So what does putting the word "the" in front of the word "me" actually do in your mind? More than being an exercise in improper grammar, it creates some internal distance for you in your mind between your conscious awareness and the false identity of {self} within the mind that causes us all your heartache. Or more accurately, it **points out** the internal distance between your conscious awareness and your false identity of {self}. When you use the verbal tool "THE me", it objectifies THE me of the {self} into an entity you can talk about and look at from a short distance. It reminds you that THE me of the mind isn't actually you, but just a process in your mind connected with the natural tendencies of your physiology. Using the words THE me distances you from THE me, thereby distancing you from the negative stuff that is generated by THE me. And in learning that there can be some distance between your conscious awareness and THE me, you remind yourself that in all likelihood you (i.e. your conscious awareness) are not THE me. You learn that you are not your mind's construct of {self} that causes your pain and suffering. Thus it is in these intentional moments of awareness that you can start to understand the true nature of your mind itself.

You want to know one of the biggest secrets about your mind and your {self}?

The simple fact is that if you can look at your mind from some inner vantage point and see it working, you are proving to yourself that you are not the sum of your mind at work. Just as your eyeball cannot look at itself because your eyeball is not separate from itself, and a single olfactory receptor in your nose can't smell itself because it is not separate from itself, and your fingertip cannot feel itself because it is not separate from itself, neither can you see your mind working from some alternative internal vantage point unless that vantage point—that conscious awareness—is not sourced from your mind.

If you just had a holy shit moment, awesome. If not, keep reading, we'll get you there.

What I just said is that in the universal model of awareness, being able to perceive something requires a bit of separation from it. So if you can observe your mind, whatever is observing your mind is not your mind. So in reality, if you're able to observe your mind, which every chapter in this book has shown is possible, then **your conscious awareness** (the thing you consider is "you") **cannot be the totality of your mind**. We're going to present some neuroscience in the second book that really supports this observation, but let's move forward for now, because we're starting to move into the territory of digging in earnest beneath your mind's {self} into the deeper truth behind your real identity. As we peek into the truth underneath the illusion, not only do you prep yourself to ditch the illusion and all the pain it has caused you, you now can start asking the question, "If I'm not my mind, then who am I?" Or more accurately, "If I'm not my mind, what am I?" And the answer to this question is actually your answer to the biggest secret in the universe. More on this later.

Hacking the Minds of Others Using {Self}

Depeche Mode once sang that people are people. Sounds legit to me. Seriously though, it's because people are people that we can count on the physiology of the brain to work the same way in most folks, especially when it comes to the core functions of {self} preservation and serving the needs of the {self}. So what can you do with that knowledge? Well, you can use it to get things done, of course, and even laugh as it works. And there are already some great examples to show you exactly how that's done.

Dateline: Australia, 2007

Traffic authorities in Australia were having problems with road safety, particularly as it pertained to the speed at which males were driving along public motorways. Officials tried numerous ways to reduce the speed of traffic, increasing patrols, and increasing speeding fines, but nothing was seeming to work. Speeding was still occurring and crashes were still happening. Until they started a very interesting advertising campaign. In 2007, authorities hired an ad agency to create a number of video and print ads suggesting that the reason that male drivers were speeding around was to compensate for the fact that they had small penises. And they made no to efforts to hide that this was exactly what they were suggesting. The ads actually contained a woman holding up a pinky finger as a male driver sped past in the background. There was no ambiguity there for any adults paying attention to the ads. Did it work? To quote officials in Australia, the campaign was "very successful." While the ads did attract complaints of sexism, a government commissioned survey found that 60 percent of young male drivers did indeed reflect on their personal driving habits, and the statistics showed both speed and crashes were reduced as a result.

Why did this work? Because of the target individuals' {selves}, of course. The ads attached the idea of {speeding} to the idea of a man {having a small penis}. Penises are, of course, a portion of the body that falls in the center of the {self} map. It's the primary connection to a man's sexuality and virility, which also both fall onto the {self} map, and most men wish to have others see their penis as something to be admired and cherished, not ridiculed. So if speeding was now connected with a man's penis being somehow deficient, that is not an idea men wish to have connected to {self}, thus more men avoided speeding as a result. So the speeding problem was solved by devaluing a disposable attachment (speeding) within a group's sense of {self}.

Dateline: Colombia, 2013

In the little town of Barbacoas, the roads were bad. Or should I say . . . the road was bad? There was only one, which had only one lane, and it was horrible, and dangerous, making the trip to the local hospital a fourteen-hour drive when you needed to go. As a result, people were dying in transit, including women in labor. But as much as the people complained about the road situation, the local government never had the political will to improve it. Until, that is, the women figured out how to influence the {self} maps of the men in charge. And what they did was genius. They started a "crossed legs" campaign.

The women of Barbacoas banded together and denied sex to the men of Barbacoas until they agreed the road would be improved. So the women collectively said, "Gentlemen, talk to the hand." As a result, it didn't take long for authorities to act. A little over a month without sex, and the men in charge mysteriously found it in their best interest to get the road improvement process initiated. Reporter John Otis told UPI in October of 2013, "Just this month, the Army Corps of Engineers has announced, 'Yes, we are rebuilding that road,' and the bulldozers are in there, and they're getting going on it. So there appears to be a happy ending this time."

Heh-heh. He said "happy ending." Shut up, Beavis.

When you look to improve the world in some small way, where actions of people around you are required to assist in making that improvement, you now know the first thing you should address is what label, or attachment, or idea can be applied to influence others to take positive action in support of that effort. This has huge implications in the science of leadership and running businesses, where large groups of people sometimes need to be attached to a common goal. It certainly plays a role in how politics and political movements can be more effectively managed, or circumvented. It even has implications in how to be a better parent, and how to get the best out of our kids who will be the leaders of tomorrow. We will discuss more details on a few of these topics in Chapter 12, but first I'm going to show you some deep mind hacks.

Chapter 10 Takeaways

In order to improve our emotional output and increase happiness overall, you can do any or all of the following:

1. Before any negativity even occurs, you can proactively alter your expectations regarding upcoming events to hot-wire your mind for higher happiness responses and lower negativity responses.

2. You can alter your Perceptions of events as they happen or after they've happened, looking for a Perception which most reduces your inner turbulence.

3. You can use affirmations to fire your vagus nerve and calm your minds to prime your happiness pump.

4. To remove negativity in the moment, you can use the Equation of Emotion Review to throw yourself into meta-awareness, and enable the hardwired name-it-tame-it functions of your brain to reduce your negative responses.

5. You can stay in the moment, allowing life to simply be as it is without the judgment which could raise negative responses from your subconscious brain activity.

6. You can use tools like THE Me to subjectify {self} and distance yourself from {self}, thereby distancing yourself from the negative responses of the {self} and reducing your inner turmoil.

Chapter 10 Reflection

1. What quick mind hack can you see yourself starting tomorrow to increase happiness levels in your life?

11. The Deep Mind Hacks

To understand truth one must have a
very sharp, precise, clear mind; not
a cunning mind, but a mind that is
capable of looking without any distortion,
a mind innocent and vulnerable.

—J. Krishnamurti

At this point, I trust that you are really starting to see just how useful even a small peek into your own mind can be, and how not exercising these disciplines of the mind in the past has really gone a long way in screwing up our individual lives, our societies, and also the current state of our world. In just our short review so far, with only cursory peeks into our mind's consciousness, we've learned how our minds see our identity, and how and why that flawed identity creates the negative crap in our minds. We've learned how these same influences drive our daily behavior. And we've learned some pretty easy preemptive and reactive mind hacks to take back control from the false {self} within us.

We need to get our brains back under control, at the very least because our new technological world has changed our brains in a large number of very bad ways. As mentioned in the introduction of this book, our human attention span has now dropped to below that of the common goldfish. The attention span of a goldfish is nine seconds on average. Humans are now measuring an average 8.5 seconds. This is horrible news for our human brain health. Mode shifts in the brain create wasted brain cycles, and quick attention shifts create a more chronic condition of stress. So our shorter attention spans could literally be killing us. So it's here that we should look even a bit deeper into mind, and into other mental disciplines we can use to strengthen our meta-awareness muscles to take back control of our minds, improve our brains, and even maybe reveal some deeper truths about our true identity within that still lies hidden to discover.

Mind exercises come in an amazing array of flavors, so if one particular mind exercise leaves a bad taste in your mouth, the good news is that you won't be stuck with just the one. Just as when you're eating ice cream at Baskin-Robbins, there are numerous options to taste and even mix together to create your own personal practice that works for your unique bubble-gum-mixed-with-mint-chocolate-chip preference. Regardless of the type of mental discipline that is practiced, when you focus on something in particular, it breaks the pattern of thoughts in the brain that compares everything in relation to {self}. And that's an awesome thing.

Meditation

The first deep mind hack is one with a history older than written history itself. Meditation was first mentioned in writings from ancient Asia around 1500 BCE, but some scholars speculate that its roots may date back fifteen hundred years before that, to 3000 BCE. Meditation has long been considered within most religions as a practice that can bring one closer to God, truth, inner peace, and liberation of self. Science has confirmed that meditation is one of the best ways to improve brain and body health, decrease stress dramatically, and maximize happiness and well-being. And the most recent science shows it can indeed deepen any spiritual practice.

Scientifically speaking, meditation has been shown to be a miracle drug with little to no negative side effects. It improves brain function, immune system function, and memory function. It's been shown to improve focus, alertness, and emotional awareness. It can enhance sensory processing, so your food tastes better, your music sounds more awesome, and you notice more cool stuff in the world. Meditation has been shown to physically increase gray matter in the good areas of the brain where you need more brain, and shrink negative emotion and pain centers in the brain where you could use less brain, such as in the limbic system. Meditation has even been shown to elongate the end caps on our chromosomes called telomeres, which researchers at Stanford found is directly correlated with how long we live. When our telomeres shrink, our DNA gets damaged during replication and we get sick and die. When our telomeres get longer, our DNA is protected, and we wind up living longer, healthier lives. Meditation has been shown to make our telomeres longer; so, meditation can literally postpone death and make our later years healthier years. In addition, meditation lowers blood pressure, lowers heart rate, and drastically reduces the inner mind wandering that's been shown in multiple studies to result in clinical depression. In short, meditation is awesome.

Meditation even makes your brain work faster. A study done on attention blink rate in the brain showed that after just eight hours of training in the meta-awareness practice of meditation, study participants' brains reacted faster to attentional cues. In that study, a computer flashed a series of letters in quick succession on a screen for participants to view. In the midst of this stream of quick single letters however, the computer would randomly also flash numbers in the sequence every now and then. It was the study participants' job to register seeing those numbers as fast as they could, making sure to pay attention for any other numbers that may also momentarily appear. Some of those numbers came pretty quickly. After meditation training was completed, participants reacted faster to the intermittent numbers in the sequence than before their meditation training, and they also missed fewer of them. Pre-training testing showed many people just missed some of the numbers entirely. Not so with the meditation-trained brains. The meditation-trained brains were simply faster and more attentive.

A healthier brain makes for a healthier body. One ten-year study from the Institute for National Medicine and Prevention measured the impact of meditation vs. eating right and exercising. Researchers split study participants into two groups. The first group they told to eat right and exercise, and had them keep logs to record their activity. The second group they told to meditate for twenty minutes per day, twice per day, for a total of forty minutes, and also log their progress. After ten years, the meditation group had experienced two thirds fewer heart attacks and strokes than the eat-right-and-exercise group. And of the people in the meditation group who slacked off and only meditated twenty minutes per day, they still experienced almost 50 percent fewer heart attacks and strokes than the eat-right-and-exercise folks. As a bonus, the meditators reported dramatic reductions in anger issues. To be fair, people who take care of their mind and body health by engaging in meditation probably don't tend to eat a lot of fast food on their couch in front of the TV. So, even if this study is basically a comparison of eat-right-and-exercise folks who don't meditate vs. eat-right-and-exercise folks who do, it still shows the meditators had two thirds fewer heart attacks and strokes over the non-meditators over ten years. SO, ROCK ON, MEDITATORS!

Personally speaking, I appreciate how well my brain works during the portions of my life where I'm meditating. In my fifteen years of meditation practice, there have been a couple times I've intentionally stopped meditating just to see what happens in my mind as a result. Admittedly, there have also been a few times when I've unintentionally fallen off the wagon for a month or so because "I was too busy to meditate", only to find I needed to return to meditation because my mind didn't work as well as when I was meditating. When I'm meditating, my health feels optimal, my focus feels exceptional, my patience with others goes through the roof and remains there, and frankly I feel smarter. My brain seems to put things together more quickly, which helps my daily work. I appreciate the work benefits as much as I do the physical and emotional health benefits.

In today's world, your work environments provide an opportunity for you to become distracted every eleven minutes on average. And if you pull your attention to whatever is distracting you, be it that last e-mail that came in, your Facebook app on your phone, the latest sports scores at ESPN.com, or even where you're thinking about going to lunch that day, it takes an average of twenty-five minutes to get back to your original task. A study coauthored by Gloria Mark at UC Irvine showed interruptions like these result in significantly higher stress levels in the body. David Meyer at the University of Michigan showed us that higher stress levels dramatically inhibit short-term memory retention, memory recall, and cognitive function. That's all bad ju-ju for getting work done and remaining healthy. Meditation has been shown to help all of that.

My son started on meditation to help with his schoolwork via a popular mobile meditation app called Insight Timer. He loves relaxing before bed with the guided body scan meditation. The good news is that kids who meditate have been shown to get better grades in school, get higher standardized test scores, have higher emotional intelligence, have fewer bullying issues, and receive higher leadership scoring from their teachers and their peers. That's some awesome stuff right there. I am completely supportive of schools that start mindfulness meditation programs to help their kids learn. Teachers are reporting that mindfulness programs are transformative to their classrooms.

Meditation Is Not Against Your Religion

Even with all this awesome science surrounding meditation, there's still one topic we need to discuss before moving into all the options we have when considering a meditative practice. Because for some people reading this book, there's a little voice in the back of their minds being suppressed at this moment, and it's asking a really important question:

"Doesn't meditation come from a religion other than my own?" There's a big misconception in some religious groups that meditation is not, or should not be, a part of their religious practice, or that meditation is a part of other people's religions, and therefore should be avoided at all costs. Their EoE sees it as a threat to their religious practice. "I have not been taught that meditation is a part of my religious beliefs, so meditation is part of someone else's religion, not mine. Therefore, I should not engage in it."

The truth is meditation has long been a cornerstone of most world religions, including Buddhism, Taoism, and Hinduism, but also Judaism, Islam, and yes, Christianity. I put an emphasis on Christianity, because I currently live in the southern United States, where many {self} identified Christians believe falsely that meditation is not deeply connected with Christianity. Frankly, I don't know where this mistaken belief comes from, because the Bible itself mentions meditation a number of times from Isaac meditating in the Book of Genesis, all the way through to the New Testament, where Jesus Himself spends 40 days fasting and meditating in the wilderness. Heck, Jesus even said himself, "If you do not fast from the world, you will not find the kingdom." The fact is, although it's different today, meditation used to be a huge part of Christianity. So don't think if you're a Christian that you need to skip this section. You may be refreshingly surprised to learn that true Christianity is inclusive and welcoming of meditation, not exclusive or critical of it. In my opinion, people who say Christianity isn't connected with meditation are simply ignorant of the history of their own religion.

A few years ago, I got to talk with a great scholar of world religions, who I also consider to be one of the world's most powerful masters of mind, and one of the greatest meditation teachers alive. His name is Shinzen Young. He has an audio book which is basically a recorded talk where he riffed on every major religious practice and how they utilize meditation as a tool to deepen their spiritual practice, regardless of what practice they've chosen. In his talk, titled The Science of Enlightenment, Shinzen extolls the extent to which Christianity was once focused on meditative practices as the primary tool to becoming closer to Jesus Christ. In his talk (if you're not already a member of audible.com, you can get a free copy by using my affiliate link at www.mindhackinghappiness.com/audible), Shinzen notes,

> If you've ever been to Europe, you know how many monasteries there are, and that's only a small fraction of the number of monasteries there were at one time because wars and revolutions of different kinds have destroyed many of the monasteries of Europe. What few people really stop to think about is what function those monasteries played. They were absolutely at the center of Christian tradition. The monastic movement was started by St. Benedict, and it was called the Benedictine Rule. And St. Benedict said that the reason to go into a monastery . . . was one [reason] and one [reason] only; to attain the prayer of quiet.

He then added, "It was absolutely central to the Christian tradition."

I can say as someone who grew up with some connection to religion, this really made sense to me the first time I heard it. It had always been confusing to me to think, "If God knows everything, including what is in our hearts, why would God make us verbally ask for things? Indeed, why would we ever need to say anything to God if he can read our minds?" So after hearing Shinzen speak, and talking with him about it later, I thought it made sense that prayer is a time to listen and not to speak.

Ironically, although the prayer of quiet is not taught amongst the Christian flock in most local churches, that same tradition of praying with mental stillness still exists today at monasteries around the world. And it's still one of the most sacred practices taught to the highest level male and female monks of most religious orders, Christianity especially. Today it's called contemplative prayer. It's not a speaking-to-God type of prayer, but more of a silencing of the mind to listen for God, so that whatever is going on in your head won't stand in the way of connecting with God. Legendary African American Baptist Minister and author Howard Thurman, who was an influential figure in the life of Dr. Martin Luther King Jr., said in his later years that even his own personal Baptist prayer had changed from that of talking to God, to being more of a practice of becoming silent of mind and "listening for God." Of course, if you're not sure whether to take Reverend Thurman's word, we could always look back to Martin Luther, who started the entire Christian Protestant movement away from the Roman Catholic Church in 1517 when he said, "The fewer words, the better the prayer." Even today, Greek Orthodox and Russian Orthodox churches, which are the closest things the world has left to ancient Christianity, utilize meditation and quieting the mind as a way to achieve thesois, which means "becoming like God."

The reason meditation practices have been associated with world religions for seemingly forever is because of what can happen in the mind when the mind falls completely silent: as the great Taoist philosopher Laozi (aka Lao Tzu) said, "To the mind that is still, the whole universe surrenders." We will circle back around to this special secret connection in Volume II and review how many historical and religious figures spoke of this same secret in their teachings. Incidentally, it is also why the first female Zen monk approved to bring Zen meditation to the west, Jiyu Kennett, once humorously said, "If you're afraid of being grabbed by God, don't look at a wall. Definitely don't sit still." What these and other masters of mind were speaking of is a rare but magical state of mind which can be brought on by meditative practices as well as other mind focusing activities. And while we'll reserve that conversation for Volume II, where we will discuss the brain science connected with it, this ancient occurrence is the reason almost all religions added meditation as a core practice to deepen their faith and become closer to God. So no more thinking that meditation is against your religion, whatever your religion is. It isn't.

Meditation Practice Options

There are literally dozens of types of meditative practices you can engage in, most of which wind up doing the same basic thing in the brain, and thus, the mind. Admittedly, different types of meditation have small variations in approach, so I would suggest exploring as many types of meditation as you can, to find which one or two perfectly fits your mind, your aspirations, your religious beliefs, etc. We'll cover the general types of meditation here so we don't get too bogged down in the complete additional book that could be written about all the options in meditative disciplines. If you would like to learn more, we'll provide more specific information and resources at MindHackingHappiness.com for your internal spelunking needs. Here, we'll paint with a broad brush.

Science typically classifies meditation into two general types. The two classifications are focused attention and open monitoring. Focused attention is just what it sounds like. In a focused attention meditation, you focus your attention on something in particular and hold it there, such as your breath, a particular passage from a holy book, a mantra, or even sometimes your intentional physical body movements, such as with yoga, qigong, or martial arts katas. Open awareness meditation is a bit different, but it also requires us to take our attention and focus it, just not on any one particular thing. In open awareness meditation, the focus of your attention is held on whatever arises within your mind from your senses or thoughts. You don't necessarily feed those sense experiences or thoughts with more thinking, but you do notice the internal noise, you acknowledge it, you sometimes name it, and you release it just as quickly as it arose in your mind. The effects of meditation have proved to be very positive for specific operations within the brain. Let's discuss that for a moment.

Science has so far identified a small number of specific networks of activity in your brain that provide different functions for you. The two main networks of activity that meditation is connected with are the default mode network (DMN) and the task mode network. The default mode network is the internal activity that's firing when you're not focusing on doing an activity. So when you're chilling out, or doing something that doesn't require your focused attention, your brain falls back to its default mode circuits.

When your default mode network is fired up, you can be sure a couple things are going on in your mind. First, you're thinking about something that's not happening right now. So you're thinking about something connected with future, or past, or an imaginary scenario such as a daydream or fantasy. Second, your default mode network thoughts are always about things associated with your {self}. The thoughts are always about you, including all the things that make up the idea of you in your mind. So if you're remembering your past or imagining your future, you're thinking about {you}. If you're thinking about your sports team and its chances at winning the big game, that's thinking about {you}. If you're thinking about what you're going to say to your boss when you see him later, you're thinking about {you}. Default mode network thoughts are always {self}ish in nature, and if you didn't set an alarm to think about a certain thing at a certain time, rather you let the thoughts arise naturally, letting your mind dictate where you go next, they are most always considered by science to be **mind wandering**.

So your default mode circuits are ego circuits. They are {self} circuits. They're your inner narrative and imaginative thought patterns connected with your personal human existence that fire when nothing else is firing. Your default mode network feeds your inner voice, generates your imaginative life scenarios, and to a large part, feeds your inner emotional turmoil engine (a.k.a. your bullshit engine).

In contrast, the task mode network in your brain fires when you're focused on something in particular. For instance, dealing out a deck of cards requires the activity of your task based circuits, as does cleaning out your e-mail inbox, or cooking a new meal. If you're focused on doing something, your task based circuits are firing to help you to get it done. It's important to note you can have {self} thoughts which are intentional and which fire your task mode network. For instance, if you set an alarm to think about how to better your relationship with your significant other by going through the specific categories of thinking about how to spend more time together, find more common interests, and spice things up in the bedroom, that focused thought will fire the task mode network instead of your undirected default mode network. The two networks of default mode and task mode rarely fire together for long periods of time. It's usually either one or the other taking up the energy of the brain at any particular moment. And this is key for us to understand when we're talking about understanding the benefits of meditation.

Matt Killingsworth gave a TED Talk where he broke down the numbers for us. He said our default mind wandering {self} circuits are firing about 47 percent of the time. This is bad news for us, because studies show when those circuits are firing, we are about 20 percent less happy than we could be if they weren't firing. So if we allow this mind wandering to happen, basically half our lives is spent at a C+ in happiness rather than at an A. Matt even went as far as to say that mind wandering is the cause for unhappiness, and not the result of unhappiness. And he may be right.

Dr. Charles Raison at Emory University has found through his research that people with a hyperactive default mode network usually wind up depressed. He suggests when the default mode network fires too often, it connects too strongly to our attention and fear centers of the brain, which rewires you to pay attention to your {self} related thoughts more and more through neuroplasticity. True to how the body works in general, those negative brain muscles get stronger when used. This process continues until finally you are so wrapped up in your {self} crap, a profound depression can arise within you. So creating more balance, where our default mode network isn't firing as often, is probably a good idea.

This is why meditation is critical for maintaining good psychological health. Because meditation is a focused activity that turns off the default mode network and turns on the task mode network in the brain as proven in fMRI studies. Participants in meditation studies have been shown to have down regulated default mode network activity and more reactive focus circuits. Focus-based activities give your brain something to do other than stew in its own {self} stuff processing. But unlike other focus-based activities such as driving a car, or doing a simple puzzle, where you can actually split your attention while thinking about your inner narrative as you do the task, the act of meditating doesn't leave any room at all for splitting your attention and getting absorbed in {self} stuff, because the whole focus of the task of meditation is to focus the mind on something other than your mind's default mode activity.

Think of it as a workout for our mind without all the sweat.

Regardless of how you choose to meditate, controlling your attention with purpose flexes attention muscles in your brain, which strengthens them. This is probably why science shows gray matter increases in the attention centers of the brain in meditators. In addition, focusing your attention on things that don't cause you stress allows for a deep but focused relaxation to occur in the mind. This may be what helps increase gray matter in the positive emotion and emotional regulation centers of the brain in meditators, and why science shows emotional pain is reduced by almost half in those who meditate.

Personally, I think all these health and well-being benefits are secondary to the primary reason that people should meditate. That reason is firmly connected with what meditation does for your understanding of your personal consciousness. When you practice a meditation which allows you to watch what is going on in your mind or in your body, that gives you insight into the fact that you are not those things you are watching. As we discussed in the last chapter when introducing the mental tool of THE Me, a separation must be present for you to observe something. So if you can watch something mentally, you are not that thing. Your conscious awareness is the observer. Thus, meditation reminds you through experience that you are not your body, and you are not your mind. This is one of the biggest mini-realizations regarding the deepest secrets of Self the world's leading luminaries were trying to tell you.

Journaling and Free Writing

A really good way to clean out the cobwebs of the mind and get your brains functioning more efficiently is to dump your mind stuff out onto a sheet of paper.

The science on journaling is pretty cool. Studies show journaling helps health and well-being, but also creativity, business effectiveness, achievement of personal and professional goals, and according to yet another study by Matt Liebermann at UCLA (of our name-it-tame-it fame), writing in a journal even helps the emotional regulation portions of your brain. Could it be that dumping your inner most thoughts and feelings out onto a piece of paper allows for your subconscious processes **to be heard**, like John Gottman showed was the primary determining factor for marital relationships to stand the test of time?

The British journal Advances in Psychiatric Treatment reports that health outcomes for what they classify as "expressive writing" include fewer stress related visits to the doctor, improved immune system functioning, reduced blood pressure, improved lung function, improved liver function, improved working memory, improved sporting performance, higher student grade point average, reduced absenteeism at work, quicker re-employment after job loss, and a feeling of greater psychological well-being, just to name a few.

Just as there are many types of meditative disciplines, there are equally as many writing disciplines. You can keep personal journals, gratitude journals, weight loss journals, idea journals, travel journals, parent and child journals, religious journals, etc.

Many people enjoy keeping daily journals using prompts to get them started with their writing. "The three things I was most thankful for yesterday were..." and then you're off and running, talking about three positive things that require you to think about the good things that happened yesterday. This brings into your Perception things which balance your Equation of Emotion. Reflecting on the positives in your life fires off the positive hormones and neurotransmitters that improve your health and well-being. This can be a bonus side effect to the act of journaling if this is your selected approach. But just getting feelings out, regardless of whether they are good or bad, can be really helpful, too.

One study showed that journaling for just two minutes for two days using the simple prompts like "What hurts me is...," and "Others are . . ." caused study participants to measure higher on standardized well-being tests. That's with just four minutes of writing. Another study showed in out-of-work groups where participants wrote to themselves about their feelings for just 5 consecutive days for 20 minutes per day, 68.4 percent of them had jobs within 8 months vs. only 27.3 percent of the non-writing control group getting jobs. So the writers had three times the success in getting a new job. Both groups got the same amount of interviews, but the people who journaled for one hundred minutes wound up getting the job offers. Again, we don't know why, but we could speculate that you are clearing the subconscious emotional noise that inhibits your brain from doing more productive activities and allows for better outcomes to arise as the result. Dr. James Pennebaker, who is one of the field's leading experts, and who was connected with these first two studies (among many others), tells us that some of his students who wrote about their most meaningful experiences for just fifteen minutes per day wound up not only feeling better about life overall, but also got higher grades, and had healthier blood work than their non-journaling counterparts.

The concept of journaling is simple: just let out whatever is in there that wants out. There are thousands of prompts on the Internet for people who want to try journaling (and we'll even provide some good ones on our website), but as long as you're speaking from the heart as if no one will ever read what you are writing, and you're not censoring yourself through the filter of your mind, then I think you're on the right track.

Check out MindHackingHappiness.com if you're interested in journaling.

Physical Exercise

Personally, I don't like running. I know some people do, but I just can't get there. I do like playing team and individual sports, especially sand volleyball and sometimes racquetball. Thankfully, there are tons of exercise options for us.

A lot of us hate hearing the e-word, but the fact is that exercise is the single best activity you can engage in to maintain your brain health. Wait. Exercise helps brain health? While physical exercise is great for maintaining physical health too, it turns out exercise also helps the brain in tons of awesome ways. We used to think the brain never grew any new cells after we reached adulthood, but it turns out science has proven that super-wrong, and along the way science has also shown that exercise is the most effective way to maximize new brain cell growth, called neurogenesis. As adults, we only get an average of about 700 new brain cells per day, and in comparison to the 85 billion or so neurons up there, that ain't much. An average slap to the head can kill 20,000 brain cells. So admittedly, we need all the help we can get in maintaining brain health as we get older. We need exercise almost as much as we need food and water.

Specifically, exercise increases neurogenesis in the hippocampus, which is the memory center of our brain. In addition, hundreds of studies and over thirty meta-studies (which are studies that are summarizations of a bunch of other studies) show exercise fights anxiety and depression, improves self-esteem, mood states, increases resiliency to stress, and improves sleep. If you want to stave off dementia and cognitive decline in later years, exercise now. 700 neurons a day isn't a great number, even if you get that amount every day, which you won't. Just find some activity to move your body and breathe. Even just walking around outside counts.

Probiotics and Diet

This hack is a bit non-standard, but I promised you more than just weak sauce in the beginning of the book, and science is just starting to understand that our gut has a lot more to do with our emotional landscape than we once assumed. Along with our brain being filled with neurons, inside our body we also have brain-like neurons around the areas of our heart, and all throughout our gut. So along with having a brain-brain, we also have a heart-brain and a gut-brain. It turns out that phrases like "trust your gut" and "I have a gut feeling about this" have a substantial foundation in science. Our hearts and guts actually think. In fact, 95 percent of the serotonin found in our bodies, which is a hormone linked to hundreds of positive functions around the body, but especially beneficial to the brain and nervous system and our positive emotions, is housed in and around our gut.

Interestingly, your gut is mostly made up of bacteria that is not officially part of your body, and which could scientifically be classified as parasites, if it weren't for the fact the activity of these parasites is essential for your survival. It's a simple fact that you would die without the parasites in your gut doing their thing. You have roughly ten times more parasitic cells in your body than you do cells that actually make up your body tissue itself. When it comes to the DNA those cells carry, the fact is that you are only 1 percent human. The amount of foreign DNA that exists in your body outnumbers your human DNA approximately 99:1. If that weren't strange enough, scientists have found that a full 37 percent of your actual human genes originated from outside bacteria, and that indeed your internal body temperature of 98.6°

F is the result of the most efficient temperature for bacteria to operate being 100° F. Science is now showing those little single-cell bacteria actually play a role in dictating your emotional health and mood as well as your physical health and digestion. So although we're not sure how it works, it turns out the mood of these little bacteria, partly determines your emotional landscape.

To oversimplify absolutely everything in the gut, we have good bacteria, neutral bacteria, and bad bacteria. It's obviously better to have more good bacteria than bad bacteria, and one of the things that can help create a positive gut environment down there is adding good bacteria to your diet, and eating a diet which is prosocial to the good bacteria. Although the science of the supplement industry is dubious at best, good bacteria diet items such as probiotic supplements and yogurt have been shown to improve digestion and immune system function, and can deliver good bacteria straight through our stomachs into our gut where it can go to work. By the way, if you've taken antibiotics in the last four years, add some yogurt to your diet. Studies show it can take four years to rebuild a healthy digestive tract after taking antibiotics. Another good general rule is to eat a diet higher in vegetables and lower in carbohydrates. Bad bacteria love carbs. Ditch the doughnuts, pick up the froyo.

Beyond what I've shared here, pick up Dave Asprey's book Head Strong, if you'd like to know more about how to adjust your body science to best benefit your brain. He goes into great detail of how your brain works at a cellular level and what you can do with diet and exercise to maximize your brain and happiness potential.

SDT / Float Tanks

Okay, so in a previous chapter I told you I was a little weird, right? So it should come as no surprise to you when I reveal that I have a sensory deprivation float tank in my home office. So your first question might be, what is a sensory deprivation float tank? It's a big tank of lukewarm salt water that you float in, which has been shown to have numerous physical and psychological health benefits, and where you can calm your mind more effectively than almost any other approach available. If you remember, I mentioned float tanks earlier in the book when we talked about the mind gym of the Navy SEALs. In a sensory deprivation float tank, it's easy to float effortlessly, and when it's kept at a perfect lukewarm temperature, it dissolves the perceived barrier between you and the water. It sounds simple, but the effects on conscious awareness are actually a pretty big deal.

And before you ask, "where the heck could I ever float in a sensory deprivation float tank", spas all over the country are adding them to their list of health maintenance services, so you may already have one available just down the street. Let me now explain what you might experience if you found one.

If you take a moment, right now as you're reading, to shift your attention slightly to also be conscious of the sensations of your skin, you'll probably start to feel things touching your skin as you read this book. Maybe you can feel the physical matter of the book you're reading, or the headphones you're using to listen to it. What you are feeling through your skin is where your body supposedly stops, and where the book, or the headphones, or the clothes covering you, or the air around you, or the seat/floor/ground/bed supporting you start. There's a clearly defined point of demarcation where your body stops and the rest of the world begins, and when you're listening to your touch senses carefully, you can feel where that occurs. You can feel where your body ends. It's a function of the physical portion of the {self} map in your brain. This function allows you to know where your body parts are when you're not actually looking at them. It allows you to feel your feet and know where they are as they press onto whatever is below them. It allows you to feel your arms and know where they are while they hang down or rest on whatever they're touching. It's what allows you to focus in on pretty much anywhere on your skin at any time and feel what's going on there, even if there's nothing going on. Without touching it, is the back of your head still there? How do you know? Crazy cool, huh? You can feel it now, can't you? Where just a couple moments ago, you were ignorant of the whole skin sensation process, you can now feel where your body ends and where the world starts. Congratulations on controlling your attention for a moment there. That was a meta-awareness moment for you.

In a tank of temperature-controlled salt water, that line of demarcation, that sense of separation between you and the rest of the physical world, goes away. It dissolves the line between your body and other. So if you're sitting in a chair at the moment reading this book, you feel the weight of your whole upper body pressing down onto your butt, which then is supported by the seat, right? Floating in a tank of water is much different. The body feels weightless and unsupported by anything on the Earth. This is because the water completely and evenly supports your body from every individual point the water touches you. And if that water is at skin temperature, there is no temperature difference for the skin to perceive, and no single pressure point for the skin to feel, so after a few minutes of getting situated in the tank and floating, the water seemingly disappears, taking with it the very line of demarcation where your body seemingly ends, and the rest of the universe seemingly begins.

Because of the tank's controlled environment, senses of sight, hearing, touch, taste, and smell are all attenuated. What this environment provides is an amazing space where your sensory input is minimized (hence the name sensory deprivation), and where the mind can fall into a space of complete silence. It's actually quite refreshing and rejuvenating. I highly suggest you try it if you're up for new experiences.

The Science of Floating

There has actually been a fair bit of research done on floating. From a study perspective, floating in a sensory deprivation tank for as little as a single hour resulted in increases in scores on standardized creativity tests, and studies also show that floating can enhance performance in athletic and musical tasks that require high levels of concentration and visual-motor coordination. Benefits were seen in tennis players, basketball players, archery, and in artists performing jazz improvisation. In one study, music performers who floated just four times showed an enhancement in their technical performance ability, even after a full week out of the tank, suggesting long term effects are in play. In other studies, researchers measured decreases in blood pressure and stress hormones both in and out of the tank between float sessions, and a meta-analysis of multiple studies confirmed floating was more effective in reducing stress than many other relaxation exercises, biofeedback therapy, and even kickin' back on the couch.

Some amazing things can happen in the mind when it's left to operate in the absence of the senses it normally needs to scan for threats. In the float tank, there's nothing going on, and nothing to do but float. This unique situation changes the patterns within the mind for a while and gives it more free space to organize and put things away, store memories from short term into long term, and finally, give it a bit of time to roam around and play, which if we're paying attention, provides us an amazing peek under the covers of our own subconscious existence. If you meditate in the tank, it results in the most effective meditation sessions you'll ever experience. I really love the level of quiet my mind can achieve when floating in a tank. I experience deeper, quieter meditation sessions in a shorter amount of time than if I'm sitting or walking in meditation. I was once told a story of a Zen monk who reported the same thing. After an entire lifetime of practicing sitting meditation, he said his tank sessions allowed him to go deeper and more effortlessly into the state of Samadhi than he ever had before, which is a period of a sustained peaceful bliss which is also very healing to the body. He reported his float sessions were more profound than any he had ever experienced sitting on a zafu (a zen meditation butt pillow - don't go sniffing those). If this idea even interests you a little bit, you might find yourself a day spa that offers floatation sessions. Spas that rent time in float tanks are popping up all over the place.

The Best Deep Mind Hack: Forgiveness and Compassion

How do we consciously practice forgiveness and compassion? Candidly, I'm probably supposed to stop talking after posing that question and just let you sit in silence with it. That's the type of question that is amazingly powerful when left to your internal pondering faculties. You might do well to revisit how you personally answer the question, "How do I practice forgiveness and compassion in my life? And how might I intentionally practice more of it?"

—

It's tough to forgive sometimes, isn't it? There's always that one thing that happened, or that one person who so egregiously intentionally hurt us or someone we love, that we simply just want to walk away forever and never look back, allowing ourselves to hold ill will for them indefinitely because of whatever happened. For many of us, this can come in the form of a past relationship partner, or previous friend. Heck, sometimes we even make mistakes for which we don't want to forgive ourselves. For some of us, we pile up mistakes, life events, and people for which we hold grudges for years. For lifetimes even. Before I understood life to the level I do now, this holding onto anger thing happened in my own life. And if you'll indulge me this next personal story, I think it may shed some light on the process of forgiveness for all of us.

A Personal Story

The anger that begged forgiveness was targeted toward my mother. And in fact, I did walk away and not speak to her for about five years of my life. Now, the story I'm about to tell you will not hurt her feelings, because she passed away a few years ago. Everyone else in my family agrees it's okay to tell it, so I'm just gonna lay this very personal story out the only way I know how to tell it, because it's a real life example of forgiveness.

Growing up, my family was very dysfunctional. My dad was an absentee father who lived out of state most the time, so I lived with my Mom. She had multiple issues that were never completely addressed, which created challenges for everyone around her. Her days of living through the Great Depression as a young child caused her to be a closet hoarder. Her stuff was her world. And she measured life by the stuff she could accumulate. Subsequently, if she wanted something new in her life and couldn't afford it, she rarely let her lack of funds stand in the way of acquiring it. I think my mom stole from everyone she met in life, even her own family, stealing from my aunts and uncles, my sisters, and even from me when she took thousands in cash that my paternal grandmother had gifted to me when I was young. When relatives came over, there would always be a few items that she needed to "put away" first before they arrived. I had no idea what was going on at the time. To me, Mom was just being Mom.

Because my mom had so much internal stuff going on, my childhood was tainted with some instances of neglect. I remember being left alone when I was three years old after being put down to take a nap. I climbed out of my crib and wound up falling down the basement steps, knocking myself unconscious. When I awoke a little later, cold and scared in the darkness of the basement (I couldn't yet reach the light switch), I started crying. Then I remembered seeing my mom's car driving away, before I'd fallen down the steps and remembered I was alone. I had no idea I was not supposed to be alone, I just figured I'd screwed up being alone, so I climbed back up the steps and coincidentally met my mom and sister as they came through the front door. My mom had gone to pick up my sister from band practice at school. The hug I got from my sister healed my emotional boo-boos. My mom simply told me that was why I needed to stay in my crib.

It wasn't until my parents' divorce proceedings however, that my mother finally crossed the line to an extent I couldn't forgive. Because of the emotional and behavioral challenges I had developed, neither my mom nor my Dad really wanted custody of me. It was a bit of a reverse custody battle, fighting to see who would not be stuck with me moving forward. Don't feel bad for me. Everything's all good now as you'll read later in the book. But this was my reality back then.

In an effort to bolster her argument for not taking me, my mom told the court that I was incorrigible and beyond help, and that I should be put into a juvenile detention center at the age of thirteen. The judge, who was given copies of my ninety-ninth percentile scores on early standardized tests, thankfully disagreed. It was at that point my father, who was basically broke and homeless at fifty-eight years old, agreed to take custody. He did love me, and taking me would save him from paying child support at least. In the court's final ruling, my Dad was awarded his Ford pickup truck, some personal belongings that could fit in his truck, and custody of me. And that was it. My mom got the house and every item I had ever touched. My dad and I moved into his mother's two-bedroom, one-bath home (that was the grandmother who would later help me turn my life around).

I didn't speak to my mom for years. My grandmother was the person who convinced me it was probably a good idea to connect with her, for compassionate reasons above any other. I had not picked up the phone or seen my mom for four years, but even in her self-absorbed world, she was probably missing me. Frankly, I was ready to go the distance on the silent treatment, having written my mom off completely in my mind. And even when I did relent to restart a relationship with her, I'd only somewhat forgiven her. It would be another fourteen years before I was able to forgive her fully.

Let's talk about what I finally discovered all those years later that opened the door to full forgiveness.

As humans, when we get hurt, we seem to forgive others more easily when we perceive the offending party didn't intentionally take the actions that hurt or offended us. An example of this is when someone bumps into us accidentally in a crowd. They didn't really mean to do it, so we can easily forgive them. Excuse me. No problem. Similarly, when others do take intentional actions that accidentally hurt us, we seem to be able to forgive that easily as well. An example of this would be if someone throws a ball that goes off course and accidentally hits us while we aren't looking. Oh, I'm so sorry. No problem. We even throw the ball back while easily forgiving the accident.

It's this same forgiveness-of-innocence spirit that makes it easy to forgive kids' mistakes. We know they have a lot to learn, and they don't yet completely understand everything there is to know about life, or how to handle their negative emotional reactions. There have even been times my son has become very angry with me when I've been forced to restrict his privileges because of some other behavior independent of his anger. When he gets upset at the punishment, he sometimes says or does things he doesn't really mean as part of his reaction. He's six. I don't hold his negative reactions to his punishment against him at all. I know he's just reacting to how he sees things from his limited perspective. In those moments, he's a victim of his anger. He's just doing his thing as a kid, reacting to what his mind is giving him at the moment. I know although he may be angry for a minute, he doesn't truly dislike me or not want to be around me, even if he is growling in frustration at me and stomping away to ignore me. It's cute. I try not to giggle. I know the beauty of his true existence underneath that anger, and I know the anger will eventually pass.

It wasn't until my spontaneous awakening to the true nature of mind (a story I present in Volume II) that I was able to start seeing adults in this same light of uneducated, inexperienced innocence. With this epiphany, I was able to see the adults around us - and by that I mean **all** the adults around us, from Pershing, Iowa to Beijing, China, including the adult I see in the mirror - as the innocent victims of our mind's {self} defending mechanisms. The fact is that none of us who are caught in the mind's endless loop of defense of {self} realize we are caught in that {self}ish loop until we somehow catch an outside glimpse of our mind. When we act in ways that are destructive or harmful to ourselves, or other people, or our world, we don't truly know what we are doing or why we're doing it. We're not conscious of the damage we're causing, or what's causing us to inflict that damage. By our very nature, in the strictest sense of the word, we are what the Epicurean poet Lucretius called 2,000 years ago, "the sick man ignorant of the cause of his malady." We can't look at ego from ego. We can't look at {self} from {self}. Unless we are educated to the mind's process, and can look at it from meta-awareness, we are blind to it, and a slave of it. And so as an entire race, we are the victims of the very ignorance we create, which causes us to hurt ourselves, and others, and our world.

With this understanding of the true nature of mind, I started seeing everyone in the world who is stricken by this same malady of {self} and the Equation of Emotion, as infinitely and effortlessly forgivable. They were forgivable regardless of what egregious action they may have taken to hurt me or others because of the uneducated and uncontrolled operation of their minds. They are the innocent childlike victims of their minds' pain and suffering, acting out in a reactive and immature constant {self} defense. I could see this entire world of people as deserving of compassion for our collective internal struggle, playing victim to our own minds, blind to the deeper more profound truth that can be uncovered within us. It was at that moment I understood Plato's aphorism, "Be kind, for everyone you meet is fighting a great battle," and where another statement, made with a dying breath, took on a whole new meaning; "Forgive them, Father, for they know not what they do."

It was in that single moment of clarity, I was able to completely forgive my mom. My mom became the child saying and doing things she didn't mean without knowing what she was doing. She and everyone else in the world were simply victims of what their minds were giving them. They could not pull themselves out, because they were uneducated about the pitfalls of mind and how it moves Heaven and Earth, and even creates false realities sometimes, to defend {self}. How could I be angry or hold a grudge against absolutely anyone, when the bad actors are only bad because they don't understand anything about the beautiful true nature that underlies their mind's false understanding?

Even though we all look like adults, really we are innocent and overly reactive children. We have to forgive each other for this. We must forgive each other. We only hurt ourselves and each other accidentally, even though sometimes it certainly looks and feels intentional. We do it intentionally, accidentally. This realization is the deeper root of the profound secret the world's ancient luminaries tried to tell us about {self}. This is the type of observational awakening that allows for us to grasp the underpinnings of unconditional love, devoid of our {self}'s conditions for giving love. This is the revelation that allows for the flourishing of pure altruism within a very flawed, but very controllable, human mind.

So it was clear to me that every one of those actions my mother took was an action of defending of her false {self}, which had its hands around her throat. When she stole from me and my family, she did so because her mind was in the grips of defending the ideas and attachments connected with her unstable sense of {self}. When she neglected to provide the care a mother should provide her children, she did so to defend and serve her mind's {self}. When she testified to the judge that I was incorrigible and beyond help in court, the act that I saw as a massive betrayal, she did so to defend her mind's {self}. The other alternative for her would have been to admit to her{self} that she was a less than perfect mother who held a lot of the responsibility for how her son was turning out. Her {self} wouldn't allow her to take a hit for where I was headed. Now that I could now see her as a victim, I completely, and permanently, and inclusive of all future transgressions yet to come, forgave my mother. She was a victim of a mind that put her personal existence closer to the center of her {self} map than even her youngest child and only son. Most parents I know put their kids first, including me. I'd die in a second for my kids, biological or otherwise. She simply couldn't. And with my new insight, she could now be effortlessly forgiven for her blindness to her mind's {self}.

I believe this is what the Roman philosopher Lucius Annaeus Seneca meant when he said, "A physician is not angry at the intemperance of a mad patient, nor does he take it ill to be railed at by a man in fever. Just so should a wise man treat all mankind, as a physician does his patient, and look upon them only as sick and extravagant." It was also Seneca who said, "The first step in a person's salvation is knowledge of their sin." My sin was holding my mother responsible for taking human actions while being a human.

It comes down to this: If we would look to settle every score of every transgression ever made against us, we would spend our entire lives in the act of revenge. And revenge or holding ill will against someone is the ego's folly. It's a function of the mind's false {self} needing to re-validate itself. This is the very subconscious activity from which we wish to free ourselves. The great philosopher Confucius once said, "Before you embark on a journey of revenge, dig two graves." He said it because chasing around looking to vindicate the wounds of the {self} wastes the awesome life you could have if only you were to ditch the needs for the {self}'s payback. Forgiveness and compassion frees us from this loop. And forgiving my mom wound up being more liberating than any act of retribution could have ever possibly been.

Even though my mom was more affected than most, we all fall victim to the same process within the mind that revolves around {self}. We're all sickened by it to a certain degree. None of us goes untouched by it. It's a physiological process. It's exactly why Einstein said the value of a human being can be measured by the extent which they are liberated from the {self}. We're all stricken by the same disease of mind, from which most of us never recover. But maybe it's time to start forgiving ourselves and our harmful reactions, and start to exercise compassion for ourselves and each other, so that we can help ourselves out of this local and global mess our minds have put us in. Maybe it's time to get our {self} out of the way so it stops causing us pain and suffering, and forgive those who haven't been able to do the same. Maybe it's time to truly change the world by breaking the pattern, and not letting our children fall into the same trap of mind we fell into.

Maybe? Maybe. By the way, regardless of what happened in our human history, and how people who came before us did things, it's our world now, and we can change it if we want. We can change our governments, our monetary systems, and our cultures if we wish to be less {self} serving, and more loving and helpful. We can change how our human minds work. It's a choice of not being a slave to what was, and creating and embracing what's next.

The Brain Science of Forgiveness and Compassion

I think the science of forgiveness and compassion is best exhibited by the monks of Tibet, who make forgiveness and compassion a daily practice for themselves, and who under the gentle suggestion of His Holiness The Dalai Lama, have made their brains available for scientific study. The Buddhist Monks who live in Tibet make it a life practice to pray and meditate for all of us daily. They practice two scientifically proven meditations that have been shown to have the most profound positive effects on the brain, one called Dzogchen (with a silent d), and the other called Metta, also known as Loving Kindness Meditation.

Dzogchen means "highest perfection." It's used interchangeably with the term ati yoga, which means "primordial yoga." The practice goes back thousands of years. In practicing Dzogchen, one falls into a state of a mindless bliss, which can only be attained after years of practice, but which provides a space of pure awareness where the true nature of mind (a state of no-{self}) can be effortlessly experienced for as long as one wishes to experience it. It's a pretty friggin' amazing space (or non-space, officially) to hang out in for a while if you can get there.

Loving Kindness Meditation is more of a self-guided practice that anyone can do, where complete love and compassion starts with one's own existence, then slowly expands outward to other life in an ever expanding sphere that eventually consumes the whole infinite universe. You wind up expanding your loving wishes that every life form in the universe be happy and free of pain and suffering, including the weeds in your garden, the germs on all the doorknobs, and that asshole down the street.

That's quite a different thought pattern than our minds typically create for us, isn't it?

Loving Kindness Meditation is a really cool practice to experience if you can find someone who is well versed in leading that type of meditation. The key is to really try and feel that love and compassion for every bit of life within the sphere, which you are willingly ever-slowly-expanding. If you can feel the compassion and love for absolutely everything, the practice becomes very powerful because while we're doing it, we get separated a bit from the regular patterns of {self}, and our consciousness gets expanded out beyond the confines of our skin, just like other meditative practices help us do, and just like what we might experience while floating in a sensory deprivation tank.

Scientists have discovered that Tibetan monks who practice things like Loving Kindness Meditation and Dzogchen have different patterns of activity in their brains than other people do. Specifically, the default mode network in the monks' brains is quieter than it is in other people, and the monks' brain waves are distributed a little differently as well.

Dr. Charles Raison at Emory University, who spotlighted the connection between the default mode network and depression, is one of the researchers who discovered the Tibetan monks don't have as many problems with depression and negative rumination. Because much of their time is spent giving their mind something to do, which quiets their default mode network, and raises their happiness levels through the roof.

One of the other effects compassion training has in the Tibetan monks is that their gamma brain waves are off the charts. Let me oversimplify the science of brain wave patterns for a second: There are six main types of brain waves that are most common in our human brains. From slowest to fastest, they are; slow cortical waves, delta waves, theta waves, alpha waves, beta waves, and one type most recently reclassified, which was previously thought to be noise, gamma waves. Our slow cortical waves are basically just a timing signal or drum beat which the brain uses to synchronize messages. Think of those as the brain's clock that allows everyone to arrive to the party at the same time, like we do with our wristwatches. Delta waves are the slow powerful waves that arise in parts of the brain when we sleep and which can arise in the deepest of meditations. These have an amazing healing and restorative effect on the body, and its why doctors say we all need to be getting eight or so hours of sleep each night. Theta waves are also sleep-time waves, but are more common when we find ourselves in that relaxed twilight state in between wakefulness and sleep, where our waking consciousness is either on its way in, or on its way out. These can also increase during meditation. Alpha waves occur when we are relaxed and alert, when thoughts are flowing with ease but not at a high pace. I call these the Jimmy Buffet waves; alert, but chill. Beta waves are our action waves, when our brain is in its most active state. This is when we seem to be firing on all cylinders, getting a lot of work done, or figuring out a lot of things in a short amount of time. While beta waves are great for the office, they can also occur in many alert states of stress, and they take a lot of energy and resources to maintain over time. So they kinda stress the brain out a bit, and even wind up harming the brain if it doesn't get the right amount of focused relief, with sleep or through some sort of meditative practice. Last are the gamma waves. Previously, gamma waves in the brain were dismissed as by science as "spare brain noise." But then researchers discovered gamma waves actually relate to the simultaneous processing of information from multiple brain areas. So for lack of better terms, those are the waves that put the big picture together for us in our mind. Although they are the lowest amplitude waves in the brain, they are also the fastest, and carry the most information of all our brain waves. They are kicking ass when the brain is being its best most efficient self. Gamma waves are so fast and efficient, their frequency is quicker than the rate at which our neurons fire, so how they even exist is still a mystery to neuroscience. But maybe not coincidentally, they are also the most highly active brain waves when the mind is in states of universal love, altruism, and the 'higher virtues'. And in our Tibetan monks, who practice empathy and compassion as a way of life, these highly efficient super waves are measured the highest compared to any other group of people on the planet.

So maybe if we want a better brain, a happier brain, and a healthier brain, what we should do is learn to see into the mind of ourselves and others, to raise our empathy and compassion levels. Maybe what we should do is learn how our {self} maps and Equation of Emotion works to be able to better understand the {self} maps and Equation of Emotion in others. Learning how and why other people feel the way they do increases our empathy and compassion naturally. Learning why people react the way they do and why they take the actions they take delivers us an amazing level of understanding and patience with their actions, even if their actions are somewhat harmful to us at the moment. In addition, seeing our own propensity to react without conscious awareness throws a wrench in our own unconscious process to want to lash out in return of some perceived sleight and cause even more harm, more pain, and more suffering in the world.

I'd say that's a pretty good mind hack.

Chapter 11 Takeaways

1. Numerous deep mind hacks work by utilizing conscious awareness to engage in activities which assist the subconscious mind into reducing its noise.

2. Beyond meditation, journaling, diet and exercise, and maybe

even floating in a float tank, one of the deepest mind hacks is consciously practicing forgiveness and compassion.

3. All deep mind hacks require effort, but they all have extremely positive effects.

Chapter 11 Reflection

1. What deep mind hack can you see yourself starting tomorrow to increase your happiness?

2. Do you see an opportunity to forgive someone for a deep pain they caused you while they were in the unconscious space of defending their mind's {self}?

12. More Amazing Hacks to Improve Life

Everything should be made as simple as possible,

but not one bit simpler.

—Albert Einstein

In Section I of this book, you learned how your human mind works, and in Section II, you learned about the general tools and control mechanisms within your mind that can be applied to change your life in a general sense. But we haven't yet fully covered all the awesome benefits that can come from throwing back the covers of our conscious and subconscious minds. There are some last, both infinitely profound, and not-so-profound-but-really-useful things we can do to increase our life's happiness. Let's discuss some of those now.

Hacking Your {self} Map for a Better Life

In learning how the {self} operates in our minds, one of the most useful things you can do for your day-to-day happiness levels is to hack your {self} map. If you decide to move some things around, or even move some things off your {self} map altogether, you can reduce the number of opportunities you have to experience pain and suffering, and you can also reduce any inner turmoil you do experience when some inner bullshit eventually arises. This sounds more complicated than it is. Actually, moving things around on your {self} map is pretty easy to do, and when you decide to do it, the results can be amazing.

Simplifying Life Consciously

Mark Manson wrote a wonderfully entertaining book called, The Subtle Art of Not Giving a Fuck. Despite its edgy title and frequent cursing, it's a great book on how to decide what to give a fuck about, and how we might reduce the number of things we do give a fuck about. His point is that many of us give a fuck about way too many things, and that if we reduced how many fucks we had to give, our lives would be much happier for it. And while I disagree with Mark's assertion in other parts of his book; that a complete and lasting happiness can't be attained (it actually can and we explain it in Volume II), he's exactly right that giving too many fucks about too many things is definitely the path to pain and suffering.

The items and ideas on your mind's {self} map are the things your subconscious mind cares about defending. That's just a function of your brain. You know your mind automatically creates Expectations/Preferences about your {self} stuff, which then feeds one side of your Equation of Emotion. These pre-made Expectations/Preferences then sit waiting to be compared to any Perceptions which happen to float through your head at any given moment. In addition, you know the level of attachment you have to particular {self} items partly determines how powerfully you experience your reactions to your Perceptions. Therefore, it stands to reason, as well as it being aligned with common sense, that if you decided to pick up a few things and toss them off the map, you'll have fewer negative emotional reactions from that moment forward as a result. And if you grab a few things you've been way too attached to and toss them out toward the edge of your map without giving them up altogether, when you do experience negative emotions about those items (because they're still on the map), then at least it won't destroy your world.

Mark Manson would call this having fewer fucks to give.

Moving Stuff Off the {self} Map

Whether you want to call it having fewer fucks to give, or simplifying your {self} map, the mechanism is exactly the same. You release stuff you don't need to care about. You loosen your grip on some of the things you do care about but which aren't as important as your life's most important stuff. And you leave the most important stuff alone and continue to care deeply for it. So it's not about caring about stuff less, it's about caring about less stuff.

For instance, one of the best things my wife ever did to increase my daily happiness levels was to remove {cable TV watcher} from our {self} map. We haven't had TV for almost a decade, including most forms of the network news. This has improved life dramatically because it slows my mind's flow of unnecessary Perceptions that the news tries to convince us are important. Fewer Perceptions from the news means fewer negative reactions from my internal Equation of Emotion. Fewer negative reactions creates less cortisol, which equates to a longer life for me and my family. With the aid of Internet technologies, we haven't yet missed one major news story or weather alert that has mattered to us since.

Beyond saying good-bye to the manufactured drama called the news, although I joked about it a few times previously, I also consciously removed the idea {I hate spiders} from my {self} map, as well as all attachments to the idea {government should function properly}. Consciously removing both of these ideas has allowed me to watch both spiders and Congress simultaneously without the smallest motivation to freak out. In fact, you could drop a million spiders on an open session of Congress, and I wouldn't bat an eye. Although it would make a lot of news!

When you decide to move things off your {self} map, that gives you more attention and energy for the things you consciously leave on your {self} map. For instance, I consciously decide to be very connected to the idea of {wanting to help people raise their happiness game}. I think that's a beneficial {self} item that might make a difference a few years down the road. Leaving that particular item on my {self} map helps my brain create the drive for me to take the actions to defend that {self} item. That means I have the motivation to write this book without having to fight to remain motivated. It means I have the drive to put out a podcast, to pay to have a mobile app developed, etc. Knowing how my {self} and Equation of Emotion works, I can consciously choose what items to leave on my {self} list, and thus shape how I live my life every day. That not only keeps me motivated to take actions that are well aligned with my core existence, it keeps me happy that I am now in alignment with the stuff that is most important to me. It's the stuff I selected to keep. And this can happen for you too. Now that you know how your mind works, it simply takes conscious effort to decide what {self} stuff you want to keep and what you want to pitch. While this may be a bit of common sense, at least you now understand the underlying mechanisms which make it common sense, and you can use that information to pinpoint the stuff that maybe shouldn't matter as much to you as it presently does.

You can consciously edit your {self} map regularly. And in doing so, you are now literally sculpting your life to what you want it to be. For instance, it's okay to still love your favorite sports team without letting that attachment hold a solid center position on your {self} map. There's absolutely nothing wrong with having your favorite sports team's logos on everything you own, and to keep up with your team's wins and losses and latest news. But if you're going to do that, just do it consciously. Do it knowing the whole process of attachment to the team is a big game within your mind, not just a game down on the field of play. Enjoy the wins, but don't let the negative results ruin your day. Reviewing and placing your {self} items on your map consciously allows you to control, even at a subconscious level, the amount of turmoil that any one {self} item can generate. Not everything has to be something you care about. Not everything you care about has to be of utmost importance. Take a look at what you might grab from the center of your {self} map, and nudge it out toward the edge a bit. You'll be happier as a result.

Trial lawyer and podcaster Mike Deblis put this concept into very elegant terms for us when I was a guest on his podcast for trial lawyers, called Theater of the Courtroom. We were discussing the benefits of reviewing the Equation of Emotion for those who experience high levels of stress in their jobs (such as lawyers), and how the {self} map feeds half of that process, when Mike pointed out a simple truth about the Equation of Emotion process; that it reminds us to hold onto only the most important things. He said, "It's almost going back to something very, very, basic and simple; that we shouldn't get so absorbed in material items, and we have to value the things that are more important in life, which is the health of our family. And it really puts things into perspective, because so many of us today really do hold onto projects and things [we've] got going on as tightly as we hold onto our spouse, son or daughter, and this really teaches us how to mind shift, and realize what is most important in life."

Frankly, I couldn't agree more with Mike's statement. It kinda fits Mark Manson's idea not to give a fuck about unimportant shit. Or Richard Carlson's idea in Don't Sweat the Small Stuff, and It's All Small Stuff. If you consciously clean off your {self} map of the things that are less important to you, by default your happiness levels will certainly increase as a result. Who cares what negative political bullshit people are posting on Facebook, or Instagram, or Twitter? That phenomena is never going to end, and no one cares about your opinion on it but you, so don't waste your life responding to it. Why waste your life writing e-mails and making posts about your favorite television show getting canceled, when you can stop watching other people live their fake lives on a screen, and go start living your real one? Who the fuck cares if you got a B in some certain class in school instead of an A? Take all that shit off your plate. Remove that you need to be [this] or [that], or that people need to think of you [this way]. If too much stuff bothers you today, consider moving some things around on your {self} map. It will reduce how much bothers you tomorrow.

If you might need help visualizing your {self} map to better understand how you might more easily adjust your map, we plan to have a mobile tool for you. Check the website for more information.

Creating Lasting Motivation with a {self} Item

Every one of your conscious actions in life is connected with defending or promoting a {self} idea in your mind, or you wouldn't take that action. It's simply how your nervous system works, which is inclusive of your brain, the very thing that creates your initial motivations to take action. When you go to work, it's to get the money that allows us to eat and put a roof over your head, or maybe it's because you enjoy the work. When you give a compliment to someone, it's because you are responding to a thought that has arisen in your minds, and your need to communicate that thought. When you take a drive, or plant a garden, or go to church, or even watch a television show, it's because you have a {self} motivated interest to do that particular thing. Most the time, your motivations rarely surface, leaving you to the explanation of why you did things to just, "because I wanted to," or "I had to."

But sometimes you identify things that you think you **should** do, and you consciously try to place them onto your {self} maps, and then try to create the motivations necessary to accomplish taking the actions to make it happen. An example might be that you believe you need to lose some weight, because you know it will make you healthier and look better. So {lose weight} then gets added to your {self} map, and attached to the ideas {improved health} and {better body shape}. {Improved health} and {better body shape} are now your anchors for the new attachment of {lose the weight}.

The only problem is that your new attachment to the idea {lose weight} doesn't automatically get a spot close to the center of your {self} map, and if all three of your ideas {lose weight}, {improved health}, and {better body shape} all fall farther out from the center of your map where {your love of cheesecake} sits, the fact is you're doomed to lose that race right out of the gate. As we saw in Section I, when two or more {self} items come into conflict with each other, the one closer to the center always wins that battle—if you value your child who is falling into the pool more than you value the personal electronics in your pocket, you dive into the pool after the child, electronics be damned.

Since you know only the most centered items on your {self} maps win all our battles of action, when you add a new {self} idea of something you should do, it can dramatically increase your chances of success of acting on that new {self} idea, if you anchor the new idea to another {self} idea that falls more toward the center of your {self} map. Let's stay with the example of wanting to lose weight. It usually isn't until your doctor tells you your extra weight is literally killing you that you find the motivation to alter your diet and add some exercise into the mix. What is happening is that the idea {losing weight} is being directly connected to {health of the body}, which is something which falls dead center on your {self} map. So where moments before, the idea {losing weight}, and maybe also {exercising}, were destined to live a lonely unnoticed existence out near the edge of your {self} map, losing out to {your love of cheesecake}, after our doctor asks a question like, "Would you like to have your heart attack here, or wait until you get home?," now {losing weight} gets attached to the {body} and so {losing weight} starts to get your full attention.

I use this same method to motivate myself to watch what I eat, and exercise more often than I have in the past. I attach that {self} idea of {staying healthy} to the {self} idea of {my kids}. Specifically, I use my attachment to the idea that {I want to be around longer for them} as the real motivator for staying healthy. I don't want to leave my kids before a time where they can be done needing me. I want to give them a good start, and a solid foundation of being able to understand life to the level I believe I do. I want to be there to answer any questions they may have earlier in life. So that's my real motivation for staying healthy. Without that associated attachment, the {self} idea of {staying healthy} would die a slow lonely death in my mind. It's only because {being healthy} is anchored to {my kids}, something which falls dead center on my {self} map, that I'm able to take actions on a regular basis to stay healthy. When it comes to {my love of cheesecake} vs. {the love for my kids}, there's no contest.

In the business world, some of the top coaches for new entrepreneurs are calling this {self} association exercise "finding your single motivating purpose." Being an entrepreneur is tough, especially when it comes to maintaining a high level of motivation to develop product offerings and do what's necessary to develop a real business. But they say if you can find a single motivating purpose, that motivational hurdle can often be removed entirely, and doing the things required to be a budding entrepreneur can become a breeze. That's the activity of anchoring your new business to something very important on your {self} map.

Making changes to your {self} map, which is one of the variables which feeds the Equation of Emotion, changes the output of all the instances of your Equation of Emotion itself. This can result in changes to your entire emotional landscape, by changing the processing patterns of your mind, which can then result in dramatic changes to our motivations to make life exactly what you want it to be.

Using the {self} and the EoE in Business—Your Side

There are two sides of the coin when it comes to using your knowledge of the {self} map and your Equation of Emotion in business. The first side has to do with using knowledge of your own {self} and EoE process, and the other side has to do with using the knowledge of the {self} and EoE of others. Let's talk about using the knowledge of your own {self} and EoE process first.

Optimizing Your Brain and Maintaining Motivation

You are most effective when your brain is operating at full capacity. So it goes without saying you would probably prefer it if your thinking brain wasn't being turned off by your emotional brain during those times you need to be getting a lot of work done. One solid way to ensure this doesn't occur is to keep any potential negative emotional reactions you might have in the workplace to a minimum.

The first tool in your bag for reducing your workplace turmoil is to hold onto your business goals rather loosely on your {self} map. I think it was the rock band .38 Special who said, "hold on loosely, but don't let go." I think this is a sound piece of business advice. Of course, most employers won't like that I'm giving you this same advice, but that's only because they have yet to read the next few paragraphs on how to maintain a solid high effort level, and how this same science can be used to properly motivate employees and promote the development of truly amazing leadership skills.

We all have to create an income for ourselves in this civilized world we've based on monetary trade. But nothing says you need to buy into it so much that the process of work itself ruins your emotional life and health because of it. Holding onto your business goals loosely is something that requires focus. It requires strength. It requires a positive mental attitude to still be able to deliver quality work while at the same time not getting too caught up if things don't wind up going exactly to plan. Ironically, the farther you can nudge your business attachments out from then center of your {self} map, the more effective you can be in attaining your business goals in a particularly challenging business environment. Isn't that just weird? But it's completely true. The more you hold on loosely to your business goals without letting them go, the better you can do at obtaining your business objectives. When you make your business goals too large a portion of your {self}, then you can't get {self} out of the way. This means you can never gain entry into the super-efficient mind state of flow, which only happens when {self} gets out of the way.

This is one of the reasons Google has pledged its ongoing support for Meng Tan's internal mindfulness training program Search Inside Yourself, taught at Google campuses worldwide. That program pushes employees toward releasing their focus on their business attachments, becoming more mindful and more compassionate about the people with whom they work. It's the most popular program Google has ever had, and they credit the program for having what they call "the happiest, healthiest workforce on the planet." It raises their employees' emotional intelligence, which has been shown in workplace studies to increase productivity by 20 percent. And there's certainly no arguing about the level of Google's success in business.

Setting Expectations in Business

We touched on this in Chapter 10, but setting expectations

consciously in ourselves and others is one of the best ways to prevent future turmoil from surfacing. One of the best companies I ever worked for had a company motto that integrated setting expectations as part of it's culture. That mottos was, "Under commit and over deliver." They focused on utilizing this motto in dealing with their customers, but frankly it seeped into the core culture of the company, so it was a bit difficult to find people working for that company who weren't dedicated to under committing and over delivering in employee-to-employee relations as well. It was an amazing place to work. This company, a small tier-2 data center provider named Inflow, had a 100 percent customer satisfaction rating for multiple years running because of this very motto. And it's not hard to see how they did it.

They did it by setting realistic expectations of good quality service, and then working to exceed those expectations by over delivering on the promises that were made. I would even throw in last minute unexpected discounts when the price for services had already been agreed upon. The operations team would follow up by providing well above average implementation services and unexpected perks. And by now we all know what happens in the human mind when an Expectation or Preference gets met or exceeded by a Perception. That Equation of Emotion result creates positive emotions. So Inflow's customers absolutely **loved** the company. And you might easily guess what happened after they started accumulating customers who loved them. Those customers made referrals of their colleagues at other businesses. They became not just brand loyalists, but brand evangelists. The happiness level of Inflow's customers was legendary in the data center market space. And I made sure every one of my new prospective customers knew it.

A friend of mine, who was the sales manager for the largest competitor in our space, a company named Exodus, later told me at a poker game at his house that no matter how confident his sales rep was in closing a deal, when he found out they were selling against me at Inflow, he would report that deal as a low probability deal to Exodus sales management. It seems he was setting some internal expectations as well. This certainly spotlights the engine for success that Inflow created by making it a company policy to properly set expectations (and then exceed them) with the customers we did indeed win. And we won a lot of them in a major market against the biggest players in that market. After the tech bubble burst in 2000, Exodus and a few other major providers went out of business, while Inflow was acquired by SunGard, a data center company that is still in business today.

Creating the Right Perceptions in Business

We can't yet abandon the topic of how {self} and the Equation of Emotion can be a benefit in business without discussing how conscious changes in your Perceptions can also make life easier for you.

I used to hate sales. I was always more partial to engineering and science. Before I decided to go back to college after having served in the military, I held a couple jobs in sales, and absolutely hated both of them. The first sales job I had was at the electric organ store in a mall in Florida, where we tried to sell electric organs to old people who were looking to rediscover their love of music, without picking up a more challenging instrument like a guitar. I'm not bashing organs. I learned to play an old Hammond B-1000 when I was a kid. But these new fancy ones had one finger chord capabilities and automatic symphonic accompaniment with complex rhythm percussion. It basically played everything for you. I sucked at it, and never sold a single one. I think they hired me out of pity and because it looked good to have another warm body in the store.

My second sales job was easier. It was selling TVs, stereos, and appliances for my brother-in-law at a regional outlet. I listened to his interactions with customers and mimicked him, and I actually sold a bunch of electronics and made a little money. And while I loved working with my brother-in-law, and was grateful to have the job, I hated being in sales there, too. But at least selling TVs was easier than selling organs. It wasn't until after college, when I was picked up as an engineer for a super computing company, that I had my first great Perception shift about sales.

As a pre-sales engineer, I accompanied the sales reps on sales calls and spoke about the technical details of the supercomputers they were considering purchasing. In one short ten-minute conversation, I was able to convince an executive at Time Warner they needed to buy yet another $750,000 refrigerator sized computer, which netted the sales rep a $60,000 paycheck for the one sale. The sales rep could have been a fly on the wall in that conversation, and for reference, I wasn't even making $60,000 a year at the time. It was that conversation, along with the fact that I noticed the most successful sales reps were the ones who were climbing the corporate ladder more quickly than all their colleagues, that my Perceptions about being in sales changed.

So of course, I moved into sales. And because I took the time to learn the science of sales, and had the benefit of being my own pre-sales engineer, I started to succeed in selling supercomputers beyond my wildest dreams. One of the area managers told me I had a 91 percent closing ratio for qualified customers, even in competitive deals against Sun Microsystems and the eight-hundred-pound gorilla in the space, IBM. That said, there was still one thing I hated about sales. And that was the part of the sales process called "prospecting," the finding of new potential customers. The cold-calling into offices to people I didn't know, asking if they had any interest in buying more supercomputers. That part just sucked. I hated hearing the word, "no". Until my Perception about that changed as well.

The secret here is that sales is ultimately all about math. Here's how it works: When you call a certain number of people, only a very few of them will have interest in your product. And from that small number who have interest in your product, even fewer of those folks will have a real need for your product, a budget to purchase your product, and a defined timeline in which to do so. You need all of those forces to align to have a properly qualified customer. Having a properly qualified customer is the key to being successful in sales. Because if you don't properly qualify your prospective customer, you could waste your time sending information and answering questions to satisfy their personal interest. They're never going to actually buy. And in the meantime, you've wasted valuable resources potentially missing your next big sale because of the time you've wasted with the non-buyer. So as a result of this truth, I learned to love the word "no".

Getting to the "no" quicker meant I could get on to the next potential customer, and be that much closer to the mathematically probable "yes" I knew would be certain to come. And I was always right. The yes would eventually come. In the meantime, that meant finding out earlier rather than later that a new prospect had need but no budget was not a disappointment for me. It was a relief. It was a win. I could tell them to definitely call when they were allocated some budget, and get off the phone with them and either onto the next sales call, or into the car which I parked at the golf course for the rest of the afternoon. The big thing that allowed for my success in sales was a change in my Perception regarding the word no. I raced to it. I loved hearing it. Because that was the one word that I knew would eventually lead to another "yes".

So what Perceptions about your business existence can you change? What Perception changes could alter the patterns within your mind and thus change the course of your career or increase the levels of your success? You may want to think about it, because the answer to that question sets the very foundation of thought that can make or break your success in business. All because of your one simple equation.

Resilience in Business

Resilience is defined as "the ability to recover from, or adjust easily to, misfortune or change." So resilience in business is obviously defined as the ability to recover from, or adjust easily to, misfortune or change . . . in business. Or if you read about resilience from a fortune cookie, resilience is the ability to recover from, or adjust easily to, misfortune or change . . . in bed. Forgive me, I digress.

Resilience isn't a topic exclusively reserved for business, but it is certainly something business executives and those in the workforce need, so they can stay grounded and calm in the midst of what is a constantly challenging environment. Whether it's the latest sales forecast numbers, the fact that your unread e-mail count just topped one thousand, that next internal deadline for whatever is looming, the fact the boss just chewed you out for something that wasn't your fault (or maybe it was), or simply the fact that Gladys is clipping her damn toenails at her desk again (does she not have time to do that at home?), resilience in dealing with challenging situations in the workplace is one of those things absolutely everyone needs in business. Resilience is also one of those latest buzzwords that has become en vogue in boardroom discussions about maintaining a healthy, productive, and creative workforce. One of the reasons Emotional Intelligence is so hot amongst the top business leaders in the largest corporations in the world is specifically because high EI helps deliver high levels of resiliency within those leadership teams. They love that EI science stuff.

Resilience is what allows you to react to bad news quickly and formulate an intelligent response without letting your negative reactions shut down your thinking brain. Resilience is what allows you to experience a tough day, a tough week, or tough month, without it sapping your energy levels down to the point it negatively affects your performance. Resilience is what allows you to quickly adapt to disruptions, while maintaining the empathy and insight to safeguard the people, assets and brand equity which then provides for organizational resilience. Organizational resilience is the keystone to staying in business.

Leading training programs designed to increase Emotional Intelligence in executives teach that resilience can be trained in your mind on three different levels. From my perspective, these three levels have very blurry lines between them, and I think they can actually be combined into one process (which will be included in an EI for Business training offering from Mind Hacking Happiness), but let's discuss the three anyway.

The first way to train resilience is by building inner calm. We've spoken in this book about how you can reduce your inner turmoil dramatically by understanding the variables that come together to create your mind's pain and suffering. This also applies to your business pain and suffering. As you understand your Perceptions as compared to your Expectations and/or Preferences in the business environment, your emotional fall-out about things not going perfectly at work naturally subsides. This harkens back to Spinoza telling us, "Emotion, which is suffering, ceases to be suffering as soon as we form a clear and precise picture of it." What is a moment of turmoil at work but an internal emotional reaction to something you want to see differently than you are currently seeing it? That's entirely emotional. This is why I'm confused when other leadership programs suggest emotional resilience is the second and separate level at which resilience can be trained. This is when my mind asks, "what interrupts inner calm but emotion, and the thoughts which then follow that emotion? What other reaction from the body is happening besides the nervous system comparing one thing to another?" The third level is what is called cognitive resilience, which I think makes a little more sense. Because your thinking brain is what you use to resolve many of your work-life challenges, increasing the resilience of inner calm does indeed open the door to increasing the ability to think better.

Resilience in business comes from an ability to let go of both success and failure equally. It's best not to dwell too long on either your failures or your successes. The mindfulness teacher Shinzen Young has a great teaching for this, which he calls, "**gone.**" Reminding yourself constantly that each moment is there and then gone, allows you to remember each following moment comes anew, and can bring with it great new things if we completely allow the last moment, either good or bad, to disappear. Gone. "I just closed a big sale for us." Gone. Onto the next opportunity so we can thrive and exceed sales expectations. "We just experienced a big failure in our web presence going down." Gone. What can we now do to quickly resolve that issue rather than fret about it? This very practice also works exceptionally well in meditation practices. When a thought interrupts you, gone. When a noise distracts you, gone. From an MHH standpoint, having the ability to resolve emotional turmoil creates an amazing capacity for a tool like "gone".

My resilience in my sales career came from being able to see the small fails of being told "no" as part of the big win of getting the eventual "yes." So when I experienced the small fails, I immediately left them behind me. Similarly, when I got that big "yes" from an international juggernaut that made my whole year, I didn't sit on my laurels too long celebrating it. I processed it, did something fun as a reward, and got right back into action. I exceeded quota every year of my sales career but one, making the President's Club trip numerous times entirely because of resilience.

Using the {self} and the EoE in Business—Their Side

We've discussed the benefits you can glean from digging into your mind's {self} and understanding how the Equation of Emotion works within your own mind. But equally as powerful and equally as beneficial can be your understanding of the {self} of others and their potential Perceptions which fill their Equation of Emotion and influence their mind's activity. The simple fact is that understanding others is the key to being successful in business. Whether it's understanding your teams, your customers, or even your competitors, understanding how to get people to do what you would prefer they do comes down to understanding what it is that will make them **want** to do what you would prefer they do.

Knowing Other's {self} Maps

Carl Jung once said, "Knowing your own darkness is the best method for dealing with the darknesses of other people." And while you don't necessarily apply the idea of darkness to potential challenges you face in the workplace, a good question might be, "why the hell don't we use the word darknesses when we're discussing challenges in the workplace? That might make work a hell of a lot more entertaining."

Seriously though, as much as we humans can all be different from each other, and with all the variances of genetics, age, culture, heritage, background, and attachments of mind which can cause us to act differently in very similar situations, the basic functions of the human nervous system are the basic functions of the human nervous system. And the comparisons our nervous systems use and the differences it perceives in its defense of {self} mechanism pretty much works the same way in all of us. That said, your mileage may vary, past performance is not an indicator of future results, and all celebrity voices were impersonated. Void where prohibited.

Seriously though, you can never really know every little thing that shows up on someone else's {self} map. It could be argued that you may never really know every little thing that gets plotted onto your own {self} map. The {self} in the mind is a pretty darn complex thing. Along with your regular ideas of identity, your {self} map includes conscious and subconscious memories, conscious and subconscious thought patterns, experiences that you've had which you may or may not completely understand, and even your perception patterns can loop back around and become {self} items which then need to be defended themselves, making perceptions fill both sides of the Equation of Emotion simultaneously. Our minds are friggin' cray-cray, y'all.

As you attempt to learn more about others' {self} maps, you first need to know that you're really only looking at the bigger more obvious things that we can identify to help you get along with people better, to understand other peoples' basic reactions to things, and maybe if you get the time, to go out of your way to make someone else's life a little better through your intentional actions. But that said, there's a lot of practical things you can do with better understanding someone else's {self} map and their Equation of Emotion process.

By better understanding the people around you, you can better know what motivates them to do what they do. You can better know how they see them{selves} which can inform you how to better interface with them to grease their internal wheels so they can grease the wheels of the business. For instance, if you know Harry in engineering is someone who likes to know the logical reasons for things before giving you any buy-in or real effort on something new, you can lead with the logical reasons for a policy change or new task for Harry. "Harry, we've discovered an issue with our customers not understanding how to best utilize our new web service in relation to the old interface. We know how its better, but now they need to know too. So I'd like you to work on a written script of how you would explain to someone how to use the new system, section by section, so we can make a video for them to resolve some of the confusion." This is going to give Harry everything he needs to buy in internally and move forward with your request. But if we're talking to Lisa about the same software transition, who is much more a people person and who is working the customer support lines, we need a different approach. "Lisa, you may hear a bit of frustration on the other end of phone and through e-mail with this new roll-out. Listen and be compassionate with each and every complaint. This is a big change for them. Tell them that we've identified the challenge, ask them what they'd like to see better explained in a video, because producing a web video for them is our current plan." That speaks Lisa's language of compassion and connection with other humans. It sets her expectations for dealing with a tougher crowd, which will create more balanced Equations of Emotion for her in her job, creating more resilience during this more turbulent time for customer support. And in either case, you've given clear instructions to the person you're dealing with in a way that sets them up for success.

Knowing the {self} and likely Perceptions of your coworkers can certainly help deal with issues inside the walls or virtual walls of your office, but they can be critical in dealing with your customers as well.

The rise of General Motors in America was entirely due to understanding the {self} of their customers. In the early 1920s, car sales in the United states hit a ceiling. It seemed that everyone who needed an automobile, and who could afford one, had one. And as a result, sales fell flat. Enter the influence of then GM CEO Alfred P. Sloan, which took hold of the American public and got them buying cars again. Sloan introduced a concept called the annual model change. Unlike his main competitor Ford, which made the same old reliable Model-T year after year without substantial non–engineering driven changes, Sloan ordered GM to change their cars' appearance every year for no reason whatsoever. This made it easier for their customers to identify who was driving the latest model, and thus who was most affluent among their neighbors. This made them want the latest model as an addition to their {self} map. And so even though the old black Ford out front still drove great, GM car sales took off, Ford and other makers soon copied GM's approach, and the entire industry for reliable used cars was born as a result of knowing how their customer's {self} worked.

On the opposite side of understanding {self}, the Hillary Clinton Campaign for President found out the hard way what it means to misinterpret the {self} of their potential customers, the American voters. They made the critical error that most failed entrepreneurs make when they flounder in reaching enough customers to remain in business. They assumed they knew what their customers wanted instead of understanding their target market's {self} maps. They failed to connect with the correct attachments which fell near the center of their voters' {self} maps, and which work the exact same way in most voters. They failed to take the science of human physiology into account, and as a result failed to real emotional connections with large swaths of voters. Clinton's supporters voted reasonably. Her opponent Trump's supporters voted emotionally. Had Clinton been able to capture even 2 percent more emotionally-motivated votes, she would have been President of the United States.

Seeing the {self} and EoE in Others for Better Relationships

Along with being able to improve your business relationships as you see into your {self} and the {selves} of others around you, you can also improve your interpersonal and romantic relationships with this stuff as well.

Having Better Romantic Relationships

People with higher levels of Emotional Intelligence have better romantic relationships. Period. They understand each other better. They anticipate each other's emotional needs better. And as John Gottman's Love Lab studies show, when they get the noise of their own minds' {self} out of the way, to truly listen to their partners in a way that their partners feel heard, that type of thing can be a predictor of relationship success with over 90 percent accuracy. And this is one of the most powerful tools within this book. Actually taking the time to **hear** people and what they are trying to communicate to you. So how can you bolster this process of making your relationships better with your new knowledge?

First, whether you're dating someone new, or whether you've been married for multiple decades, it might be healthy to ask, "what is on my romantic partner's mind at the moment?" And even further, "what does that reveal about what is on their {self} map?" In other words, what is important to them in the moment and long term? What things are dear to them? What do they consider a portion of their mind's {self}? You should ask them if you can't figure it out for yourself. For instance, one of the things on my wife's {self} map that she communicated to me once is the idea of living in a clean house.

In an effort to meet her EP, I make a conscious effort to get the countertops wiped down, and get the kitchen table cleared, and run a quick Swiffer on the floors. When these things are done, you can literally see it in my wife's body language as she enters the house. There's a particular sway she has that suggests she has an obvious mindgasm of joy for the cleanliness and organization around her. We're 13 years into our marriage, and I think I can speak for both of us when I say we still kinda dig each other. I feel blessed. But consciously ensuring that happiness is a big part of the process.

Better Family Relationships and Being a Better Parent

This new perspective has changed my life, because I can now see into my family's minds, especially with regard to what role I play on their minds' {self} maps. Because of my role as son, brother, uncle, cousin, husband, and father, as Jim Coan showed us in his lab at the University of Virginia, I make up a small chunk of their mind's {self}. I am actually an internal part of them. This new perspective puts a whole new spin on how my actions and communications influence their minds and lives. It especially highlights for me the potential inner turmoil I could cause for them if I wasn't mindful of their {self} maps. This comes to mind all the time when dealing with my wife and son, but it particularly came to mind in being able to deal with my mom in her later years as dementia took her memories and identity.

A Personal Story

After years of living in northern Indiana, where the winters can be harsh, and where one slip on the ice could result in a broken hip or worse, my family and I decided that it was time for my mom to sell the two-bedroom house she'd been living in and move to a warmer climate. So we moved her down into my house in Atlanta for a time, then eventually got her accommodations at a local retirement home. The food was great, their little bus ran regular trips to the store, she made a lot of new friends, and of course, she hated it. I stopped by to see her regularly to check on her, to ensure the service standards hadn't slipped, and just to say hi and chat. Then that one day came.

On one of my visits, I knocked on her door, and just like every time I had visited before, she opened it. She looked up at me. There was no look of recognition in her face. In a kind but curious tone, she asked, "Can I help you?" Wow. I'd heard things like this could happen, but you never think it can happen to you until it actually does. It was the first day my mom had looked at my face and didn't know who I was.

The processing in my mind was swift and precise. I saw all the potential emotions which could occur in me before they were even generated. At that moment, my mother, who at 45-years-old, had been told to abort me for medical reasons, who had waited her whole life for a son after having four girls previously, was now looking out her door at a complete stranger. I could have felt devastated in that moment. My mother still made up a large portion of my mind's {self} map. And now the portion of {self} my mom represented had just lost her side of all the fond memories we shared. She'd also just lost the potential future positive emotions that can only come from sharing time with a son.

In that moment, I had forever lost a mother's love. That's a special kind of love that can't ever be replaced. I had lost all future instances of a gleam in her eye, which would likely be forever extinguished when interacting with me. I had lost the special mutual bond of understanding, patience, and forgiveness, that can only be shared between a mother and her child. I was no longer her child. I was a stranger. So that moment could have been completely devastating for me. And for many people in similar circumstances it is.

But thankfully, my mind processed and acknowledged every bit of the emotional fallout preparing to explode, before the fuse could even be lit. In the cycle of one full breath standing outside that doorway, I used the deep understanding of the source of any pain I could experience in that moment to set aside my potential negative reactions. It was like my mind saw all the implications of what was happening in that moment, and before the various Equations of Emotion could even fire off the negative emotions which would then attempt to hijack my mind and emotions, it gave me the opportunity to simply say, "Nah, I'll pass on all that pain, thanks." My deeper understanding of Self beyond the mind's {self} gave me the power to completely sidestep the pain and suffering which could have at that moment started ruining the time I wanted to spend with my mom. And while that may sound weird or inhuman, that little super-speed processing of emotion in my mind is actually what allowed me to be completely present for my mom from that moment, and completely human in serving her needs rather than being mired in my own.

I could have spoken up and said, "Mom, it's me!" But making that kind of statement would only be serving my own need to be recognized and validated. It would be serving my own needs for everything to be status quo. It would not be embracing the state of constant change in the universe, and would have been harmful and confusing to my mother. Would she have enjoyed the embarrassment that she had just forgotten who her only son was? Would she enjoy the fear of being reminded her mind was giving up her memories and identity? Would she enjoy knowing what she may have just done to her son by forgetting him, even if in the next moment she were reminded? No, no, and no. Sometimes ignorance is bliss. And in this moment, her ignorance was going to be bliss for both of us.

I wanted to leave the next moments open and act normal in case her memory did kick in, so I formulated a response that could fit both scenarios for her. "Hi, I just wanted to stop by and say hi, and see how you were doing." She opened the door invitingly, said, "okay," and walked back into her suite as I entered, asking a general question of how things were going for me. I could tell in her tone she wasn't going to remember me as her son, but she always tried to be a nice lady to strangers. So I played the role of the friendly stranger who just stopped by for a bit to talk for the rest of the time. And we had a nice chat. By my setting aside of the needs of my false {self}, I could be completely present and compassionate to her. For curiosity's sake, when she did say I looked familiar, I did offer her an out by asking her about the handsome boy amongst the pictures of grandkids and great-grandkids next to her bed. It was my son's picture. "Oh, those are my people. Aren't they just cute?" was all she said. "They certainly are," I replied. "They obviously love you a lot to send you such nice pictures." And at that point I excused myself, gave her a warm hug, and left.

I never needed any more emotional processing of that visit than what occurred during that single breath of understanding in her doorway. It's not like I swallowed hard, fought off the tears long enough to talk to my mom, then broke down as soon as I got out the door, or back to the car, or back home. The whole situation was resolved completely in that one single moment. And as a result, I was able to get past my own inner bullshit to be able to completely serve her. What I felt during that whole visit and all the visits which later followed, was the joy of being with my mom. I felt joy that she seemed generally happy, even if she couldn't remember me, or my wife, or my son. So instead of experiencing sadness in such a potentially sad moment, I experienced joy instead. Wow! Was this the name-it-tame-it affect of immediately down regulating a set of negative emotions on steroids (or on fleek, if you're under thirty years of age)? Had the effects of becoming quicker and quicker at processing the negative crap of my brain finally created a plastic effect which made it automatic for me?

The great master of happiness Matthieu Ricard proved in an fMRI machine that after years of practicing the meta-awareness discipline of meditation, the startle reflex itself can even be negated. The startle reflex is the most basic and quickest responses of the limbic system which also causes our negative emotions. So was this same phenomenon what was happening in my own brain, and thus my own mind? Up until that moment, I had certainly noticed the smaller mental crap of life bouncing off my mind like it was wearing a Superman suit. But how could such a potentially powerful emotional situation be handled just as easily and quickly as someone cutting me off in traffic? We'll talk more about this in Volume II, but after that one encounter in which I chose whether or not I wanted to experience a strong negative emotion, I grasped the benefits of the mind discipline I had been practicing. This realization was life-changing.

When you want better family relationships, it's a great exercise to look at your relationships through the lens of your family member's {self} map and their Equation of Emotion. Ask yourself how you appear on other people's {self} maps? What is your role for them? How can your actions create potential pain and suffering because you are a variable in the Equation of Emotion in their mind? How could you alter your behavior in such a way that it creates more happiness for people in your life? These are some of the most important questions you can ever ask of yourself. Because if you can get your {self} out of the way, and figure out what role you play in their {self}, you can deliver some amazing moments for them from inside their own minds. Applying this vision has even made me a better parent.

Declan and I were playing a game of air hockey recently. Even at six, he's really good, and I have to play at a high level to beat him sometimes. I try to create a healthy mix of him winning and losing so he can experience the joys of winning, and also be forced to deal with the pains of losing. This particular time, he got an early 7-3 lead, but I was able to come back and win the game 10-9. I looked over at him when I had scored the last goal. I smiled and said, "Good game, Declan!" He said nothing. I repeated my statement, this time with a little emphasis. "Good game, Declan." I was waiting for his response back to me, trying to teach him that regardless of whether we win or lose, we must be gracious to our opponent.

"I don't wanna say good game," he finally replied. "I didn't play my best game."

I had to take a breath. First, there is no way I could just walk away from this situation. He needed to understand a few things about winning and losing, and he needed to be able to deal with either situation immediately after the result of the match has been concluded. Second, I needed to be very careful about how I handled this teachable moment, because I'm his Dad, and I needed to be really mindful that I fill a rather large part of his {self} map. So if I started out with firing simple criticisms at him, like, "you should say good game," or "that's not the way this family handles losses," those statements could be seen by his mind as something on his {self} map (Dad) attacking something else on his {self} map (his behavior after losing), which would make this a way more complicated situation than it needs to be. Telling him what he should or shouldn't do would have caused more negative emotion and shut down his thinking brain. I might well have been talking to a brick wall in that case. So I took a moment and mindfully decided how to proceed.

Instead of going a route that could wind up being confrontational, I took stock of what was going on in his mind at the moment. He'd just experienced a loss in air hockey. So he was dealing with a little sadness, and maybe even a bit of anger, depending on how much he thought he should have won that game, which he had at one point been leading by a wide margin. So rather than saying anything critical, I validated him and helped him feel secure. "Come here," I said, as I sat down right where I was standing on the floor. Removing height differences for kids is critical in talking with them. When he arrived, I gave him a hug. "You know I love you right?" He nodded. When he leaned back to sit in my lap there were tears in his eyes. He knew he was supposed to say "good game," but he didn't want to, and he was conflicted by why he couldn't resolve the issue. So I sat on the floor with him, and was just really honest. "I know you're frustrated, and I'm trying to figure out a way to explain things to help you, so can you give me a moment?" This gave him a sense of control. Now he was helping Daddy figure out how to help him. Now he was listening.

I started with the obvious. "Losing just sucks sometimes, doesn't it?" "Yeah, I didn't play my best game," he said. This was his mind trying to reason its way into not accepting the {self}'s devaluation of the loss. It was saying, "I'm still good at air hockey. I can still consider myself a winner even though I lost, because I didn't play my best game." I had to directly respond to this and then figure out how to tie it into the larger lesson in a minute. "Well, sometimes we just don't play our best games, buddy. Sometimes as hard as we try, we just don't live up to our own expectations, and our mistakes cause us to lose, and it just sucks."

I paused. It was time to show him the tool of meta-awareness and the usefulness of looking into other people's minds.

"But do you like playing the game? Is it fun for you?" This question required him to look into his own mind for the answer. He nodded affirmatively, wiping away some tears. I continued. "And in order to play the game, do you need someone on the other side of the table to hit the puck back and forth with?" Again he nodded. "So it's good to be thankful for our opponent regardless of whether we win or lose, right?" He nodded. I could tell he was really thinking about it. I continued. "But let's imagine they lose. We want them to feel good about playing, and we're thankful they played, otherwise we couldn't have won, so we tell them 'good game' right? So they might feel okay playing with us again?" Again a nod. "But what about the times we lose and they win? It sucks for us to lose, but do you think they enjoy winning?"

"Yeah," he said. I was glad he was following along. His mind was engaged.

"So let me ask you a different question. What if Daddy was playing against someone else and Daddy won? Would you be happy for Dad if I won playing against someone else?"

"Yeah," he replied.

"So in that moment you and I could share in that joy of daddy winning, right?"

"Yeah," he said.

"And you could be happy for one of your friends if they won a game against someone else, right?"

"Yeah."

"Okay . . . so here's the deal: When Daddy or someone else plays against you and wins . . . and you lose for whatever reason... whether you played bad or you played your best and just were second best that day... right at the moment you lose and your opponent wins, you have a choice. You can focus on what it feels like to lose . . . how does that feel again?"

"Bad," he said.

"Yeah, so you can focus on your loss which makes you feel bad . . . or . . . you could focus on your opponent's win and how your Dad, or Mom, or your friend or whomever you're playing feels about winning. And even though it was you they beat . . . you can choose to share in their joy with them. Because we already said we can feel good about the successes of our family and friends, right?"

"Yeah."

"So let me ask you one more question. When your opponent wins, do you think they want to hear that you didn't play your best game and that they only won because you weren't playing your best, or do they want to feel good and have you share in their joy of winning against you as a good player, and share in the joy of playing the game regardless of who won?"

He thought about that for a second. "They want to feel good," he finally said.

I added one last quick question. "So do you want to focus on your loss, which kinda sucks, or do you want to share in Daddy's win?" And this was the moment of truth. This was asking him in kid terms if he could put aside the needs of his {self} and enter the mind of someone else, and be happy along with them for their win against his {self}. And I will take this next memory to my grave. He looked me in the eye, smiled with happiness, and in a very genuine but quiet tone, said, "Good game, Dad." And then he gave me a hug.

Good game, buddy.

As a follow-up, just before I sent this book to the editor, about six months after our talk on the floor that day, my son helped create a poster about how to share love with others. His addition to the poster was a drawing of telling the other team "good game" on the soccer field. Parenting for the win. I don't mean to brag about that, but the fact is that with the parenting modeling I had as a child growing up, I would never have come up with that teaching moment without the aid of the insight of Mind Hacking Happiness. So I'm not bragging on myself as much as I'm bragging on what we can all do with our minds if we just stop and learn how our minds work.

Better Knowing Our False {self}, to Open the Door to the True Self

The ancient message "Know Thyself" inscribed at the Oracle of Delphi, and found within every major religion globally, and communicated by many of our world's leading luminaries, has two large components to it. The first component is being able to identify and understand the thing within us which masquerades as our true Self but isn't really our true Self. When we discover and understand this first Know Thyself component, that opens the door to being able to search for, and uncover, the second large Know Thyself component, which is the actual truth regarding our Self. We'll discuss this second component soon.

Knowing about the false {self} and being able to see it working within us is the first big step we need to take, and by reading this book, you're taking that step.

This concept of better understanding your mind as the first step to liberation from your {self} was spoken of by Jesus, Muhammad, the Buddha, and many others, but I think it may have been best summed up by the great philosopher and father of Taoism, Laozi (aka Lao Tzu). He wrote an amazing book of wisdom called the Tao the Ching. In Asia, it's simply titled as his name, Laozi. Along with the Bible, and Qur'an, it's one of the best-selling wisdom books of all time. Laozi was a really wise dude. In a short saying, not included in the Tao, he made one of his most profound statements, summing up the plight of humanity in only three simple lines. "To know that you do not know is the best. To think you know when you do not is a disease. Recognizing this disease as a disease is to be free of it."

In the first line, "to know that you do not know is the best," Laozi delivers a good piece of general advice, and also a deeply concealed coded message. First, it's true to know you don't know some particular thing is good. Because then, if you want or need to know that something, you can go looking for it. But Laozi isn't talking about just any nonspecific something here. He's talking about the most profound secret in the universe connected with Self. He's saying that to acknowledge we don't know the true Self is the best. And by telling us it's best to know that we don't know, he's confirming that there is indeed something more for us to know. I equate this first sentence to what Jesus said in the Gospel of Thomas about people who do not know themselves living in poverty and being the poverty.

Laozi's second line brings the deep wisdom. "To think you know when you don't know is a disease." I love both his selection of the word 'think', and also the word 'disease'. Because "to think you know" in regard to Self is literally the mind's {self}, the portion of {self} the mind thinks into existence. So what he's speaking of there is our ego. Our false {self}. And so in the one short line, "to think you know when you don't know is a disease," Laozi is telling us that the {self} we think is our existence really isn't our existence, and that the false self is a disease. So in those 11 simple words, Laozi provides us a very literal explanation of what I've now taken the better part of a book trying to explain. [Thanks a lot, Laozi. ;-)]

His use of the word disease is even better than his use of the word think. Because that one word disease delivers three distinct truths. First, what is a disease but an illness of the body that harms us in some way? Our {self} certainly does that, as referenced in Section I. The mind's {self} is the integral piece of mind which creates negative emotions and causes us humans to treat other people horribly in defense of {self}. Second, what is a disease, but a sickness which is oftentimes unintentionally passed from one person to another? We certainly train our children, even if accidentally, that it's okay to accept our false {self} as our very identities. And the last reason 'disease' really fits; do we humans always know we have a disease before it kills us? Nope. And this disease of mind that we all have, this mind's {self}, kills us quite regularly without us even knowing we have it. Most of us die with our false {self} still completely in tact, letting it kick and scream through our very last breath.

As far as I'm concerned, Laozi can drop the mic and exit stage left at this point. But instead, he's got one more thing to say, which shows us the cure for our disease. In Laozi's last line, "recognizing this disease as a disease is to be free of it," he points directly to our mind's control room of meta-awareness, and being able to see our mind's process from a distance for what it is; a self defense mechanism of our body. This last line also points to the exit door of enlightenment, which is something we cover in Volume II.

By simply understanding how to see our mind's {self} and why it does what it does, we've actually taken a huge step away from being completely controlled by it. This is awesome! But frankly, this also introduces a big quandary for us. Because although we may no longer be fooled by this internal magician of mind when we've learned how its tricks work, ultimately the {self} in the brain is a hard-wired neural component that doesn't quit working just because we can now see it for the illusion it is. The {self} processing within the brain continues as a function of the body. The processing of the Equation of Emotion doesn't quit. It's been hard-wired into our bodies through millions of years of the evolutionary mechanism. That is why it's said that getting rid of the ego is like trying to get rid of your own shadow. It's impossible to do, because it's a function of the brain. This is why the great Zen master Dogen, in an attempt to teach the true nature of the mind to the Buddhists monks who believed that the same divine nature flows through the foundation of all beings, asked, "If all beings are Buddha, why all this striving?" It's because our {self} is a boomerang function within the mind. It keeps coming back.

13. Sympathy, Empathy, and Compassion

Keep me away from the wisdom which does not cry,

the philosophy which does not laugh

and the greatness which does not bow before children.

—Khalil Gibran

It was a beautiful sunny day, and we had gone down to a local park to take in a free summer blues concert sponsored by our city. The event had a good family feel. The stage looked out over a sloped and shaded grassy area where people could spread out their blankets in clear view of the band. There was a small paved area in front of the stage that served as a dance floor for the few who felt brave enough. There were some food trucks lined up a short distance away, and there was enough space near the edge of the park where the kids could run off their extra energy without bothering the adults who were there to hear some particularly good blues music.

My son had wasted no time in making some fast friends, with whom he was now throwing balls with and playing chase games.

My wife and I set out a picnic and had him stop by every couple laps to grab a bite of food. It was fun. After the picnic, we got up and played with the group of kids for a while until it was time for some ice cream. After all, how can you have a summer music concert and not include ice cream as part of that experience, right? There was just one problem, however. I saw that in the group of kids, there may have been a few whose parents may not have the means to buy them an afternoon ice cream treat. Now, I remember what it was like as a child to be the one kid going without something everyone else had. It sucked. So rather than skip the ice cream, or make some weak-sauce move of calling Declan back to our blanket to hand him an ice cream cone in clear sight of everyone else, which would prompt the other kids to go ask their parents for the same, possibly putting the parents and kids in an awkward situation and spoiling their fun rather than adding to it, I just ponied up and bought a bunch of ice creams for all the kids. (Note: I did have them to ask for their parents' permission.)

As I was handing out the ice creams, there was one little girl at the back of the line who was waiting very patiently. She and Declan had hit it off rather well during playtime, and they were treating each other very kindly all afternoon. They were both about four years old at the time. She had been one of the kids I worried would wind up with no ice cream if I didn't just get some for everyone. As I handed over her ice cream, my suspicions were confirmed. She accepted her ice cream with a big smile, and with an innocent honesty of oversharing that many four-year-olds have, she looked up at me with her big blue eyes, and shyly said, "Thank you. My daddy's in jail."

My heart sank. I wanted to buy her the whole ice cream truck in that moment. I wanted to scoop her up and hug her and tell her there were a lot of people in the world who loved her whether she realized it or not, and that she should not worry if her life was different than her friends lives. But I couldn't find the courage.

Instead, I stumbled through some comment about how mommies and daddies sometimes make mistakes, and just because he couldn't be with her right now didn't mean he didn't lover her. I didn't know if that was true. Some daddies don't love their daughters. I wish I could have said something better. But I failed. The feeling of wanting to give that little girl more than just ice cream stayed with me through our picnic repack, our walk to the car, and throughout our entire drive home. My wife must have sensed what was going on in my mind, because on the way home she reached over, grabbed my hand, and reminded me, "That's why we're going through the fostering classes, honey."

Fast forward about nine months later. It was Friday night. We had just been called to receive our first foster placement, an eight-month-old baby and his older sister. The spare bedroom was ready. Whitney and I hoped we were ready. We felt nervous, but prepared. We had clothes for both genders for kids up to age five, diapers, bottles, and related baby items. We had a lot of toys ready, and we had prepped Declan to be very kind and welcoming, because the kids who were coming to our house didn't expect to be sleeping at a stranger's house when they woke up that morning. The doorbell rang. I opened it. And who peeked through that door, but that same little girl Declan had made friends with at the music concert and who I had wished to be able to help in a more meaningful way all those months ago! Life is really weird sometimes. And sometimes in a really weird-good way.

Compassion is a requirement to being a good foster parent. We've provided a lot of lip service to compassion in this book. But there are some important differentiations in the twigs on the branch of human caring about which you need to be aware, so that you ensure you deliver compassion when looking to help others relieve their pain and suffering. Let's discuss that in earnest for a moment.

In the branch of human caring, there are three twigs that represent your reactions to other people's pain. They are sympathy, empathy, and compassion. Now, to discuss these individually, we could break down the Greek origins of the words, and discuss a bunch of semantics and philosophy, but in keeping with our "what you need to know" spirit, I see sympathy, empathy, and compassion as follows: Sympathy, empathy, and compassion map directly onto our cognitive, affective, and motivational reactions to other people's pain.

First is the cognitive twig, which is the "I understand what you're feeling" twig. That's basically sympathy in a nutshell. Sympathy is the ability to understand that someone is in pain and feel sorry for them in their pain, without putting on that same cloak of pain with them. For instance, when someone you know loses someone they loved who you never met, sympathy is the typical reaction. You can feel sorry for them, but you can't really share in their personal loss. Having sympathy for someone's plight is better than not caring at all, but it typically doesn't motivate you to help someone without one of the other two twigs. Sympathy is the more "sucks to be you" reaction people have that doesn't do anyone any good. But it is a requirement for the next two twigs to exist.

The cognitive sympathy twig feeds into a second larger twig of affective understanding. Affect is the term scientists use for our emotions, so the affective component is the ability for us to understand on a feeling level. This is where you can identify on a feeling level with the pain someone is experiencing, and maybe even feel that pain a little bit with them. This is empathy in a nutshell. Empathy is both the cognitive understanding of "I understand your pain," mixed in with the affective understanding of "I feel your pain." When you know someone who loses someone who you also knew, you can feel a bit of their pain in your heart as well. Or maybe if you've gone through a similar situation in the past to what someone is going through, you can also share in their pain a bit. This is the feeling of empathy. It can be strengthened by putting yourself in other people's shoes mentally on a regular basis, and imagining what they're going through. Imagining their {self} ideas and seeing their Equation of Emotion also helps you practice this.

The thing to notice with empathy is that there's an emotional component to it. Emotions drive you into action, so depending on the amount of empathy you generate, this can actually drive you to take action to assist others in dealing with their pain. And that's helping someone else, which is awesome for both them and you, according to studies.

Compassion is the strong branch of caring that is created where a third twig join both sympathy and empathy. This last twig is one of motivation. It's the "I want to help you" component. This is the more {self}less component, and it's exactly how compassion expert and language translator to His Holiness the Dalai Lama, Dr. Geshe Thupten Jinpa, sees compassion. He says, "Compassion is a mental state endowed with a sense of concern for the suffering of others and aspiration to see that suffering relieved." So when we take sympathy, the "I understand your pain" twig, follow it to where it joins empathy, the "I feel your pain" twig, and follow that into where it joins the "I want to help you" twig, that makes up the tree branch called compassion. That's where the branch of human caring really gets its strength. That's its core. It's in this space of "I want to help you" where most firemen live. It's where most EMTs, nurses, and doctors live. It's where most police officers live. And it's certainly where most foster parents live.

Frankly, compassion is where we all need to live if we wish to make this a world in which the evils mentioned in chapter nine are finally stamped out. This is why you need the ability to look into your own mind and feel where your caring comes from for others, so you can increase your levels of compassion, if necessary.

14. A Unique Story of Compassion

> I know not with what weapons
> World War III will be fought,
> but World War IV will be fought
> with sticks and stones.
>
> —Albert Einstein

Coming off of the preceding inquiry into compassion, I could not close this book without sharing an amazing one-of-a-kind story that has never been told anywhere before, about two incredible moments of compassion during Word War II. This story almost doesn't quite fit the book, but after you've heard it, you'll probably agree it has a solid lesson that aligns with decreasing the world's pain and suffering and increasing overall happiness.

Personally, I abhor the idea that violence should ever be required to settle differences between people or governments. However, as a veteran of military service myself, and a student of history, and knowing of the human atrocities that were uncovered during the aftermath of the defeat of the Third Reich in Germany, I have immense respect for the men and women who stood in harm's way and used force to overthrow the Axis forces which promised to deliver more chaos, bloodshed, pain and suffering, had they been allowed to continue its push across Europe, into Africa, Asia, and potentially the Americas. It was a different time then, before we had the global communication technologies that connected us and showed us we as humans are more alike than we are different, and that we all face the same basic life challenges. I was told almost every generation of my family from the American Revolution forward served the military forces of United States of America, including my 5th great-grandfather, who manufactured the muskets for the Colonial Militia that fired the 'Shot Heard 'Round the World' which started the American Revolution, and my 3rd great-grandfather, who was in charge of the army for the part of the U.S. territory that is now Indiana and Michigan, where I would later grow up. My hope is that my children are among the first generations in our family not to have to ever serve a military force. This amazing story is about, and told for, for my uncle Jim.

Uncle Jim's Story

My uncle Jim was an amazing man. I remember him as an incredibly funny, kind-hearted, soft-spoken, and intelligent man who always had a smile and a hug anytime you needed one. He was a man of impeccable character with a strong moral compass. He worked as structural engineer on some rather well known projects, including the Chicago Skyway and Willis Tower, formerly known as the Sears Tower, which stood for decades as the world's tallest building. To me, uncle Jim stood as one of the world's tallest men. He stood six foot one, which isn't exceptionally tall and is the height from which I also see the world, but even though I looked over at him during family gatherings and not up, to me he was still a giant. He was one of the 16.1 million Americans asked to fight for the United States and its Allies during World War II.

Back during that time, he was also an exceptional man. Uncle Jim started his Army enlistment at the age of seventeen, where he then volunteered for the additional duty of being a paratrooper and member of the 517th Parachute Regimental Combat Team. The 517th PRCT was an independent unit that wound up seeing action in six different countries in some of the most historic turning points of the war. Basically stated, the 517th was one of the specific groups of badasses you wanted around when there was a particularly tough job to do, or when the shit was about to hit the fan.

Every member of the 517th PRCT was a volunteer. But they didn't accept just anybody. They screened every applicant looking for the best the U.S. Army had to offer. Every member was required to qualify as "expert" with their primary weapon, "sharpshooter" with another, and "marksman" with every other weapon used by the platoon. Their physical fitness requirements were higher than other Army units. And being an Airborne unit, they were also expected to jump out of planes into the middle of enemy territory quite regularly. They were part of the elite of World War II. The 517th completed jump school at Fort Benning, NC without a single wash-out, supposedly setting a record that still stands to this day.

During his service with the 517th PRCT, my uncle Jim fought in North Africa, Italy, France, The Netherlands, Belgium, and on the final push deep into Germany. His war experiences read like a Hollywood movie. He dropped into France a month before the D-Day invasion, tasked with destroying communications infrastructure and a munitions depot that supplied Normandy. The mission went awry when, upon leaving the exploding munitions depot, four members of his six-man team were killed in a firefight after being surprised by a German patrol who were alerted by all the explosions. My uncle and another man were wounded, captured and tortured in an attempt to gain information about the invasion which Germany had a high suspicion was coming. They blew out his kneecaps with a pistol and replaced them with artificial ones inserted during a surgery that was done without anesthetic. They forced him to witness the execution of

Frenchmen every day of his capture, with the threat he would soon be next. Not once did he or his teammate give up any information.

After being liberated from the POW camp in Ste. Mere Eglise, he lied about not being tortured so that he could go rejoin his unit. At the time, as far as the U.S. Army was concerned, being aggressively interrogated was good enough to receive a quick ticket home, or at the very least a re-assignment to a non-combat unit. But the easy road wasn't Uncle Jim's selected path. He wanted to go back to his brothers in the 517th.

During his time in the war, his actions were heroic to say the least. He walked into enemy fire to pull soldiers to safety who had been hit by enemy snipers, he single-handedly neutralized a number of German machine gun positions on multiple combat operations, and he even took out an enemy tank by himself during the Battle of the Bulge after the 517th was called in to help recapture the Belgian village of Manhay. He was part of the team that took Nijmegen, which a historian later characterized as a battle that redefined the meaning of the word courage for all time. That battle later inspired the book and subsequent movie, A Bridge Too Far. He was one of the 18 surviving men of his company who were surrounded and pinned down by German forces at Bastogne when his unit was sent in to assist the 101st Airborne, which was also surrounded and cut off by the Germans. This very operation was the one which would prompt General George S. Patton to deliver his famous prayer for good weather in December of 1944. During that operation, my uncle's unit was cut off, out of food, and they were literally freezing to death from the feet up, having been dropped in with no winter equipment beyond two blankets each, which most of them wore on their feet. If that weren't bad enough, after experiencing some of the toughest fighting in Europe, they were also out of ammunition. Uncle Jim had saved one last bullet for himself in case the Germans ever made the final push into their position. My cousin, Uncle Jim's son, who would later follow in his father's Airborne footsteps, still has that single round magazine to this day. It was one of my uncle's most prized possessions from the war. Thankfully, Patton's Third Army broke through German lines and captured Bastogne only hours later.

While fighting World War II, Uncle Jim had his pack shot off his back, his helmet shot off his head, and even had a shell explode so closely it blew part of his uniform off his body, leaving only a couple scratches on his skin. He helped liberate Italy. He helped liberate France. And he helped liberate the death camp at Buchenwald, which affected him greatly, and was probably his most indelible experience of the entire war. He couldn't talk about it without tearing up, and when he did talk about it, oftentimes his sentences would be interrupted midstream by long moments of silence. For his acts of valor, he was awarded a number of military decorations, to include a Silver Star and the Croix de Guerre of Belgium, which was pinned on his chest by Prince Charles himself at the same ceremony he awarded General Eisenhower the Order of Leopold and a sword. As he told it, my uncle Jim "wanted a sword too goddammit, but no such luck." For his lesser amazing exploits, Uncle Jim was awarded a Bronze Star, Six Bronze Battle Stars, a Bronze Arrow Head, a Presidential Unit Citation, and of course, a Purple Heart with two bronze clusters.

His acts of war saved lives and were awarded recognition, but his biggest impact on World War II may have actually been a quiet act of compassion. And it's here that I am going to tell you a story that not many people know. Not many people know it, because like most other WWII veterans, my uncle Jim rarely ever talked about the war. When he did talk about it, he only did so if you met three unspoken conditions. First, you had to be a veteran (which I am). Second, you had to be male (ladies, don't judge, Uncle Jim grew up in a different generation). Third, he had to trust you. I guess me being a nephew with military experience passed muster with Uncle Jim regarding his willingness to speak candidly about his war experiences, because what I am about to share with you, he told me directly (and to the other male veterans in my family). Now, that said, I have no other sources for this next story besides my uncle Jim. So please take that into consideration when reflecting on it. Frankly, I believe its true. I believe its true because (1) Uncle Jim never found reason to lie about anything, and (2) when Uncle Jim told me this story, he didn't make a big deal about it, and right before telling this tale, he was speaking about how horrible the experience of war is for the men and women who fight them. So it was framed in neither a positive nor negative light. It seemed more of an example to make his point. To me, it just seemed like Uncle Jim telling me in a matter-of-fact tone about what happened when his friend came close to reaching the end of his rope because war is hell. You'll understand why I am providing all of this preamble for this story momentarily. Here is the story:

One of the other members of the 517th PRCT was a Private First Class named Melvin "Bud" Biddle. Bud and my uncle Jim were very good friends. They ate together, played cards together, joked around a lot, and basically watched each other's backs in combat. I have a picture of them standing together posing in Italy on my Facebook page.

As my uncle Jim told the story, it was sometime in the late spring of 1943 that he and Bud were talking, when Bud told my uncle Jim that he was having a crisis of conscience about killing people. "I just can't do it anymore, Jim," he said. And then he told my uncle that he was thinking about walking away from the war altogether. Now, for any of you who are not veterans, one of the big things you learn in training is that desertion in time of war is one of the most serious offenses a soldier can commit. It's almost worse than murder. In times of peace, desertion can land you in Ft. Leavenworth prison doing hard labor for twenty years before they even consider letting you out. But during wartime, the customary punishment for such an offense is a quick court-martial and immediate execution via firing squad. If you were exceptionally lucky, maybe, just maybe, you could get away with a life sentence of hard labor, but either way, you will most likely never see another day of freedom for the rest of your natural life. That's how serious this conversation between Bud and my uncle turned in an instant.

Uncle Jim immediately started trying to convince Bud it was a bad idea. This was a time before conscientious objector status even existed. And this was World War II. The Germans were coming, and they were serious business, having already rolled into controlling most of their neighboring countries. He tried and tried to convince Bud. But Bud was resolute. He just couldn't kill anymore. They talked for a while, my uncle Jim hoping and praying he had changed his friend's mind. But to my uncle Jim's disappointment, the very next morning after that conversation, Melvin "Bud" Biddle was not present for the regular morning muster. He was gone. "I was the only one he told," said my uncle Jim. Even fifty years later, he had a look of helplessness on his face when he said those words to me. "I think he just didn't come back from that night's patrol, but I don't know. He just wasn't there."

In the confusion of war, it was very common for men to become separated from their units. On my uncle's first mission into France, they were dropped 163 miles from their intended target and had to steal a car to get to where they were going. Night patrols would lose soldiers who wouldn't know how to get back to their unit. Some would get captured or killed. Some would just get lost for a day or two before finding their way back. So knowing that fact, when Bud didn't show up for morning muster, my uncle did something that would touch the lives of hundreds of men before the end of the war; he showed compassion for Bud Biddle's crisis of conscience, and reported Bud as Missing In Action (MIA) on the unit roster instead of as a known deserter. Uncle Jim's actions were certainly a no-no in the eyes of the Army, but he did it anyway. Without clear evidence that Bud deserted, he was hoping if Bud did walk away, he would soon come to his senses and return to the unit. But frankly, after their long conversation, he wasn't sure if Bud was ever coming back.

Uncle Jim said he thought Bud was gone for about a week, or maybe a little more, but certainly less than two weeks. But he did finally come back. "Then one day, he was just back," my uncle Jim said. "He looked at me. I looked at him. I gave him a nod. He gave me a nod. And that was it. I didn't ask him about it." Bud would later tell my uncle about the family he stayed with, the girl with whom he had started a romance, and about that family's fear of the German war machine rolling across their homeland. In his time away, Bud had come to a realization: "The sooner we can get this war over with, the sooner we can stop the killing," Bud said. And so after a short break from the war, Melvin "Bud" Biddle went back to being a soldier in an elite paratrooper unit of the U.S. Army.

And this is where the delicate nature of this story becomes clear. Because Melvin "Bud" Biddle wasn't just a normal soldier who took a short break to clear his head and then return to finish the war in anonymity. No, instead, Melvin "Bud" Biddle turned out to be a genuine war hero, and was one of the eighteen men from the original 160 of the 517th PRCT who survived the whole war. His bravery in action even earned him the Congressional Medal of Honor, the single highest honor a U.S. serviceman can receive. He was one of only 464 soldiers out of 16 million to receive this award, only 198 of whom survived to ever wear it. Most men receive the award posthumously because their brave actions actually result in their own death. Part of Melvin Biddle's Medal of Honor citation reads as follows:

> He displayed conspicuous gallantry and intrepidity in action against the enemy near Soy, Belgium, on 23 and 24 December 1944. Serving as lead scout during an attack to relieve the enemy-encircled town of Hotton, he aggressively penetrated a densely wooded area, advanced 400 yards until he came within range of intense enemy rifle fire, and within 20

yards of enemy positions killed 3 snipers with unerring marksmanship. Courageously continuing his advance an additional 200 yards, he discovered a hostile machine-gun position and dispatched its 2 occupants. He then located the approximate position of a well-concealed enemy machine-gun nest, and crawling forward threw hand grenades which killed two Germans and fatally wounded a third. After signaling his company to advance, he entered a determined line of enemy defense, coolly and deliberately shifted his position, and shot 3 more enemy soldiers. Undaunted by enemy fire, he crawled within 20 yards of a machine-gun nest, tossed his last hand grenade into the position, and after the explosion charged the emplacement firing his rifle. When night fell, he scouted enemy positions alone for several hours and returned with valuable information which enabled our attacking infantry and armor to knock out 2 enemy tanks. At daybreak he again led the advance and, when flanking elements were pinned down by enemy fire, without hesitation made his way toward a hostile machine-gun position and from a distance of 50 yards killed the crew and 2 supporting riflemen. The remainder of the enemy, finding themselves without automatic weapon support, fled panic stricken. Pfc. Biddle's intrepid courage and superb daring during his 20-hour action enabled his battalion to break the enemy grasp on Hotton with a minimum of casualties.

This is only one of many heroic stories of Melvin Biddle. Heroic stories of Melvin Biddle can be found all over the Internet. He was awarded a Bronze Star for one of them, which is another very prestigious award for bravery in battle. From the sound of it, he probably could have been given ten of those. "Oh gosh, he was a real hero," my uncle said. This, from a man who didn't consider himself a hero, even though he himself received a number of the highest military honors awarded to U.S. servicemen.

Melvin Biddle personally saved hundreds of lives during his time as a paratrooper for the 517th, and I think no one should ever consider that his initial crisis of conscience demeans his accomplishments in any way. I believe he left the war for compassionate reasons, and returned to it for equally compassionate reasons. He was never proud of his violent exploits. One story of his heroism tells of a time he single-handedly took out 20 German soldiers who were dug in over a hilltop, where he threw multiple grenades, eliminating all the enemy fighters. One of his fellow soldiers stood at the top of the hill, calling out, "Hey Bud, come look at what you did." "I don't want to see it" was Melvin's reply.

Personally, I think if Congressional Medal of Honor winner Melvin "Bud" Biddle did leave his unit willingly for a short time (we have no official proof because only Biddle himself could have confirmed this before his death in 2010), it makes his story stronger because of what he overcame to be able to put himself into a mind-space of doing something he desperately didn't want to do for the sake of others who were suffering under the oppression of a clear threat to the whole world. Biddle hated killing. That was a large part of his {self} that he sacrificed by becoming one of the bravest and most effective soldiers of WWII. Something that will never be lost on me is that it was my uncle Jim's compassion for his friend that played a role in that outcome. (If you're interested, you can view an edited news piece, followed by the unedited footage of an interview my uncle James T. Dorman did for a local news station where he speaks of his time in the war, on YouTube.)

We might do well to remember that patriotism and fear started the war in Europe, and with the cessation of violence under treaty, and the liberation of the Nazi death camps, kindness and compassion finished it. I'm sure the men who fought in WWII would agree with me when I say (as a veteran myself) that I hope we start with kindness and compassion before the next great war ever comes to fruition. Jimmy Carter, a man I greatly respect, said it best. "We will not learn to live together in peace by killing each other's children." It is my hope that this book allows us to see the mechanisms in our minds which cause us to wage war so that we may some day make more courageous decisions. At the very least, if we share the ability to take control of our minds and quell our subconscious fears, the type of mass emotional manipulation that is required to build the political will for making war may be nearing its end. Maybe it's now time for all of us to learn the deepest secrets of Self which free us from being emotional pawns for our{selves} and others. Maybe it's time to liberate ourselves from the destructive patterns of {self} that cause our{selves}, and the world, so much pain. Maybe it's time to uncover the amazing true Self within us, and reveal the real purpose of our time here on Earth, which is not of creating conflict, internal or external.

15. Using Our Minds as a Tool for Improving Life

> Don't play what's there,
>
> play what's not there.
>
> —Miles Davis

My uncle Jim's decision to not report his friend to Army Intelligence was one steeped in meta-awareness. Uncle Jim was able to look into his own mind and see his internal reactions to the situation, but then also measure what was going on in his friend's mind to balance the two perspectives and come to a rational decision based on the facts that lay before him. Uncle Jim knew how the Army would judge the actions of his friend, and that they would not likely take into serious consideration his friend's mindset or deeper motivations for taking the actions that led to his alleged temporary absence. His use of meta-awareness in a critical moment indirectly saved hundreds of lives in the war, and it's my hope that in retelling the story I might inspire other people to use their minds in a similar fashion.

The act of using your mind to control your mind is not an easy task to master. But the fact is that your physiology is indeed built to help you accomplish that difficult feat if you practice the disciplines that get your brainpower working for you. Raising the consciousness levels in your mind is a surefire way you can employ to not being controlled by your mind and its destructive and unproductive processes connected with the mind's {self}. When you're able to see your mind operating from the internal space of your mind's Control Room, called meta-awareness, you're able to control your mind and make more sound decisions with your mind. With practice, thanks to neuroplasticity, your ability to control your mind gets stronger over time and changes the quality of your life as a result without maintaining the original effort it took to get you there.

Learning and understanding how your subconscious mind processes your Perceptions vs. the Expectations/Preferences connected with the ideas on your mind's {self} map, you gain the ability to see that internal process in action and can take control of it. In addition understanding it employs your name-it-tame-it brain circuits which, to a guaranteed result, turns your inner turbulence down and makes it more manageable. While your emotions will always probably remain a subconscious process in your mind, you can still take control of the variables that your subconscious mind uses to create your emotions in the first place, and use your understanding of the process to gain access to the volume and frequency knobs of your emotional processing, This allows you to turn down the creation of any negative stuff that arises at will. Is happiness and enjoyment of your existence shining through at the moment? Leave it turned up to 11. If it's some temporary negative bullshit coming through your speakers, take the controls and turn that shit off.

Reducing your inner turmoil makes you a better colleague, a better business professional, a better leader, a better parent, a better friend, a better lover, and a better more aware human being in general. In short, it makes you a better person. It makes you powerful because you are no longer having to fight the challenges within your own mind before taking action to address the challenges presented to you by the world. That's important. But maybe most importantly, taking control of your mind also just makes you happier. And isn't that what life is all about?

When you take control of your mind, you take control of your whole life. You take control of how you see things, of how you react to things internally, and of how you respond to things externally. This puts a whole different energy into play within your mind and also a different energy of what you put out into the world as you take action on your altered thought patterns and more positive emotions. This changes your {self} and changes the world. Gandhi once famously said, "Be the change you wish to see in the world." This shift of awareness in your minds accomplishes both in one smooth action.

Entering the mind space of meta-awareness where you can see your mind operating in real time allows you to see your{self} more accurately than you had seen your{self} previously. This becomes a life changing shift almost immediately. If you use only this portion of the science of raising your conscious awareness, this small shift will serve you for the rest of your life, and will provide benefits you never knew were possible. You may find it will reduce your pain and suffering overall, and increase your overall happiness as a result. And if this is all I can ever do for you, I will be forever grateful. Because a happier life for you means we've bumped the happiness meter for the world a tiny fraction as well. And that stuff becomes exponential over time with the people you touch and make happier because of your happy presence. And this helps us become the change we wish to see in the world.

Now... all that said, at this moment we also need to acknowledge that other people still exist, and we need to acknowledge that some of them are assholes. And some of those assholes will try to either inadvertently or deliberately ruin your day from time to time. And how do we battle this challenge? We recommend this book to them, of course.

Seriously though, how many people do you know who would love the benefit of being able to see their mind a bit better? Who would love to understand how their mind worked, or better yet, understand how the mind of a difficult person around them worked? How many people do you think would appreciate knowing where their mind's Control Room was, and how easy it was to step inside and take control of their mind?

So if you agree that I've shown you the process of how to take control of your mind, and you've even maybe experienced being able to take control of your mind a little bit while reading through this book, please go... right now... and do just a few quick things for me:

First, write a quick review of this book wherever you got it online.

Second, take an extra second to "Like" and link us up on social media. That will help other people find Mind Hacking Happiness down the road. You can find the links for our social media accounts on MindHackingHappiness.com.

Third, share this book in one other way to someone. Buy a copy and gift it, or be like a couple corporations and get a set for your whole business team. Or if you can't think of another way to share it with others, stop by MindHackingHappiness.com and make a quick donation to the cause so that we can use your contribution to share the mind hacking message out to people who need it.

Let's positively change the world one person at a time.

Lastly, if you simply use the basics of what you've learned here, you're ahead of the happiness game. But if these insights have helped you, don't forget to sharpen them. Plasticity works both ways, and if you don't employ these tools, you will lose them. We've created ongoing education options and exercises at MindHackingHappiness.com if you need help there.

Thanks in advance for your reviews and online shares. See you somewhere soon.

Hugs.

Your New Friend,

Sean Webb

Made in the USA
Lexington, KY
02 April 2019